THEORIES AND APPROACHES TO LEARNING IN THE EARLY YEARS

The Critical Issues in the Early Years Series

This series provides both national (UK wide) and international perspectives on critical issues within the field of early years education and care.

The quality of Early Childhood Education and Care (ECEC) has remained a high priority on government agendas in recent years (OECD, 2006). This series reflects this developing early childhood context which includes professionalizing, and up-skilling, the early childhood workforce. In particular, the series brings a critical perspective to the developing knowledge and understanding of early years practitioners at various stages of their professional development, to encourage reflection on practice and to bring to their attention key themes and issues in the field of early childhood.

Series Editor

Linda Miller is Professor Emeritus of Early Years at The Open University. Since 2005 Linda has been co-director of international project 'Day in the Life of an Early Years Practitioner' based within the European Early Childhood Research Association (EECERA). She is currently on the Expert Advisory Group for an EU study on Competencies in Early Childhood Education (ECE) and is co-lead researcher for the England case study. She has been a member of government stakeholder groups and working parties concerned with workforce development in the early years. Linda has written and co-edited a wide range of books for early years practitioners, and has published in national and international journals.

Reference

Organisation for Economic Co-operation and Development (OECD) (2006) *Starting Strong II: Early Childhood Education and Care*. Paris: OECD.

Titles in the series

Miller and Cable, *Professionalization, Leadership and Management in the Early Years*
Miller and Hevey, *Policy Issues in the Early Years*
Miller and Pound, *Theories and Approaches to Learning in the Early Years*

THEORIES AND APPROACHES TO LEARNING IN THE EARLY YEARS

Edited by
Linda Miller and Linda Pound

Los Angeles | London | New Delhi
Singapore | Washington DC

First published 2011

SAGE Publications Ltd
1 Oliver's Yard
55 City Road
London EC1Y 1SP

SAGE Publications Inc.
2455 Teller Road
Thousand Oaks, California 91320

SAGE Publications India Pvt Ltd
B 1/I 1 Mohan Cooperative Industrial Area
Mathura Road
New Delhi 110 044

SAGE Publications Asia-Pacific Pte Ltd
33 Pekin Street #02-01
Far East Square
Singapore 048763

Library of Congress Control Number: 2010926223

British Library Cataloguing in Publication data

A catalogue record for this book is available from the British Library

ISBN 978-1-84920-577-1
ISBN 978-1-84920-578-8 (pbk)

Typeset by C&M Digitals (P) Ltd, Chennai, India
Printed and bound in Great Britain by TJ International Ltd, Padstow, Cornwall
Printed on paper from sustainable resources

Education at SAGE

SAGE is a leading international publisher of journals, books, and electronic media for academic, educational, and professional markets.

Our education publishing includes:

- accessible and comprehensive texts for aspiring education professionals and practitioners looking to further their careers through continuing professional development

- inspirational advice and guidance for the classroom

- authoritative state of the art reference from the leading authors in the field

Find out more at: **www.sagepub.co.uk/education**

CONTENTS

ABOUT THE EDITORS AND CONTRIBUTORS

Editors

Linda Miller is Professor Emeritus of Early Years at the Open University. Since 2005 Linda has been co-director of international project 'Day in the Life of an Early Years Practitioner' based within the European Early Childhood Research Association (EECERA). She is currently on the Expert Advisory Group for an EU study on Competencies in Early Childhood Education (ECE) and is co-lead researcher for the England case study. She has been a member of government stakeholder groups and working parties concerned with workforce development in the early years. Linda has written and co-edited a wide range of books for early years practitioners and has published in national and international journals.

Linda Pound has worked in universities and was an LEA early years inspector for 10 years. She has been head of a nursery school and deputy head of a primary school. In her current role as an education consultant, she provides training, advice and support for early years practitioners both nationally and internationally. She is also an assessor for the National Professional Qualification in Integrated Centre Leadership (NPQICL). Linda has written extensively – her most recent book is the third in a series entitled *How Children Learn* (Step Forward Publishing, 2009). Her major areas of interest are learning and curriculum in the early years.

Contributors

Deborah Albon has worked in a variety of early childhood settings as both a nursery nurse and later a teacher. She now works across a range of early childhood programmes at London Metropolitan University as Senior Lecturer in Early

Childhood Studies. Deborah is currently engaged in research looking at 'food events' in four early childhood settings and has published a number of articles in this area as well as the book *Food and Health in Early Childhood,* co-written with Penny Mukherji (Sage, 2008).

Sarah Blackwell is the Director of Archimedes Training and has been pioneering Forest Schools programmes and training in the UK for the past 10 years and is both managing director and lead trainer. Sarah was the first practitioner to deliver Forest Schools in urban environments across South Yorkshire in the early 2000s and has worked extensively with children, young people and families, including those with additional needs. Sarah's passion is to provide high quality training and through her work seeks to inspire all learners to take Forest Schools into their own settings with confidence and enthusiasm.

Martin Bradley is currently chair of the Montessori Schools' Association and a member of the Montessori Evaluation and Accreditation Board. He was one of Her Majesty's Inspectors of schools for 23 years, for three years of which he was seconded to manage the Department for Education's Early Excellence Programme. Besides continuing to work on inspections, he is a governor of Hereford Steiner Academy.

Tina Bruce, CBE, is an honorary visiting professor at Roehampton University, having originally trained as a teacher at the Froebel Educational Institute. She also trained to teach children with hearing impairments, and taught in both special and mainstream schools. She was head of the Research Nursery School, later becoming Director of the Centre for Early Childhood Studies, both located in what is now Roehampton University. She worked with the British Council in New Zealand and Egypt, and was awarded International Woman Scholar by the University of Virginia Commonwealth. She is involved with training and consultancy for the early childhood phase in the UK and abroad. She has published many books and articles, and her books include *Early Childhood Education* (1987), *Time to Play* (1991), *Cultivating Creativity* (2005), *Developing Learning* (2004), the edited textbook, *Early Childhood: A Student Guide* (2003), and, with Carolyn Meggitt and Julian Grenier, the co-authored *Childcare and Education* (2010).

Margaret Dillane has Montessori Diplomas levels 1, 2 and 3, a BEd and MA. She has owned and run Happy Days Montessori School for the last 20 years. Margaret is the head of Montessori Education UK (MEUK) mentoring and assessment. She is a placement and teaching practice tutor for Montessori Centre International and is currently studying for the Early Years Professional Status(EYPS) at Middlesex University.

Ann S. Epstein is the Senior Director of Curriculum Development at the HighScope Educational Research Foundation in Ypsilanti, Michigan in the USA, where she has worked since 1975. Her areas of expertise include child and youth development, curriculum development (visual arts, mathematics, literacy, intergenerational), child and programme assessment, professional development and programme evaluation. Ann has published numerous books and articles for professional and practitioner audiences, including *The Intentional Teacher* (2007) and *Me, You, Us: Social-Emotional Learning in Preschool* (2009), and is co-author of *Educating Young Children* (2008), *Supporting Young Artists* (2002), and *Small-Group Times to Scaffold Early Learning* (2009). She is also the principle developer of the Number Plus Preschool Mathematics Curriculum.

Barbara Isaacs is the Academic Director of the Montessori Centre International, the Senior Accreditation Officer of the Montessori Evaluation and Accreditation Board, and author of *Bringing the Montessori Approach to Your Early Years Practice* (2010). She owned and managed a small Montessori school in Oxfordshire for 15 years and her two children attended a Montessori nursery, successfully progressing into mainstream education at the age of five.

Serena Johnson has worked in the field of early years education for over 30 years. Her career has included the headship of a nursery school and work as a Local Authority Early Years Inspector. She is a former director of HighScope UK where she developed training materials and courses. She has published widely, and contributed to the Early Years Foundation Stage guidance. She has worked as an educational consultant in the UK and abroad. Now retired, she is Senior Adviser to HighScope UK and Chair of Governors at an Early Excellence Children's Centre.

Pam Lafferty worked in Nursery and Primary Education, including the Deputy Headship of a Primary School, before becoming a Consultant Trainer and subsequently Director of HighScope UK. She has undertaken training and workshops in many countries. She has written widely and most recently contributed a chapter on 'Child Initiated Learning in the Early Years' to *Like Bees not Butterflies* (A and C Black, 2008).

Trisha Lee is Artistic Director and founder of MakeBelieve Arts, a Theatre and Education Company developing the creative potential of children aged 2–15. She is also a cabinet office appointed Social Enterprise Ambassador. Trisha pioneered the 'Helicopter Technique' based on the work of Vivian Gussin Paley in schools throughout the UK. She has lectured both nationally and internationally and was commissioned by the Childhood Cultural Centre of Qatar to develop creative reading training for teachers. She is currently writing a joint anthology on developing Spiritual Intelligence (Crown House), and *Teaching Mathematics Creatively* (Routledge) with Linda Pound.

Louise Livingston is an Association Montessori Internationale (AMI) Montessori Teacher Trainer at the Maria Montessori Institute in London. She has worked for many years with children under 6 in a Montessori Children's House. She is a council member of Montessori Education UK (MEUK) and editor of the Montessori Society AMI (UK) publication *Direction*.

Julia Manning-Morton is Programme Director for Early Childhood Studies at London Metropolitan University. She has also worked as an early years practitioner, manager, adviser and inspector across a range of settings for children aged 0–8 years. Her early experience of working in social care settings where psychodynamic concepts were integral to the support given to children, families and staff, has been highly influential in her subsequent research foci and teaching approach. This includes the Key Times action research project in Camden, London, and her current work with groups of centre heads and practitioners in supporting children's emotional development. In addition, Julia believes that the personal benefit she has gained from the psychotherapeutic process has enabled her to not only grow as a person but has also supported her professional commitment to promoting children's and practitioners' emotional well-being.

Dawn Nasser is Managing Director of Spectrum Montessori Ltd (Rose House Montessori School, www.rose-house-montessori.com). Dawn is actively involved with the implementation of the Early Years Foundation Stage through consultancy work and the delivery of training. She is an Early Years Lead Inspector for the Independent Schools Inspectorate, and an assessor for the Montessori Evaluation and Accreditation Board.

Anne B. Smith was the inaugural Director of the Children's Issues Centre, an interdisciplinary research centre at the University of Otago, Dunedin, New Zealand, between 1995 and 2006. Now an Emeritus Professor, Anne's interests are in the area of Childhood Studies, with a particular focus on children's rights. She is the author of *Understanding Children's Development* (1998), and co-author of *Advocating for Children* (2000), *Children's Voices* (2000), *Children as Citizens* (2009) and *Learning in the Making* (2009). She has had an ongoing input into policy developments in early childhood education in New Zealand since the mid-1970s. She has a particular interest in young children's learning; quality early childhood environments; family, early childhood centre and school influences on children's development – especially punishment and other forms of family discipline; and international policy and law relating to physical punishment in the home.

Jill Tina Taplin joined a group of parents founding a new Steiner school 26 years ago and soon found herself working in the kindergarten. Over the past five years, she has become increasingly involved in training adults in Steiner early childhood practice. She works as an adviser in Steiner early childhood settings, as a tutor on the training courses, and provides Continuing Professional Development (CPD) for practitioners, in addition to writing articles and kindergarten material.

Anne Marie True has run a Montessori nursery school in south-west London since 1987. She was a governor of a preparatory school for over eight years and since 1998 a governor of a local state primary school. She sits on various Local Authority education committees and is a member of the Montessori Evaluation and Accreditation Board. She is a committed Montessorian and sat on the UK Centenary Committee. She currently chairs the Save Our Nurseries Campaign.

CHAPTER 1

TAKING A CRITICAL PERSPECTIVE

Linda Miller and Linda Pound

Overview

The chapters in this book explore both contemporary and historical perspectives relating to some of the theories and approaches which have influenced Early Childhood Education and Care (ECEC) today. This chapter gives an overview of the structure of the book and its rationale. In the chapter, we signpost some key themes raised in the ensuing chapters and invite you to take a critical stance in relation to the identified themes and to reflect on these in the light of present day issues. The book is divided into three parts: Theoretical and Analytical Positions; Foundational Theories; and Contemporary Theories. In Parts 2 and 3 of the book, the chapters are written by 'advocates' of distinctive approaches to ECEC. One dictionary definition of an advocate is, 'a person who supports or speaks in favour of' (our italics) (Allen, 1991). Each of the chapter authors are 'champions' of, and passionate about, a particular and distinctive approach to learning and pedagogy, and each approach is underpinned by particular theoretical frameworks. However, theories are not a truth but an explanation and will

(Continued)

(Continued)

influence practice depending on the views and beliefs (based on these theories) held by the practitioner, or perhaps the ethos and philosophy of the setting in which she works. The chapters also consider change, transformation and continuity within each approach and its relevance to current policy and practice.

The purpose of this book is to encourage you to examine the different theories and approaches presented and to consider the implications for your own practice. In this first chapter, we invite you to critically reflect upon and consider your own individual position and perspective and to take a critical stance in relation to each chapter. Questions and discussion points at the end of this chapter (and also within each chapter) encourage you to examine each approach through your own particular lens. We hope that in using the framework we offer, you will have the opportunity to 'step back' and develop a critical perspective in relation to each chapter – so that you see what may be familiar with a new and critical eye. We have no doubt that some ideas you will 'throw away'; other ideas you will take with you. We hope that as a result of reading this book, new meanings will emerge and it will help you to look at practice in a different way.

In this book, we take the view that the terms early years and early years education and care should be seen as encompassing 'education' but with a care component and that it should be impossible to educate without caring, nor care without developing and promoting children's learning. We also use the term *she* when referring to individuals of both genders.

Organization of the book

We have inevitably been selective in choosing the theories and approaches included in this book. The history of ECEC is both fascinating and convoluted and to do that rich history full justice is beyond the scope of any one single book. We have, for example, *not* included a chapter on constructivism – either Piagetian or Vygotskian – since their theories are widely discussed elsewhere (Donaldson, 1976; Rogoff, 1990) and underpin so much current thinking about young children (Johnson, 2010). Constructivist theories are key to, and explicit within, for example, HighScope, Reggio Emilia and Te Whāriki (see this chapter and Chapters 7 and 10). In other perhaps less developed initiatives, such as the work of Vivian Gussin Paley (Chapter 8) and the development of Forest Schools (Chapter 9), constructivism is less explicit but equally influential.

Nor have we included anything on highly influential thinkers such as John Dewey or Susan Isaacs. Both deserve a special place in the history and philosophy of early childhood education – but neither approach is explicit in current practice in the United Kingdom, so have been omitted from this book. In much the same way as Julia Manning-Morton (see Chapter 2) suggests that psychoanalytical theories are implicit within high-quality care and education for young children, so the work of Dewey and Isaacs are implicit in much current practice. With their different but related emphases on empowerment and supporting children in making the connections that enable learning, their influence continues to be felt.

The interrelatedness of the theories and approaches is an interesting aspect of the chapters. For example, Froebel's theory, as Tina Bruce points out in Chapter 4, continues to have great influence but owed much to the work of Rousseau, Pestalozzi and Owen. We hope that these common threads and shared histories will become apparent as you read this book. As we note above, each chapter represents the views of individuals committed to a particular approach and set of theories, although each chapter offers a critique. Therefore, the views represented are not impartial but they *are* informed and knowledgeable. It is for you as the reader to consider the views presented and to reflect upon what they say to you and to form your own views.

The first part of the book is dedicated to *Theoretical and Analytical Positions*. The two chapters focus, not on a single approach or theory, but on sets of ideas which support a reflective and analytical view of work with young children. In Chapter 2, Julia Manning-Morton considers the way in which the broad raft of psychoanalytical theories underpins all practice in ECEC (or perhaps all practice in life). The chapter has particular importance for two key reasons. The first is that, aside from attachment, the full impact of psychoanalytical theories on adult interactions with young children is not always fully understood. The second reason for its importance is in inviting critical reflection on the way in which our own feelings and emotions shape the psychological well-being of the children with whom we work. The other chapter in this section, by Deb Albon, focuses on postmodern theories and offers an invitation to 'deconstruct' other approaches and theories. Albon raises interesting and challenging questions which may help you to bring a critical edge to your reading and thinking.

Part 2 focuses on what we have termed 'Foundational Theories' and begins with an overview of the work of Froebel by Tina Bruce. The remaining two chapters consider the specific approaches and clear theoretical underpinning of Steiner Waldorf schools and Montessori schools. Both have a long history but are being reviewed in the light of current thinking. Conroy et al. (2008: 16) suggest that their contribution might lie in the now 'stronger emphasis on individual capabilities and a more significant focus on the affective'. These three chapters together serve to remind us of the pioneering practice which continues to contribute much to ECEC throughout the world. The approaches have much in common and yet, at the same time, many differences (Bruce, 2005). However, in all three, the child is placed firmly at the centre of thinking and practice.

In Part 3, 'Contemporary Theories', the chapters are concerned with more recent approaches to ECEC. Chapter 7 focuses on HighScope which, although highly influential, has, when compared to the foundational theories explored in Part 2, a relatively short history. HighScope was established around 50 years ago in the United States and the longitudinal research findings which have emerged from it were the rationale for setting up Sure Start in England. In Chapter 8, Trisha Lee offers a personal account of the impact the work of Vivian Gussin Paley has had on her thinking and practice through a story-telling and story-acting approach. Sarah Blackwell and

Linda Pound in Chapter 9 provide an historical overview of the development of outdoor provision and the place of Forest Schools within that development. They describe the work of Forest Schools and discuss the benefits of outdoor experiences and risk taking in what they see as a current risk-adverse culture. The roles of culture and community are explored in Chapter 10 where Anne B. Smith describes Te Whāriki, New Zealand's early childhood curriculum, which reflects a holistic and bicultural vision for childhood. She describes a curriculum developed by Māori and Pākeha partners and which included wide consultation with a bi-cultural community and key stakeholders, and which emphasizes children's participation in shared meaningful activities.

The final chapter in the book draws together what we see as the critical issues raised by the chapters in this book.

Historical context

Early childhood care and education has a long and interesting history. Writers and thinkers from even before the 17th century onwards have influenced the way in which education, including early education, has been shaped and developed in more recent times. Although it is with the work of Froebel that the exploration of specific theories and approaches to early childhood care and education begins in this book (see Chapter 4), we should be aware of the precedents which shaped his thinking. Pestalozzi's belief that love, work and social interaction were the foundations of development shaped both his work and that of Froebel. Despite this formative and fascinating early work, it is within the 20th century that the history of early childhood care and education really begins to burgeon – but again this has older historical roots. Robert Owen's work in New Lanark is not explored in this book but it was he who established what has been described as the first workplace nursery in the early part of the 19th century. He and Froebel held different perspectives and their work had different roots but the ideals of both were to influence developments in the early part of the 20th century. The work of the McMillan sisters in England, looking at the needs of severely socio-economically disadvantaged children and communities, held the same compassion as Owen's pioneering work. Their emphasis on nature drew on Froebel's theories and approaches, as Tina Bruce points out in Chapter 4.

The interrelatedness of theories is something to be borne in mind as you read this book. Theories have roots and precedents and they go on to spark new theories and ideas. Theories are also shaped by the contemporary social context and these influence popular views of childhood, curriculum and pedagogy.

Themes and threads

In this section, we highlight some of the key themes and interrelated threads which permeate and link the chapters. We have added questions at the end of the chapter as a framework for your thinking and reflection. The themes explored are:

- children and childhood
- curricula, learning and play
- the role of adults
- the nature of research and evidence.

Children and childhood

The theories and approaches outlined in this book have at their heart careful observation, intense listening and a desire to tune into children – to understand what they seek to understand and to know. We should not forget that childhood is a construction that arises from historical, cultural and economic conditions (Kellet, 2010) and that educators can hold multiple views or constructions of children. Practitioners can recognize both the child in need of nurture and the child as agent of their own learning. It is reflection which helps us to understand and reconcile what are sometimes apparently irreconcilable views.

The way in which children are represented informs the way in which teaching and learning develop. The metaphor of a garden (or kindergarten) is key in Froebel's work – as the context for learning, needed if the plant (or child) is to thrive. If you think of children as blossoming plants in need of nurturing, then your approach will be different than if you primarily think of education as 'a process of living, not a preparation for future living' (Nutbrown et al., 2008: 43, citing Dewey, 1897). This assumes, as, is the case in Reggio Emilia nurseries (see below), that the child is a powerful and active agent in her own learning. This view of children as active agents in their own learning encompasses ideas of listening to or learning from the child (Clark et al., 2005) but is not in itself new. Each of the theories and approaches outlined in this book views children in this light and although practitioners understand and share this view, their interpretation of that may be different. This is because each of us also holds our own views of children and childhood and these, like theories, contain something of earlier views.

James et al. (1998) suggest that historical views of childhood (or pre-sociological views) include ideas of innocence and evil; natural development or the empty vessel; or the child without will or consciousness. They go on to suggest that more recent views have situated childhood within a cultural context, recognizing the impact that social influences have on shaping childhood, as well as the role that both nature and nurture play in the process. Perhaps the key point for the reader here is that awareness of these factors does not grant immunity from holding conflicting views. We talk about active learners but in practice (as pointed out in the chapter on Forest Schools), we minimize risk to the point where action and agency is severely limited. We theorize about children as unique individuals yet, as Paley reflects and seeks to understand in her writing, we jump to stereotypical conclusions about children.

Curricula, learning and play

Curricula are undoubtedly culturally shaped and cannot always be readily transferred from one environment to another. Te Whāriki presents a powerful metaphor of the curriculum as a woven mat on which everyone can stand, consisting of the principles of education, interwoven with strands or aims of learning which embrace both Māori and Pākeha culture. It also provides an example of a curriculum which was shaped through negotiation between practitioners holding different views – finally arriving at a consensus.

Curricula may also be shaped by the view of the child held by practitioners which can produce markedly different curricula; the place of modern technology offers an interesting illustration. Technology is not included in the Steiner Waldorf curriculum since, as Jill Tina Taplin points out, it is believed to be inappropriate to that stage of development. 'Instead … children use a wide range of "warm technology" such as … corn grinders, drills and whisks' (Steiner Waldorf Education, 2009: 28).

On the other hand, other curricula – such as those of HighScope, Reggio Emilia (discussed later in this chapter) and Te Whāriki – embrace modern technologies. How are these decisions arrived at? While the latter approaches may cite the need to recognize that children need to be part of the 21st century, the former (and other approaches) may cite the work of those who urge caution. A raft of dissenters from a very broad range of backgrounds suggest that information technologies may be changing the brain and learning in undesirable ways (Greenfield, 2004; Pagani et al., 2010), threatening established forms of communication and thought which require face-to-face responsive and interactive exchanges (Alexander, 2010) or failing to develop physicality and thought (Healy, 1999) while subjecting children to commercial forces (Mayo and Nairn, 2009).

A vital question here it seems is who is choosing what is to be learnt? On what basis are decisions made about what should be included or excluded from the curriculum? And, once those decisions are taken, by what means are they maintained or not? In Chapter 4, for example, Tina Bruce highlights the role of the revisionists – people who were prepared to make changes to the prescribed curriculum in order to maintain its dynamic qualities. Who are the revisionists in today's society?

Play is a recurrent theme in most chapters. From the earliest days of ECEC, play has been widely regarded as an essential part of the learning of young children. However, as is illustrated in Chapter 5, different theories and approaches are based on different views of what play is. This is of course closely linked to the view that is held of children and childhood. Froebel's view of play has some different qualities and characteristics to that held by Montessori or Paley. Montessori practitioners take the view that play and work share many characteristics – their emphasis is on practical tasks – while Paley also identifies play as work but places imaginative play at the forefront of her work with children. She writes, for example:

> The mind that has been freely associating with playful imagery is primed to tackle new ideas. Fantasy play, rather than being a distraction, helps children achieve the goal of having an open mind, whether in the service of further storytelling or in formal lessons. (Paley, 2004: 26)

The role of adults

The common ground which may be seen in relation to views of childhood and curricula is also to be found in the role of adults. Warmth and care are at the heart of all of these approaches, recognizing the vulnerability of young children which stands alongside their unique, active and curious approach to learning. However, there are also significant differences in the role considered most appropriate for adults.

Chapters 2 and 3 indicate that adults need both to be self-aware and to be willing and able to reflect and analyse from a range of perspectives. The emphasis within foundational theories is on an enabling role. This may take the form of providing structured materials or open-ended play materials. It will undoubtedly involve careful observation and analysis of what children are doing.

The adults' role in observing and analysing is also evident in the theories and approaches outlined in Part 3. This may take the form of analysing children's own stories and observing their play as Paley does; collecting and analysing learning stories as New Zealand practitioners do; or emphasizing the importance of observations in shaping experiences as Forest School practitioners do.

However, the adults' role in interacting with children may vary. Steiner practitioners, for example, frequently engage in practical activities. While children play, adults busy themselves with real tasks for real purposes, such as sewing. They are 'present' (Drummond and Jenkinson, 2009) and available but do not engage explicitly in children's play. Paley, on the other hand, describes some very active engagement in shaping play. When a teacher calms children's play focused on a hurricane, she tells the children that they are now the National Guard and must put on their hip boots. Now they are ready to clear up the storm damage, thus returning the classroom to order (Paley, 2010).

The role of the adult in HighScope hinges around structuring time – the environment is arranged so that children can act independently, while in Forest Schools a range of routines led by adults provide procedures to ensure that risks are safely managed. Many of these differences in the role of adults are subtle but they are informed by the adults' views of children and curricula. Official theories are often mediated or modified by the practitioners' personal theories.

It would be wrong to leave this section without mentioning the role of parents and carers. For Froebel, the emphasis was on mothers. As Tina Bruce indicates, this focus on the role of women was pioneering for its time. Montessori offered support for hard-pressed parents – again probably with an emphasis on mothers. A key feature of HighScope, often overlooked by politicians, was the high level of work with parents which was involved when the programme was introduced. One of the basic elements of Te Whāriki is the role of family and community in supporting children's learning.

The nature of research and evidence

A vital factor to consider, as you read this book, is the nature of research and evidence. Qualitative research methods may be subjective but may hold truth in the stories they tell. An example of this might be the work of Vivian Gussin Paley (see Chapter 8) whose theories are not based on quantitative research but on her own 'stories' – which have emerged from watching and listening to children. While this means that they reflect only her individual experience, it also means that her writing depicts 'real families' and real actions, is 'grounded in reality and risk'; and the reflection and analysis of experience explores not just successes, but failures – from which the writer demonstrates her own learning (Cooper, 2009: 2).

Quantitative research may be held up as being objective but may actually contain bias in the way in which it is set up (Mukherjee and Albon, 2009). The quantitative data provided by longitudinal follow-up studies of children who have been part of the HighScope approach (Schweinhart et al., 2005) have been highly influential on government policy in the UK, as have the findings of the Effective Provision of Pre-School Education (EPPE) Project (Melhuish et al., 1999; Sylva et al., 2004). However, research can only be useful if it answers questions relevant to culture, time and place. The values, principles and theoretical constructs underpinning the researchers' approach will determine its usefulness to practitioners.

In the sections that follow, we examine the way in which the themes and ideas discussed above may be illustrated by reference to the renowned approach in Reggio Emilia pre-schools. The chapter concludes by inviting you, the reader, to take a critical stance in relation to your own theories, beliefs and approaches and in relation to the chapters that follow.

Influences on early childhood curricula

According to Laevers (2004), curriculum is the way in which society expresses what they want from education. The OECD Thematic Review of Early Childhood Education and Care (Bennett, 2004) found that in most countries:

- there are national curricula for young children
- most agree on the utility of these frameworks
- most agree about curricular principles and aspirations
- most agree about subject areas
- most cover children aged 3–6
- there is a growing interest in curricula for children from birth to 3.

Developing curricula for young children involves making important decisions and choices about what and how they learn – as we note earlier in this chapter. Differences in curricular approaches stem from different conceptions of childhood. Most recently, there has been a trend towards a national and centralized form of curricula, for example in England. However, as we see from the chapters in this book, some approaches to curricula – both historical and contemporary – have stemmed from the vision and beliefs of one person, as in the case of the Reggio Emilia system of early childhood education. In this first chapter, we have included an overview of the Reggio Emilia approach to teaching and learning, as an example of an approach which embraces the key themes covered by the chapters in this book and as an example of a contemporary approach with historical roots. Moss (1999: 8) has discussed how looking at other approaches 'provides us with a sort of lens for looking at our own situations' – a stance we are encouraging you to take throughout this book.

Reggio Emilia

Reggio Emilia is an example of contemporary early childhood curricula with historical roots. It is a community-supported system of early childhood education and care situated in a region of northern Italy which has become internationally known for its provision for young children through 'The Hundred Languages of Children' touring exhibition (Malaguzzi, 1996) and through visits to the region from practitioners and authorities concerned with early childhood education (Abbott and Nutbrown, 2001).

The Reggio Emilia pre-schools stem from the inspiration of Loris Malaguzzi. His approach is grounded in his personal philosophy, influenced by his experiences in the Second World War and by progressive educational theorists such as Vygotsky. Malaguzzi believed strongly that a new society should nurture a vision of children who could act and think for themselves (Malaguzzi, 1995; Soler and Miller, 2003). This led to an early childhood education system founded on the perspective of the child. Carlina Rinaldi, who worked alongside Malaguzzi for many years, says the cornerstone of the Reggio Emilia experience is based on the image of children as rich, strong and powerful. Children are seen as unique subjects with rights rather than simply needs (Rinaldi, 1995).

The emergent curriculum

A key, and perhaps unique feature of Reggio Emilia pre-schools, is that there is no written curriculum; the child is seen as a starting point for an 'emergent curriculum' (Rinaldi, 1995: 102). The pre-schools have evolved from a 'ground up' and individualized approach to teaching and learning, rather than from external and national policy pressures. Malaguzzi refers to the 'hundred ways' in which he believes children learn and practitioners and other adults are urged to 'listen' to the many languages through which children communicate. Projects, which stem from the children's ideas, experiences and interests, serve as the main framework for teaching and learning.

Views of the child and the role of adults

Malaguzzi drew on Vygotsky's theory (amongst others – see Soler and Miller, 2003) which sees the relationship of the child and adult as central to the work in Reggio Emilia pre-schools. This perspective embraces the view that knowledge is co-constructed by the child and adult as they find meanings together. Listening to the child's views and ideas is key to this learning partnership. Central to the role of adults in Reggio Emilia is an ongoing dialogue which questions and challenges existing educational viewpoints and accepted teaching practices and approaches. This professional dialogue is shared with the children, parents, teachers, administrators, politicians and educators from other countries and enables practitioners to challenge dominant discourses around accepted ideas and practices; thus 'deconstructing' (i.e. taking a critical stance in relation to) existing ideas and theories (Dahlberg, 2000). Time for discussion, planning and preparation are built into the working week and other times of the day are also viewed as important. Rouse (1991: 13) describes her visit to Reggio Emilia, where during lunch time guests and teachers had 'a relaxed and delicious meal'. Time is also given to children to discuss their ideas, to develop cooperative projects with other children and adults and to research, problem solve and revisit work and ideas already undertaken (Nutbrown and Abbott, 2001).

A researchful approach

In Reggio Emilia pre-schools, adults (referred to as 'teachers') take on the role of children's learning partners. As projects develop, the teacher acts as the group's 'memory' by documenting visits and children's work through photographs, tape recordings and written notes. Such documentation has been described as 'visible listening' (Clark, 2005: 42, citing Rinaldi). The children and teachers can than reconstruct, revisit and reflect on what they have learnt. A *pedagogista* supports children's reflection on their learning and meets regularly with other staff and parents to share knowledge and ideas; she also has a co-coordinating role with many facets, including administration and training (Fillipini, 1995). The *atelierista* (artist in residence) is closely involved in project work and in the visual documentation of the children's work (Vecchi, 1995). The adult is seen as a facilitator and co-constructor of children's learning, helping the children to explore ideas and arouse their interest.

Parents are seen as central to the learning process in Reggio Emilia settings and are closely involved with their children's learning and ongoing projects. Information about their child is valued and 'feeds' the children's activities and experiences, thus keeping the child as a learner at the centre. Adults view group work as an important form of social learning and the practice of children staying with the same teachers over a three-year period creates a stable and secure learning environment and provides for continuity of learning experiences for the children. This is indeed a model of a 'community of practice' (Wenger, 2010).

The environment

In Reggio Emilia pre-schools, the environment is seen as the 'third teacher' with both indoor and outdoor experiences an important part of the learning process. The environment is intentionally visually appealing and stimulating with close attention paid to 'spaces, materials, colours, light, microclimate and furnishings' (Clark, 2007: 4). Displays of the children's work reflect ongoing projects and research, providing documentation of the learning process. Focal points are the piazza, a central meeting place where children play and talk together and the tetrahedron with a mirrored interior, where children can sit and see themselves from many angles (Nutbrown and Abbott, 2001). The importance placed on listening to children's views is demonstrated in a project where, in one Reggio pre-school, the children's views informed the architects' thinking about the kind of space needed for 'living well' in a school environment (Clark, 2007: 9).

The pre-schools of Reggio Emilia have, as Clark (2007) says, reached a global audience through 'The Hundred Languages of Children' exhibition and through publications. In Clark's own research, focusing on enabling young children to participate in decision making, the influence of Reggio Emilia is acknowledged. She posed the question, 'What does it mean to be in this place?' and asked the children, 'Can you show me what is important here?'

Critique

One criticism of the Reggio Emilia approach is that the lack of a written curriculum reduces 'accountability' to the wider community and to society and that practitioners may feel insecure about such an open-ended approach. However, advocates argue that the rich and detailed documentation through photographs, slides, film, publications and the travelling exhibition, opens practice to criticism and scrutiny. This process builds on Malaguzzi's philosophy of making the practice of Reggio Emilia visible to others in order to share and promote his vision (Soler and Miller, 2003). Another criticism is that whilst the system has aroused immense interest internationally, the 'localized' approach to teaching and learning means that it is not readily transferable and applied to other cultures or context.

Taking a critical stance

Theoretical positions are about how we understand the world. The way in which adults take on a theory or an approach depends on their own views of children, curriculum and practice, as the example from Reggio Emilia clearly illustrates. All of us have existing theories of our own and none of us give these up readily. Professional development processes which fail to take account of this may result in what has been termed 'formica' (Pound, 2000, citing Claxton, 1984) since it overlays but does not change the views and beliefs it masks; these remain untouched and unvoiced but yet continue to influence behaviour. The theories and beliefs we hold – whether formal or informal, explicit or implicit – influence practice. This is what makes reflection such a vital aspect of effective practice and enables the development of a 'researchful approach' to teaching and learning. In looking at the theories and approaches presented in the chapters in this book, you do not have to agree with them, but what you *do* have to be able to do, is to argue a case or a position.

Professionals taking a critical stance will need to consider the nature of research and evidence to be able to become reflective. Gardner (2006) argues that no one, in any profession, can be regarded as a professional unless they have developed reflective practice. All practitioners need to ask themselves whose theories they are adopting and where have they come from.

Reflecting on practice

Reflective practice involves questioning what you do and why you do it in the way that you do. Early years practitioners in their day-to-day work may have very little time to stop, think and reflect upon their practice. However, reflection based on observation is a recurrent theme in the chapters that follow. One of the remarkable features of the pioneers of early childhood care and education, such as the McMillan sisters, Susan Isaacs and Friedrich Froebel, is that they knew and understood children well. Their observations gave them great insight – insights into the nature of play as well as the role of physical action and social interaction in learning. Today, these theories are being supported through neuroscientific study and developmental psychology (Pound, 2005).

Schon (1983) talks about 'knowledge in action' – that is the knowledge that practitioners may use on a daily basis but which they may not readily articulate. This encompasses the view that knowledge is not 'out there' but within the practitioner; however, sometimes strategies and processes are needed in order to 'get it out'. This may take place when we talk through problems, ideas or situations with colleagues in what Wenger (www.ewenger.com/theory/index.htm) describes as a 'community of practice' – when we try to articulate to others what we think and mean or when we read a book such as this. For example, you will bring your own views, beliefs and present understanding to the ideas and theories presented in the chapters in this book. They may be ideas on which you routinely base your practice – but have not yet clearly articulated. The danger of this is that 'accepted practice' can become routine rather than questioning – for example, the role of play in the curriculum as a 'leading' activity. Exposing yourself to a range of different ideas, beliefs, perspectives and frameworks, as presented in the chapters in this book, can enable you to reframe your thinking or use your unarticulated knowledge to look differently at children, families, settings and practices – thus leading to greater understanding and perhaps to change. A book can be viewed as a 'cultural tool' offering you the opportunity to position yourself in relation to new or familiar ideas, to challenge your own views and beliefs and to help you to 'know what you don't know'.

The Reflective Practice Cycle

The Reflective Practice Cycle is designed to support practitioners in thinking about and exploring their practice and in beginning to articulate the 'hidden' values and beliefs that underpin their practice (Cable et al., 2007). The three-layer model of professional practice includes:

- *Thinking about practice* – the 'visible' top layer that represents what practitioners do in their day-to-day practice
- *Exploring practice* – the 'explicit' and 'articulated' knowledge, values and beliefs that are used in talking about practice (often learnt from courses, reading and sharing experiences or talking with colleagues)
- *Reflecting on practice* – the usually hidden knowledge that is not readily articulated, comprising values and beliefs and hidden assumptions and ideas about children, culture and society.

The model is designed to help practitioners understand the interactions between their day-to-day practice and how their knowledge, values and beliefs influence the ways in which they work with children. We hope that this book enables you to explore these layers of beliefs and values and encourages you to think more about some of the implicit ideas that shape your thinking and practice, and that new meanings will emerge as a result.

Final thoughts

No single book can do justice to the rich tapestry that is ECEC. No single chapter can do justice to the intricacies of the theories and approaches that seek to explain how children learn and how we can best support that learning. The human mind is complex and adults are capable of holding a number of dissonant views at the same time. Reflection is the process by which we attempt to sort out those anomalies between theory and practice, between what we say and what we do. As the practitioner and theorist at work in each of us strives to come to a heightened understanding of children, learning and effective practice, the chapters that follow may cause us to construct, deconstruct and reconstruct our ideas. While each of us must do this in our own unique way, in the light of our unique experiences, we have also to reach consensus with our colleagues. A genuinely consistent approach to effective education for young children can only be arrived at through communities of practice and shared thinking.

 Summary

- Both historical and contemporary approaches to teaching and learning in the early years can inform thinking and practice.
- Theoretical positions are about how we understand the world.
- Critical reflection is crucial to effective practice.

Questions for discussion

We hope the following questions will support you in developing a critical and reflective stance as you read through the chapters in this book.

1. What different understandings about how children learn and develop are contained in the approaches outlined in this book?
2. What are *your* views of children and childhood and how do these affect your practice?
3. How are play, learning and 'work' interpreted in the different approaches?
4. Which approach speaks to you most and why? (*Higher level question*)

Further reading

Levels 5 and 6

Craft, A. and Paige-Smith, A. (2008) 'Reflective practice', in L. Miller and C. Cable (eds) *Professionalism in the Early Years.* London: Hodder Education.
This chapter traces the role of reflection, both in and on practice, and draws on Wenger's notion of communities of practice.

Maynard, T. and Chicken, S. (2010) 'Through a different lense: exploring Reggio Emilia in a Welsh context', *Early Years*, 30(1): 29–39.
Following the staging of the Reggio Emilia travelling exhibition, this article gives an account of a project in which teachers explored Reggio philosophy and practices in order to gain insights into their thinking and pedagogy.

Waller, T. (2010) 'Modern childhoods: contemporary theories and children's lives', in C. Cable, L. Miller and G. Goodliff (eds) *Working with Children in the Early Years* (2nd edn). Abingdon, Oxon: Routledge/Open University Press.
In this chapter, Tim Waller offers an accessible and critical discussion of contemporary perspectives on children and childhoods. He examines contemporary views of the child and challenges traditional theories of child development.

Levels 6 and 7

Edwards, C., Gandini, L. and Forman, G. (eds) (1998) *The Hundred Languages of Children: The Reggio Emilia Approach to Early Childhood Education* (2nd edn). Norwood, NJ: Ablex Publishing.
This book brings together the reflections of Italian educators who were involved in founding the Reggio Emilia system and 'observers' of the system. It offers useful background material to those who wish to understand more about the origins, history and philosophy of Reggio Emilia.

MacNaughton, G. (2004) 'The politics of logic in early childhood research: a case of the brain, hard facts, trees and rhizomes', *Australian Educational Research*, 31(3): 87–104.

MacNaughton claims that early childhood education is essentially about children's rights. She regards tackling inequality as its prime task and warns against embracing simplistic theories that ignore the complexities.

Wood, E. (2007) 'Reconceptualising child-centred education: contemporary directions in policy, theory and practice in early childhood', *FORUM*, 49(1 & 2): 119–34. Available at: http://dx.doi.org/10.2304/forum.2007.49.1.119

This article argues that contemporary theories challenge aspects of developmental theories, focusing on social and cultural influences. Wood places children together with adults at the heart of contemporary educational processes.

Websites

www.ewenger.com/theory
This website offers an explanation of 'communities of practice' and provides links to further reading and information.

www.sightlines-initiative.com
This website outlines Reggio-style approaches in England, and offers a range of information and links to Reggio Children's website.

References

Abbott, L. and Nutbrown, C. (eds) (2001) *Experiencing Reggio Emilia: Implications for Pre-school Provision*. Buckingham: Open University Press.

Alexander, R. (ed.) (2010) *Children, their World, their Education: Final Report and Recommendations of the Cambridge Primary Review*. Abingdon: Routledge.

Allen, R.E. (ed.) (1991) *The Concise Oxford Dictionary of Current English*. London: BCA/Oxford University Press.

Bennett, J. (2004) 'Goals and curricula in early childhood', in S. Kamerman (ed.) *Early Childhood Education and Care: International Perspectives*. The Institute for Child and Family Policy at Columbia University.

Bruce, T. (2005) *Early Childhood Education* (3rd edn). London: Hodder Arnold.

Cable, C., Goodliff, G. and Miller, L. (2007) 'Developing reflective early years practitioners within a regulatory framework', *Malaysian Journal of Distance Education*, 9(2): 1–19.

Clark, A. (2005) 'Ways of seeing: using the Mosaic Approach to listen to young children's perspectives', in A. Clark, A. Kjorholt and P. Moss (eds) *Beyond Listening*. Bristol: Policy Press/The Netherlands: Bernard van Leer Foundation.

Clark, A. (2007) *Early Childhood Spaces: Involving Young Children in the Design Process*. Working Papers in Early Child Development.

Clark, A., Kjorholt, A. and Moss, P. (eds) (2005) *Beyond Listening*. Bristol: Policy Press.

Claxton, G. (1984) 'The psychology of teacher training: inaccuracies and improvements', *Educational Psychology*, 4(2): 167–74.

Conroy, J., Hulme, M. and Menter, I. (2008) *Primary Curriculum Futures: The Primary Review Research Survey* 3/3. University of Cambridge.

Cooper, P. (2009) *The Classroom All Young Children Need: Lessons in Teaching from Vivian Gussin Paley*. Chicago: University of Chicago Press.

Dahlberg, G. (2000) 'Everything is a beginning and everything is dangerous: some reflections of the Reggio Emilia experience', in H. Penn (ed.) *Early Childhood Services: Theory, Policy and Practice*. Buckingham: Open University Press.

Dewey, J. (1897) *My Pedagogic Creed*. Washington, DC: Progressive Education Association.

Donaldson, M. (1976) *Children's Minds*. London: Fontana.

Drummond, M.J. and Jenkinson, S. (2009) *Meeting the Child – Approaches to Observation and Assessment in Steiner Kindergartens*. University of Plymouth.

Fillipini, T. (1995) 'The role of the pedagogista': an interview with Lella Gandini', in C. Edwards, L. Gandini and G. Forman (eds) *The Hundred Languages of Children: The Reggio Emilia Approach to Early Childhood Education*. Norwood, NJ: Ablex Publishing.

Gardner, H. (2006) *Five Minds for the Future*. Boston, MA: Harvard Business School Press.

Greenfield, S. (2004) *Tomorrow's People*. London: Penguin Press.

Healy, J. (1999) *Failure to Connect*. New York: Touchstone.

James, A., Jenks, C. and Prout, A. (1998) *Theorizing Childhood*. Cambridge: Polity Press.

Johnson, S. (ed.) (2010) *Neoconstructivism: The New Science of Cognitive Development*. New York: Oxford University Press Inc.

Kellet, M. (2010) *Rethinking Children and Research: Attitudes in Contemporary Society*. London: Continuum Publishing.

Laevers, F. (2004) 'The curriculum as a means to raise the quality of early childhood education: a critical analysis of the impact of policy', Keynote lecture, European Early Childhood Education Research Association, 14th annual conference, Quality Curricula: The Influence of Research, Policy and Praxis, University of Malta, 1–4 September.

Malaguzzi, L. (1995) 'History, ideas and basic philosophy: an interview with Lella Gandini', in C. Edwards, L. Gandini and G. Forman (eds) *The Hundred Languages of Children: The Reggio Emilia Approach to Early Childhood Education*. Norwood, NJ: Ablex Publishing.

Malaguzzi, L. (1996) *The Hundred Languages of Children*. Reggio Emilia, Italy: Reggio Children.

Mayo, E. and Nairn, A. (2009) *Consumer Kids: How Big Business is Grooming our Kids for Profit*. London: Constable and Robinson Ltd.

Melhuish, E., Quinn, L., McSherry, K., Sylva, K., Sammons, P., Siraj-Blatchford, I., Taggart, B. and Guimares, S. (1999) *Effective Pre-School Provision in Northern Ireland*. Belfast: Stranmillis University College.

Moss, P. (1999) *Difference, Dissenus and Debate: Some Possibilities of Learning from Reggio*. Stockholm: Reggio Emilia Institutet.

Mukherji, P. and Albon, D. (2009) *Research Methods in Early Childhood*. London: Sage.

Nutbrown, C. and Abbott, L. (eds) (2001) 'Experiencing Reggio Emilia', in *Experiencing Reggio Emilia: Implications for Pre-School Provision*. Buckingham: Open University Press.

Nutbrown, C., Clough, P. and Selbie, P. (2008) *Early Childhood Education*. London: Sage.

Pagani, L.S., Fitzpatrick, C. and Barnett, T.A. (2010) 'Prospective associations between early childhood television exposure and academic, psychosocial, and physical well-being by middle childhood', *Archives of Pediatrics and Adolescent Medicine*, 164: 425–31.

Paley, V.G. (2004) *A Child's Work: The Importance of Fantasy Play*. London: University of Chicago Press.

Paley, V.G. (2010) *The Boy on the Beach*. London: University of Chicago Press.

Pound, L. (2000) 'Foundations or formica', paper prepared for BERA Conference, Cardiff, September.

Pound, L. (2005) *How Children Learn*. Leamington Spa: Step Forward Publishing Ltd.

Rinaldi, C. (1995) 'The emergent curriculum and social constructivism: an interview with Lella Gandini', in C. Edwards, L. Gandini and G. Forman (eds) *The Hundred Languages of Children: The Reggio Emilia Approach to Early Childhood Education*. Norwood, NJ: Ablex Publishing.

Rogoff, B. (1990) *Apprenticeship in Thinking*. Oxford: Oxford University Press.

Rouse, D. (1991) *The Italian Experience*. London: National Children's Bureau.

Schon, D. (1983) *The Reflective Practitioner: How Professionals Think in Action*. London: Temple Smith.

Schweinhart, L.J., Montie, J., Xiang, Z., Barnett, W.S., Belfield, C.R. and Nores, M. (2005) *Lifetime Effects: The HighScope Perry Preschool Study through Age 40*. Ypsilanti, MI: HighScope Press.

Soler, J. and Miller, L. (2003) 'The struggle for early childhood curricula: a comparison of the English Foundation Stage Curriculum, Te Whaariki and Reggio Emilia', special New Zealand edition of the *International Journal of Early Years Education*, 11(1): 53–64.

Steiner Waldorf Education (2009) *Guide to the Early Years Foundation Stage in Steiner Waldorf Early Childhood Settings*. Forest Row, East Sussex: The Association of Steiner Waldorf Schools.

Sylva, K., Melhuish, E., Sammons, P., Siraj-Blatchford, I. and Taggart, B. (2004) *The Effective Provision of Pre-school Education (EPPE) Project: The Final Report*. London: DfES/ Institute of Education, University of London.

Vecchi, V. (1995) 'The role of the atelierista: an interview with Lella Gandini', in C. Edwards, L. Gandini and G. Forman (eds) *The Hundred Languages of Children: The Reggio Emilia Approach to Early Childhood Education*. Norwood, NJ: Ablex Publishing.

Wenger, E. (2010) 'Communities of practice: a brief introduction', http://www.ewenger.com/theory/index.htm (accessed 24 April 2010).

PART 1

THEORETICAL AND ANALYTICAL POSITIONS

CHAPTER 2

NOT JUST THE TIP OF THE ICEBERG: PSYCHOANALYTIC IDEAS AND EARLY YEARS PRACTICE

Julia Manning-Morton

Overview

This chapter aims to explore the impact of psychoanalytical ideas on our approaches to the care and learning of babies and young children in early years settings. In it, I suggest that psychoanalytic ideas have permeated early years practice in ways that we often do not acknowledge or have knowledge of. There are strong links between the fields of psychoanalysis and early years care and education, in both theory and practice, but there is little explicit learning about psychoanalytic theories in the training of early years practitioners and most books in the field give little more than a basic account of Freud's theories of the structure of the mind and stages of personality development and some discussion of attachment theory. It seems that in this respect the early years field mirrors the historical emphasis that developmental psychology has given to the study of cognitive rather than socio-emotional development (Damasio, 1999; Dunn, 1999: 56). However, if we truly wish to develop a holistic approach

(Continued)

(Continued)

and view of children, early years practitioners need to learn about all kinds of theories of development and learning, so in this chapter I will identify some of the links that exist between developmental psychology, developmental neuroscience and psychoanalytic theory. Space does not permit a full explanation of this complex theoretical discipline so the chapter will focus on the most pertinent ideas such as defence mechanisms and the dynamics of relationships. Another factor to consider is that the focus in psychoanalytic theory is on what is underneath our everyday thoughts and behaviours. Freud suggested that our minds are like an iceberg with our motivations, conflicts and desires lying 70% below the surface (Stevenson and Haberman, 2004). This means that studying these ideas entails having to reflect on our own inner lives, which may be uncomfortable. In this chapter, I suggest that in order to better understand children we need to also develop our self-awareness, so need to look beyond the tip of the iceberg.

Psychoanalytical ideas and the formative impact of early childhood

Psychoanalytic ideas are embedded in the culture of the industrially developed world, including in relation to the development and care of children. Many ideas from psychoanalytic theory have seeped into our everyday language and thought, like 'avoidance', 'denial' and 'ego', even if their precise meanings are obscured by technical language. Yet, in the Literature Review to support *Birth to Three Matters*, David et al. (2003: 41) say that 'psychoanalysis has never appeared to have greatly influenced Early Childhood Education and Care (ECEC) in Britain', beyond drawing attention to the importance of early life and its impact on later interactions and well-being. Yet psychoanalytic theory has done far more than 'draw attention', it has hugely influenced this idea of a causal link between early experience and later life. The idea that features of a healthy adult psychology such as a secure sense of self, the capacity for intimacy and a balanced emotional life (or their unhealthy opposites) have their roots in early mental life is based on Freud's theory that personality is shaped by the person's childhood experiences, before which many aspects of personality were ascribed to physical causes (Bateman and Holmes, 1995). This concept underpins many of the values and principles that support early years practice and is the idea that is at the centre of most practitioners' motivation to work with young children; we want to give children positive experiences to support their development into well-adjusted adults. The growth of psychoanalytic ideas that have emphasized the fact that babies and young children do have an inner life, which is important for future outcomes, changed the view of the emotional life of children in the first half of the 20th century (Goleman, 1996).

The unconscious mind

Another central psychoanalytic concept that has become accepted into our thinking is that of the unconscious. Freud proposed that the mind can be divided into different levels of consciousness: the conscious, pre-conscious and the unconscious, where humans send knowledge about aspects of their lives that they either do not need or don't want to remain conscious (Freud, 1974). So the unconscious will contain repressed experiences that are too painful or uncomfortable to remain in our conscious minds and also holds sublimated (redirected) thoughts that are otherwise socially unacceptable. In the same way that the purpose of assimilation and accommodation of new experiences is to maintain mental equilibrium (Piaget, 1962), so too does the repression of negative feelings into the unconscious enable the ego (the self) to maintain psychic equilibrium. Without this mechanism, the mind would be unable to deal with the emotions arising from painful or uncomfortable external events that would threaten to overwhelm it (Bateman and Holmes, 1995).

From the concept of the unconscious arises the idea that behaviour has meaning that can be traced to psychological factors of which the person may be totally unaware. The influence of this idea on early years practice can be seen in attempts by practitioners to understand the underlying causes of difficult behaviour. This might sometimes be through specific interventions such as play therapy sessions (Cattanach, 2003) but is more generally manifested through practices such as developing positive relationships with parents in order to better understand children's emotional contexts.

Piaget (1973) referred to sensorimotor thinking, when we do things without thinking about them, as 'the cognitive unconscious', in an attempt to make a link to the psychoanalytic model of 'the affective unconscious'. This still reflects a dualist model of separate cognitive and affective domains; yet current neuroscientific thinking suggests that these processes are not separate but inextricably entwined (Damasio, 1999). In addition, as my later discussion of object relations theory shows, we also internalize the processes of our social relationships, which often emerge unexpectedly in our later close relationships (Bateman and Holmes, 1995). In order to keep these unwanted feelings and thoughts in the unconscious, we use psychological defence mechanisms, although our pre-conscious minds can also allow some expression of past processes.

Defence mechanisms

Defences are unconscious psychological configurations that play a central role in dealing with anxiety and thereby help us to maintain psychic equilibrium (Bateman and Holmes, 1995). There are several different defence mechanisms, some of which are coping mechanisms that can be developmentally necessary, as they operate like a protective shield when the outside world fails us in some way. Such mechanisms exist in all of us and will emerge in stressful situations, even in psychologically healthy people. Sublimation, the redirection of unacceptable wishes and feelings into other pursuits like art or sport, and the use of humour are thought to be mature defences, as they allow partial expression of unwanted wishes and feelings in socially acceptable ways (Bateman and Holmes, 1995).

But defences can also become a hindrance to healthy development, for example the extensive use of repression of difficult feelings in later life can lead to the separation of whole areas of emotional life from the conscious mind. In early childhood practice, this means that psychological defences against unpleasant or difficult unconscious memories and feelings in practitioners can prevent empathetic responsiveness to children's needs. Because recognizing those feelings would be too painful, they are avoided by denying or minimizing children's negative emotions and difficult experiences. Managers can also avoid difficulties in staff teams, manifested in phrases such as 'we all get along well here'!

Such a picture of an unresponsive early years practitioner will appear at odds with the image of someone in a caring profession whose aim (presumably) is to help others and do good in society. But sometimes we can adopt a psychological attitude that is the opposite of our conscious concept of self as a defence against acknowledging our true wishes. An example of this that is particularly pertinent to early years practitioners, is caring for others when one really wishes to be cared for oneself. In psychoanalysis, this defence is called 'reactive formation' and can become a generalized character trait (Bateman and Holmes, 1995).

In their study of a daycare setting in the late 1970s, Bain and Barnett (1986) identified that the early personal experiences of some practitioners, such as unresolved issues of early separation or lack of love and attention, influenced their choice of career as a possible means to fulfil previously unmet needs. They suggest that as a result, as well as deriving gratification from supporting children and families, practitioners may also unconsciously feel angry and resentful if their own needs are not met in a situation, as depicted in Table 2.1.

Table 2.1   The positive and negative feelings that can arise when caring for young children

When a child is ...	When a child is ...
happy and settled and affectionate	distressed, dependant and defiant
sociable and co-operative	rejecting and aggressive
achieving the learning goals	finding learning difficult
When ...	**When ...**
teams are communicating clearly and responding positively to innovation	practitioners sabotage our plans
parents are involved and supportive	parents criticize our provision
We feel ...	**We feel ...**
pleased, satisfied and professionally competent	angry, resentful and professionally frustrated or failing

(Manning-Morton, 2006; Manning-Morton and Thorp, 2003)

The problem here is not that the negative feelings identified in the right-hand column of Table 2.1 occur but that they are denied and repressed, either because they do not fit with our conscious public image of ourselves or because the culture of the setting considers having these emotions as a professional weakness. In this situation, defences against these difficult feelings can lead practitioners to project their negative feelings onto children, parents, managers or co-workers.

Projection as a defence against anxiety

The idea of projection comes from Melanie Klein's ideas about the mental operations of babies and young children. In Klein's theory, the internal world of the infant is populated by the self, its objects and the relations between them (Anderson, 1992). 'Objects' in this context are the mother or primary caregiver. Klein believed that very young babies do not have a concept of a whole object but only images in their minds of part objects. She developed the idea of splitting to explain how an infant will defend themselves against the anxiety that arises from internal feelings of disintegration by dividing objects into good and bad part objects. When good experiences are projected, the carer is idealized but experiences and feelings that feel bad, such as frustration in feeding or anger at the object's absence, are also split off and projected onto the carer, who is then felt to be threatening (Bateman and Holmes, 1995).

Klein's concepts of infants having feelings of annihilation and hate may sound outlandish to many early years practitioners. However, acknowledging this possibility allows us to see the complexity of babies and young children's emotional lives and can help us perhaps to understand that sometimes if a young child tells us they don't like us, or a baby rejects us in favour of a co-worker, this may be arising from an unconscious feeling that the child is experiencing as threatening to their well-being. When a child is angry with their carer, they will see them as all bad and then ally themselves with another, whom they perceive at that time to be all good. But the child's developmental task is to gradually realize that the 'good' mother and the 'bad' mother are the same person and to let go of the idea of an 'ideal' mother (Segal, 2004).

From this perspective, Susan Isaacs argued that if a child is in a setting where there is inadequate care, 'this does not mean to him the mere absence of the good he requires, a merely neutral place; it means the actual presence of positive evil' (Isaacs, 1970: 218). The implications of this statement for the need to continually strive for high standards of responsive care in settings is clear and in this particular type of scenario, the task for practitioners is to remain constant in the face of a child's anger and hate and maintain an adult caring approach. A practitioner who responds in a child-like and angry way saying 'that's not nice' or 'well, I don't like you then' is confirming to the child that their negative feelings are indeed to be feared because here is proof that they have the power to destroy the goodness of the relationship that existed before. In light of this, it seems imperative that truly professional early years practitioners and managers are able to bring a maturity of self-awareness to their job (Manning-Morton, 2006). In so doing, practitioners may be able to use their own early experiences to perhaps better understand and empathize with children's difficulties and distress rather than denying or minimizing them. This kind of personal reflection is sometimes derided as self-obsessed 'navel gazing' that is ultimately selfish. Yet if such reflection results in an understanding of self that leads to healthier relationships and a better understanding of others, surely that is positive.

Psychoanalytic theory and personal development

Psychoanalytic theory is essentially concerned with the development of the self; how we become who we are, with different strands of the discipline having different concepts and emphases. Freud set out his concept of personality development in stages but also proposed a structure of the self with three aspects: the id, the ego and the superego (Bateman and Holmes, 1995). The id is a fixed aspect of our personality and is often depicted as a kind of swirling mass of needs, wants and desires. In this state, Freud believed that infants have no separate identity but feel themselves to be merged with their primary carer. The idea of such an indistinct sense of self is now at odds with the ideas emerging from developmental neuroscience, which suggest that babies have an ability to imitate adult gestures such as tongue protrusion at birth, implying that from the first day of life babies have the beginnings of a sense of self (Meltzoff and Moore, 1983). However, it has to be recognized that this early understanding of self is just a small first step on a long road of developing personality and becoming self-aware.

As the child interacts more and more with the world, reality impacts on the desires of the id and the second part of the personality begins to develop, which Freud called the ego. The ego reconciles the instinctual demands and drives of the id with the internalized social and cultural rules that constitute the superego (Bateman and Holmes, 1995). In object-relations theory, ego development occurs through a process of (mental) separation, in which children differentiate themselves from their carer and individuation in which they start to establish their own personality traits (Bateman and Holmes, 1995).

In psychoanalytic theory, a key aspect of healthy development is when the ego understands that other people have needs and desires and that gratification of desires can be delayed. Understanding others is also seen as a positive ability in developmental psychology, in areas such as 'theory of mind' or 'social referencing' (Schaffer, 2006), which, in psychoanalytic terms, would be identified as young children paying early attention to the superego. In developmental psychology, children's ability to delay gratification is also seen as an indication of both social adaptation and future academic achievement. Eliot (1999) describes an experiment in which 4-year-olds were given a choice of one marshmallow, which they could eat at once, or two if they could wait 15 minutes. Those who did manage to hold on were the ones who in the long-term study achieved greater academic and social success. In psychoanalytic terms, this ability to accept the id's desire to eat the sweet but also to recognize the benefit of waiting and getting more, would be interpreted as a mature ego, an essential element of good mental health.

For the French psychoanalyst Lacan, individuation begins in the 'mirror stage', in which the child begins to distinguish between self and other (Homer, 2005). In this stage, the child finds an image of itself reflected in a 'mirror' of other people and their sense of self is built up through making identifications with these images (Homer, 2005).

Developmental psychology uses similar terminology to Lacan but more in relation to the external manifestations of personal development rather than the internal processes explained in psychoanalysis. An example of this is the 'looking glass self' (Schaffer, 2006), which has some links to Lacan's 'mirror' stage as it describes children's developing awareness of who they are in relation to their sex, ethnicity and position in their family. In this process, children are presented with ideas or 'images' from various sources but principally from their parents, of what a person of this age, sex, ethnicity, etc. 'ought' to be like. If this image is not congruent with their internal conception of who they feel they are, it can result in an impaired sense of self. For Klein, a fragmented sense of self comes from the internal panic and confusion that arises from bodily processes, or from discrepancies between feeling states and responses, which leads to a 'not me' state (Segal, 2004); while Winnicott developed the theory that when an infant's self is threatened in this way, a protective 'false self' develops (Winnicott, 1965).

Winnicott (1960) saw a stable sense of self arising out of maternal responsiveness and developed the idea of the 'good enough' mother (1965). A sensitive mother adapts almost completely to the baby, giving it a sense of being connected with her. This 'holding environment' allows the infant to pass to a state of greater autonomy at its own pace. Gradually, the mother adapts less completely but in tune with the infant's growing ability to deal with this, thereby allowing 'optimal disillusionment' (Winnicott, 2005: 17). This does not mean, for example, callously ignoring a baby, but allows for situations such as a feed not being quite ready when a child is hungry. This leads to a sense of 'ordinary specialness' (Kohut, 1977, cited in Bateman and Holmes, 1995), whereby a child who usually experiences consistent and prompt responses to their needs, can remain confident in the face of small instances of 'maternal failure' (Winnicott, 2005).

Related to this idea is Winnicott's concept of having an optimal amount of 'self-doubt' (1960). While too much self-doubt can cause withdrawal and a reluctance to take risks, children who have been helped to move towards autonomy at their own pace will not only have confidence in their abilities but a real sense of their limitations in any one situation. Such children will have a positive attitude to the everyday challenges of life, while those with too little self-doubt may assume they can do everything and be unprepared to deal with failure and setbacks.

In early years practice, we are careful to offer children play opportunities that are a close match to their abilities but that also offer a degree of challenge within their 'zone of proximal development' (Vygotsky, 1978), in order for children to have not only repeated experiences of success but also occasional experiences of manageable failure. But, unfortunately, it is far too often the case that the organization of groups for babies and young children do not also offer experiences that are within their zone of emotional development. Large group sizes, low staff:child ratios and institutionalized routines can impose experiences of disillusionment that many infants are not ready for. Therefore, the emphasis for early years practitioners must be on how to provide that 'holding environment' in the close relationships we develop with children.

Psychoanalytic theory and social interactions

The idea that the psychological life of the human being is created in and through relations with other human beings is the basis of object relations theory (Anderson, 1992). Melanie Klein emphasized the inner psychic structure of the infant, especially the part played by the child's 'phantasies', their unconscious representations of interactions, in personality development (Bateman and Holmes, 1995), whereas other object relations theorists such as Bion and Winnicott emphasized that the determining influence on a child's personality is their *actual* experiences of feeding and holding. These experiences then create internal representations of the relationship. The emphasis on early mother–child interactions in this perspective are encapsulated by Winnicott's phrase 'there is no such thing as a baby, only a mother and a baby' (Winnicott, 1965: 39).

The psychoanalysts writing and working within this school of thought have been very influential on early years practice and provision, both in terms of constructing a 'facilitating environment' (Winnicott, 1965) and in terms of influencing early childhood policy development. Examples of this include policies that limit the provision of early years care and education settings by the state and therefore women's equal access to employment (see e.g. Riley, 1983; Scarr, 1984).

At the micro level within settings, paying attention to the physical and psychological interactions between children and practitioners is crucial. In psychodynamic terms, the internal representations of these relationships act as templates for subsequent relationships, so babies and young children who have repeated negative experiences develop an 'attachment behavioural system' or 'blueprint' (Holmes, 1993) in which they are learning to expect little from close relationships and think little of themselves. In contrast, babies who have repeated experiences of loving responses to their signals develop a positive, worthy 'internal working model' (Bowlby, 1988) of themselves and relationships (Lieberman, 1993). Schore (2001), who has made extensive links between neuroscience and psychoanalytical theory, identifies that Bowlby's 'internal working models' are stored in the limbic system in the brain, which is crucial for the organization of new learning and the ability to adapt; while Mayes et al. (2007) suggest that the concept of an internal working model is explicitly linked to the model of schema in cognitive science.

There are three key ideas from the object relations school of psychoanalytic theory that can support early childhood practitioners in maximizing the potential for children to develop positive internal working models of relationships: containment (Bion, 1962); affect attunement (Stern, 1998); and attachment (Bowlby, 1969).

Containment

Bion developed the psychoanalytical concept of containment, in which a mother mentally and emotionally contains an infant's projected feelings of distress and discomfort, which would otherwise be too much for the baby to bear on their own (Shuttleworth, 1989: 28). When this is a positive containing process, the adult is able to perceive the baby's state and get a feeling for what they really need and the baby experiences being 'kept in mind' and emotionally 'held'. Through anticipating and sensitively responding to her child through touch, proximity and voice tone, the mother not only 'holds' the child's anxiety but also transforms it. Bion describes this as a kind of detoxifying process that allows the baby to get back their good feelings of being held and understood (Bion, 1962, cited in Bateman and Holmes, 1995). This enables the child to think about and make sense of their experience and eventually to manage their anxiety more on their own.

Affect attunement

The concept of 'affect attunement' (Stern, 1998) is similar to containment. It is the process whereby an adult sensitively reads the non-verbal signals of an infant and is then able to align their state of mind with the child to engage with them in the way they need, mirroring the child's inner state with their behaviours and vocalizations. The child experiences this as 'feeling felt' and 'being understood' (Siegel, 1999: 70). Siegel also suggests that in secure attachment relationships, this 'collaborative, contingent communication' (Siegel, 1999: 117) is the fundamental way in which minds connect with each other in order for the child to develop psychological resilience and emotional well-being.

Attachment

For John Bowlby, a child developing a secure attachment relationship with their primary caregiver is fundamental to their mental health and future ability to develop stable relationships (Bowlby, 1969). This is fundamentally an emotional process but, like Winnicott (1965) who sees a stable sense of self arising out of parental 'handling', which leads to a sense in both the mind and body of being a person, Bowlby also recognizes communications arising from gaze and touch between the adult and child as fundamental aspects of attachment processes. Bowlby suggests that the framework for mother–infant attachment communications is the co-ordination of 'care seeking' and 'care giving' (1988: 121). Care seeking is seen in behaviour that results in a child attaining or retaining proximity to a preferred individual and is a key feature of an attachment relationship (Holmes, 1993). Care giving is complementary to this attachment behaviour (Bowlby, 1988) and is focused on maintaining the equilibrium of the relationship through being caring, sensitive, available and responsive, thereby enabling a secure attachment (Bowlby, 1969).

The key person approach in early years settings

These three concepts are made manifest in early years practice through the effective implementation of the key person approach, which emphasizes developing close relationships between key practitioners and children (Elfer et al., 2003; Grenier et al., 2008; Manning-Morton and Thorp, 2003, 2006). Practitioners can support children's emotional well-being in these relationships through:

- being physically and emotionally available, thereby providing for the child's need for 'care seeking' and 'care giving' and also providing a secure base for the child to go out from to explore their surroundings
- being sensitively responsive and supportive to children's emotional expressions, thereby offering 'containment' for children and exhibiting 'attunement'
- being consistent in the physical and emotional care of children through key persons undertaking routine physical care whenever possible, thereby not only supporting attachment relationships but also supporting children in developing an integrated sense of self.

Although the concept of the key person approach may only recently have come to some practitioners' attention through the Early Years Foundation Stage document (DfES, 2007), it is not new. In the setting up of the Hampstead Nursery during World War Two, Anna Freud (Sigmund Freud's daughter) allocated a constant 'maternal figure' to each child, in order to give them the opportunity to form attachments by providing continuity of relationships. She pre-empted later research when she suggested that:

> A child who forms this kind of relationship to a grown up not only becomes amenable to educational influence in a very welcome manner, but shows more vivid and varied facial expressions, develops individual qualities, and unfolds his whole personality in a surprising way. (Burlingham and Freud, 1944: 57)

Susan Isaacs decried the 'emotionally barren life in an institution' (1970) and proposed a structure of small family groups in settings; a view and approach repeated in Bain and Barnett's introduction of 'case assignment' in a day nursery in the 1970s.

We have psychoanalytic theory to thank not only for the concept of the key person approach but also for a way of understanding the barriers that inhibit its full and positive implementation. Although the key person approach is now required practice in early years settings (DfES, 2007), practitioners frequently avoid building close relationships with the children in their care as a psychological defence against the emotional demands made on them by very young children's high level of emotional and physical needs (Elfer et al., 2003; Manning-Morton, 2006). This is particularly the case when a caregiver is preoccupied by her own difficult emotional states, leaving little mental space in which to think about the child.

Separation and transitional objects

Children's distress on separation from an attachment figure is a particularly disturbing experience for children and therefore also for practitioners. The work of Bowlby and the Robertsons' films (Robertson, 1953) on separation and loss help us to recognize the process of grief, including anger, despair and denial (Holmes, 1993) that children go through at these times. Awareness of these perspectives can help to lessen practitioners' defensiveness and denial of children's distress and has led to the development of child-centred settling in and transition processes (Manning-Morton and Thorp, 2006).These would include ensuring that children have access to their particular comfort object. Winnicott calls these 'transitional phenomena or objects' (Winnicott, 2005), which represent for the child the stage of transition from feeling merged with their mother to seeing her as separate. This object is imbued with 'motherness' and helps the child to recall a sense of comfort and security at times of stress. Winnicott also sees transitional objects as the beginning of the infant's creativity and therefore the beginning of a child's ability to play (Winnicott, 2005).

Psychoanalytic theory and creativity and play

Play and creativity may not be the first aspects of early years practice we think of when considering the impact of psychoanalytic theory, yet it is an area where psychoanalytic ideas have had considerable influence. Freud saw play as an activity in which children's impulses, which could be too dangerous to express in reality, could be worked through. So from a psychoanalytic perspective, play has a role in enabling children to explore their inner troubles and concerns, and to express or work through anxieties (O'Connor, 2000). This view of play is apparent in early years practice when we provide clay to pummel or dolls for a child with a new sibling. In a more formal play therapy session, the child's play is self-directed and takes place within a protected, uninterrupted time and space, with the non-directive but full reflective attention of the adult, similar to the process in adult psychoanalysis but with 'free play' taking the place of 'free association' (Cattanach, 2003).

It was Melanie Klein who first devised this method of play therapy, arising from her view of play as being a child's talk. Klein observed, listened to and took seriously the anxieties of very young children, being the first to recognize the unconscious processes contained in children's play (Segal, 1979). She suggested that children express their phantasies, wishes and actual experiences in a symbolic way through play and games (Segal, 1979). Symbolization through the use of books is just one example of early childhood practice that supports young children's understanding of the world, including their inner world. It was Bruno Bettelheim (1976) who identified the themes in traditional fairy stories that relate to aspects of development as explained by psychoanalytic theory, thereby developing our understanding of the power of books and stories to facilitate children's emotional growth. Practitioners today understand the power of texts such as 'Owl Babies' (Waddell, 1994) or 'Not Now Bernard' (McKee, 1984), in helping very young children to start to understand and begin to manage their feelings.

Klein suggested that an infant's phantasizing precedes the 'workings of the imagination' (Klein, 1937, cited in Steiner, 2003: 37). More recently, Segal (1991) has suggested that there is a direct link between early phantasies and adult imagination, both in everyday life and in artistic creation. Winnicott saw creativity arising from a good enough mother–infant relationship, whereby when the good enough mother presents a baby with what they need at that moment, the baby feels they have made the object themselves, which leads to the healthy development of a creative and playful self (Bateman and Holmes, 1995). For Winnicott, it is only in play that children and adults are able to be creative, not in the sense of producing works of art but in terms of being able to use the whole of our personality in discovering the self (Winnicott, 2005).

Observation

As psychoanalytically trained teachers, Anna Freud and Susan Isaacs were among the first practitioners to integrate these ideas into their educational practices. A key aspect of their practice was the frequent and regular keeping of observations of the children in their settings. Anna Freud and her colleagues collected thousands of observations as part of their training processes in the nurseries that she set up. Isaacs would observe alongside the teachers at her school and would then use her psychoanalytic training to support them in developing a better understanding of children (Graham, 2009).

This practice of using observation as a training tool has continued in the training of psychotherapists as the primary means by which they come to understand the inner life of children. In the 'Infant Observation Technique', a student observes a child weekly from birth for a period of a year (or sometimes now a 1–2 year-old too). Unlike observations undertaken in early years settings, during the hour-long visit to the child's house, the observer does not take any notes. Instead they are simply 'there', taking in everything that they see. Then, as soon they can afterwards, the observer writes up their observation in as much detail as possible. It might be thought that important detail is lost this way, but what is retained are the observer's feelings about what is observed as well as the incidents that resonate most in the observer's mind. These are then explored in a weekly seminar group, which helps the observer to understand what they have observed and also to not become too overwhelmed by any feelings transferred on to them during the visit because the group 'contains' the observer's emotional response; a practice that could usefully be adapted for use in early years settings (Miller et al., 1989).

Critique

There is insufficient space to critique all the ideas and concepts addressed in this chapter. However, as I have already noted, a common critique of psychoanalytic theory by sociologists is that the focus on the individual's inner world ignores their social and cultural context (Klin and Jones, 2007). A response to this is that we also have a 'social-affective unconscious' that consists of internalized experiences of other people and their actions.

Another criticism relates to Freud who set out his concept of personality development in stages of what he termed 'psychosexual development' (Bateman and Holmes, 1995; Crain, 1992). These ideas have been criticized both in terms of the limitations of stage theory (much like criticisms of Piaget's stage theory) and also in feminist terms, as his idea of mature development has a gender bias in favour of the masculine. These concepts and criticisms are well documented elsewhere (see e.g. Mitchell, 1974). It is also important to emphasize that 'sexual' in this context does not equate to adult sexuality but, for Freud, meant anything that produces bodily pleasure.

Feminist theory has also provided a critique of attachment theory, suggesting that it poses a biologically determinist and culturally specific view of the social roles of parenting (Singer, 1998) and that the effect of these views on policy development has been to limit the provision of early years care and education settings by the state and therefore women's equal access to employment (see e.g. Riley, 1983; Scarr, 1984).

Final thoughts

The explorations of psychoanalytic theories in this chapter show that the influence on early childhood provision is both widespread and deeply embedded in a wide range of practices. There are aspects of psychoanalytic theory, such as the concept of the unconscious, that have become so integral to our way of thinking that the impact on early years practice is diffuse and intangible at times. Other theories have had a direct effect on practice, such as the influence of attachment theory on the development of the key person approach (Elfer et al., 2003). It is interesting to note that some concepts such as this have moved more to the forefront in recent times, while other influences such as Klein's or Winnicott's views on play, have become less a part of mainstream practice.

This (hard won) recognition of the importance of relationships in early years practice and policy might reflect a resurgence of emphasis on children's personal, social and emotional well-being in early childhood, realigning early years with psychoanalytic theory, which has always sought to 'understand the human concern with relationships and our capacities for resilience across life or vulnerability to hardships' (Mayes et al., 2007: 3). Such a renewed concern with children's mental and emotional well-being may help to redress the balance of approach in early years practice and enable us to develop a holistic understanding of babies and young children. An extended knowledge and understanding of key psychoanalytic theories in our professional development would seem to be necessary for this. As I have discussed elsewhere (Manning-Morton, 2006), crossing the boundaries of professional disciplines is a key feature of being an early years professional and so understanding the links between psychoanalytic theory, developmental psychology and developmental neuroscience, as have been indicated in this chapter, would seem to be necessary to our professionalism. Not only would this enable a more holistic understanding of children, it would also greatly support the level of integrated working across professional boundaries that is currently a feature of much early childhood provision in the UK.

However, to do this effectively would mean not only understanding some psychoanalytic theories but also adopting some of the practices of the psychoanalytic tradition. In order to effectively support children's emotional well-being and develop the kind of relationships that psychoanalytic theory would suggest are necessary for children's healthy psychological development, practitioners need opportunities for developing self-awareness and reflexive practice, such as regular support and supervision. Without this, we will continue to only explore the tip of the developmental iceberg.

 Summary

- This chapter has explored aspects of psychoanalytic theory that have directly and indirectly impacted on early years practice and provision.
- It has particularly highlighted psychoanalytic concepts such as the unconscious and defence mechanisms that can help early years practitioners to develop their understanding, not only of children but also of themselves in their practice.

 Questions for discussion

1. In what ways can psychoanalytic theory support your understanding of children's development?
2. To which aspects of practice do you think psychoanalytic theory is the most relevant?
3. What do you think is a manager or leader's role in addressing the responses of practitioners to children's emotional needs? How might you/they go about this?
4. Some writers from a postmodernist perspective, such as Dahlberg et al. (2007) suggest that close relationships with a key person restrict children's creativity and relationships with others. How do you think a psychoanalytical perspective would counteract this view? (*Higher level question*)

Further reading

Levels 5 and 6

Crain, W. (1992) *Theories of Development: Concepts and Applications*. Englewood Cliffs, NJ: Prentice-Hall.
Although not very new, this is one of the few child development books that explores a slightly broader range of psychoanalytic theories alongside other theories of development.

Elfer, P. (2006) 'Babies and young children in nurseries: using psychoanalytic ideas to explore tasks and interactions', *Children & Society*, 21(2): 111–22.

Holmes, J. (1993) *John Bowlby and Attachment Theory*. London: Routledge.
This is a very thorough, yet clear and accessible exploration of attachment theory. It gives an account of the historical and social context of the evolution of this theory as well as an in-depth explanation of the concepts and critiques of the theory.

Levels 6 and 7

Bateman, A. and Holmes, J. (1995) *An Introduction to Psychoanalysis: Contemporary Theory and Practice*. London: Routledge.
This book gives in-depth explanations of a full range of psychoanalytic theories but is still accessible for the lay reader.

Manning-Morton, J. (2006) 'The personal is professional: professionalism and the birth to threes practitioner', *Contemporary Issues in Early Childhood*, 7(1): 42–52.

Miller, L., Rustin, M., Rustin, M. and Shuttleworth, J. (eds) (1989) *Closely Observed Infants*. London: Duckworth.
This book sets out the Tavistock approach to observation. As well as examples and an outline of the method, it explains the related theoretical concepts.

Websites

www.intute.ac.uk
It is very hard to recommend a website that is academically valid but still has relevant and accessible information for early childhood practitioners, but this site gives useful links to other sites.

www.p-e-p.org
The Psychoanalytic Electronic Publishing Website and Digital Archive, PEP, is a digital archive of many of the major works of psychoanalysis.

References

Anderson, R. (ed.) (1992) *Clinical Lectures on Klein and Bion*. London: Routledge.
Bain, A. and Barnett, L. (1986) *The Design of a Day Care System in a Nursery Setting for Children Under Five*. Tavistock Institute Occasional Paper No. 8. London: Tavistock Institute.
Bateman, A. and Holmes, J. (1995) *An Introduction to Psychoanalysis: Contemporary Theory and Practice*. London: Routledge.
Bettelheim, B. (1976) *The Uses of Enchantment: The Meaning and Importance of Fairy Tales*. Harmondsworth: Penguin.
Bion, W.R. (1962) *Learning from Experience*. London: Karnac Books.
Bowlby, J. (1969) *Attachment and Loss. Vol.1: Attachment*. London: Hogarth.
Bowlby, J. (1988) *A Secure Base: Clinical Applications of Attachment Theory*. London: Routledge.
Burlingham, D. and Freud, A. (1944) *Infants Without Families: The Case For and Against Residential Nurseries*. New York: International University Press.
Cattanach, A. (2003) *Introduction to Play Therapy*. East Sussex: Brunner-Routledge.

Crain, W. (1992) *Theories of Development: Concepts and Applications*. Englewood Cliffs, NJ: Prentice-Hall.

Dahlberg, G., Moss, P. and Pence, A. (2007) *Beyond Quality in Early Childhood Education and Care: Languages of Evaluation* (2nd edn). Oxon: Routledge.

Damasio, A.R. (1999) *The Feeling of What Happens: Body and Emotion in the Making of Consciousness*. New York: Harcourt.

David, T., Gooch, K., Powell, S. and Abbott, L. (2003) *Birth to Three Matters: A Review of the Literature*. Nottingham: DfES Publications.

Department for Education and Skills (DfES) (2007) *The Early Years Foundation Stage: Setting the Standards for Learning, Development and Care for Children from Birth to Five*. Nottingham: DfES/HMSO.

Dunn, J. (1999) 'Mindreading and social relationships', in M Bennett (ed.) *Developmental Psychology*. London: Taylor and Francis. pp. 55–71.

Elfer, P., Goldschmied, E. and Selleck, D. (2003) *Key Persons in the Nursery: Building Relationships for Quality Provision*. London: David Fulton.

Eliot, L. (1999) *Early Intelligence: How the Brain and Mind Develop in the First Five Years of Life*. London: Penguin.

Freud, S. (1974) *Introductory Lectures on Psychoanalysis*. London: Pelican Books.

Goleman, D. (1996) *Emotional Intelligence: Why it Can Matter More than IQ*. London: Bloomsbury Publishing.

Graham, P. (2009) *Susan Isaacs: A Life Freeing the Minds of Children*. London: Karnac Books.

Grenier, J., Manning-Morton, J., Elfer, P., Dearnley, K. and Wilson, D. (2008) *The Key Person in Reception Classes and Small Nursery Settings, Social and Emotional Aspects of Development: Guidance for Practitioners Working in the Early Years Foundation Stage*. London: DCSF.

Holmes, J. (1993) *John Bowlby and Attachment Theory*. London: Routledge.

Homer, S. (2005) *Jacques Lacan*. Abingdon, Oxon: Routledge.

Isaacs, S. (1970) *Childhood and After: Some Essays and Clinical Studies*. New York: Agathon Press.

Klein, M. (1937) *Love, Guilt and Reparation*, in M. Klein (1975) *The Writings of Melanie Klein*, Vol. 1. London: Hogarth Press and The Institute of Psycho-analysis.

Klin, A. and Jones, W. (2007) 'Embodied psychoanalysis?', in L. Mayes, P. Fonagy and M. Target (eds) *Developmental Science and Psychoanalysis: Integration and Innovation*. London: Karnac.

Kohut, H. (1977) *The Restoration of the Self*. New York: International Universities Press.

Lieberman, A.F. (1993) *The Emotional Life of a Toddler*. New York: Free Press.

Manning-Morton, J. (2006) 'The personal is professional: professionalism and the birth to threes practitioner', *Contemporary Issues in Early Childhood*, 7(1): 42–52.

Manning-Morton, J. and Thorp, M. (2003) *Key Times for Play: The First Three Years*. Maidenhead: Open University Press.

Manning-Morton, J. and Thorp, M. (2006) *Key Times: Developing High Quality Provision for Children from Birth to Three Years*. Maidenhead: Open University Press.

Mayes, L., Fonagy, P. and Target, M. (2007) *Developmental Science and Psychoanalysis: Integration and Innovation*. London: Karnac.

McKee, D. (1984) *Not Now, Bernard*. London: Red Fox.

Meltzoff, A.N. and Moore, M.K. (1983) 'Newborn infants imitate adult facial gestures', *Child Development*, 54: 702–9.

Miller, L., Rustin, M., Rustin, M. and Shuttleworth, J. (eds) (1989) *Closely Observed Infants*. London: Duckworth.

Mitchell, J. (1974) *Psychoanalysis and Feminism*. New York: Random House.

O'Connor, K.J. (2000) *The Play Therapy Primer*. New York: John Wiley & Sons.

Piaget, J. (1962) *Play, Dreams and Imitation in Childhood*. London: Routledge and Kegan Paul.

Piaget, J. (1973) 'The affective unconscious and the cognitive unconscious', *Journal of the American Psychoanalytic Association*, 21(2): 249–61.

Riley, D. (1983) *War in the Nursery: Theories of the Child and Mother*. London: Virago.

Robertson, J. (1953) *A Two-Year-Old Goes to Hospital*. London: Robertson Centre and Ipswich: Concord Films Council.

Scarr, S. (1984) *Mother Care/Other Care*. New York: Basic Books.

Schaffer, H.R. (2006) *Key Concepts in Developmental Psychology*. London: Sage.

Schore, A.N. (2001) 'The effects of a secure attachment relationship on right brain development, affect regulation, and infant mental health', *Infant Mental Health Journal*, 22: 7–66.

Segal, H. (1979) *Klein*. London: Karnac Books.

Segal, H. (1991) *Dream, Phantasy and Art*. London: Routledge.

Segal, J. (2004) *Melanie Klein* (2nd edn). London: Sage.

Shuttleworth, J. (1989) 'Psychoanalytic theory and infant development', in L. Miller, M. Rustin and J. Shuttleworth (eds) *Closely Observed Infants*. London: Duckworth.

Siegel, D.J. (1999) *The Developing Mind*. New York: Guilford Press.

Singer, E. (1998) 'Shared care for children', in M. Woodhead, D. Faulkner and K. Littleton (eds) *Cultural Worlds of Early Childhood*. London: Routledge.

Steiner, R. (2003) *Unconscious Phantasy*. London: Karnac Books.

Stern, D. (1998) *The Interpersonal World of the Infant*. New York: Basic Books.

Stevenson, L. and Haberman, D.L. (2004) *Ten Theories of Human Nature*. New York: Oxford University Press.

Vygotsky, L.S. (1978) *Mind in Society*. Cambridge, MA: Harvard University Press.

Waddell, M. (1994) *Owl Babies*. London: Walker Books.

Winnicott, D. (1960) 'The theory of the parent–child relationship', *International Journal of Psychoanalysis*, 41: 585–95.

Winnicott, D.W. (1965) *The Maturational Process and the Facilitating Environment: Studies in the Theory of Emotional Development*. London: Karnac Books.

Winnicott, D.W. (2005) *Playing and Reality* (2nd edn). Abingdon, Oxon: Routledge.

CHAPTER 3

POSTMODERN AND POST-STRUCTURALIST PERSPECTIVES ON EARLY CHILDHOOD EDUCATION

Deborah Albon

Overview

Postmodernism is a more recently developed theoretical position when compared to some of the other approaches outlined in this book. It is a perspective that has its origins in disciplines seemingly outside the sphere of early childhood, such as literature, cultural studies, politics, sociology and art. The aim of this chapter is to offer an understanding of this perspective and associated theories – post-Fordism, post-structuralism and post-colonialism – and explore how such theorizing might be applied to the field of early childhood. Whilst not a theory about learning or an approach to learning in itself, I will argue that the key contribution postmodernist thinking has made to early childhood education and care is in disrupting commonly held 'truths' about our understandings of children and how they develop and learn and, consequently, the curricula and pedagogical approaches practitioners employ in early childhood settings.

What is meant by 'postmodernism'?

The prefix 'post' indicates that there is a theoretical position known as modernism prior to the development of postmodern theorizing. This section of the chapter, then, aims to provide some discussion of this. In addition, it aims to interweave some related terms which are similar in their theoretical stance: post-Fordism, post-structuralism and post-colonialism.

Modernism as a set of ideas, or modernity as the period it encompasses, developed and pervaded thinking during and from the 17th to the 18th century in Western Europe (Bauman, 1993). This period is also commonly known as the 'Age of Enlightenment'. This period was characterized by a belief that the world is knowable and that science and technological advancement can make the pursuit of such 'truths' and the progress they promise possible. Further to this, the quest for these 'truths' can be linked to the modernist desire for certainty, order, rationality, standardization and universality (Dahlberg et al., 1999).

In the scientific world, this can be seen in positivist thinking: the search for objective and value-free 'truths' free from the relativist confines of place, culture and time (Mukherji and Albon, 2010). Associated theorizing can also be seen in the economic world, with the term 'Fordism' sometimes applied to the late modern period of industrialization, with 'post-Fordism' applied to arrangements made after this period. In brief, Fordist ideas are akin to the manufacturing practice of the Ford car industry. Fordist modes of production can be likened to modernism as they emphasize standardization of product (as opposed to niche markets), order and certainty. In addition, Fordist modes of production can be related to large-scale organizations overseen by hierarchical management systems (Brown and Lauder, 1992).

But the modernist pursuit of certainty, order and universal 'truths' came in for criticism in the latter part of the 20th century. For Bauman, the quest of nation states for order, certainty and homogeneity has legitimated some of the horrors of 20th-century events such as the Holocaust (Dahlberg et al., 1999). Further criticisms of modernism relate to its inability to allow for diversity, subjectivity, uncertainty and complexity (Dahlberg et al., 1999). Indeed, Giroux (2005) notes the way that modernism constructs borders that do not allow for diversity.

Post-colonialist thinking, which shares much of the postmodern critique of modernism, furthers this criticism by identifying modernism with the way that the ideas of minority world countries have held powerful sway across the globe, silencing perspectives that are different, seeing them as 'Other'. Cannella and Viruru (2004) draw on Said's work, which makes the distinction between the orient and the occident. The East, or orient, is conceptualized as inferior and exotic, and the occident, or West, in terms of the belief in the primacy of Western (or minority world) thought and actions. In the pursuit of progress, modernist/colonialist thinking has viewed majority world countries in terms of what they might *become* as opposed to what they *are* now (Gandhi, 1998). This, as we will see in the next section, can be applied to the way children are viewed too.

So what is meant by postmodernism? A key difficulty in defining 'postmodernism' in a clear and concise way is that it resists such easy and 'scientific' classification. Indeed, it is characterized by complexity, fluidity and heterogeneity. Although postmodernist roots can be seen in a range of movements in the 1950s and 1960s, it was really in the late 1970s and 1980s that the term 'postmodernism' became pervasive – and primarily in the minority world (Malpas, 2005). We should also be mindful that, although it could be argued that we live in postmodern times, features of modernity still abound (Grieshaber, 2004). We will see this later in the chapter when postmodernist ideas are applied to early childhood education.

Lyotard (1979) sees the modernist position as one that aims at legitimating itself through the development of 'grand' narratives or 'metanarratives' or universally held truths. Thus, he states, 'I define *postmodern* as incredulity toward metanarratives' (p. xxiv). For Dahlberg et al.:

> From a postmodern perspective, there is no absolute knowledge, no absolute reality waiting 'out there' to be discovered. There is no external position of certainty, no universal understanding that exists outside history or society that can provide foundations for truth, knowledge and ethics. (1999: 23)

In other words, knowledge, from a postmodern perspective, is socially constructed; it is contingent on culture, time and space. In addition, knowledge is not seen as derived from a position of scientific neutrality but through our own interactions and relationships with the world. Thus, knowledge can never be value-free and objective. For Lyotard (1979), by distancing ourselves from 'metanarratives' it is possible for 'micro-narratives', or little narratives, to develop, which are reflective of the thinking of smaller communities and contingent on their particular socio-cultural understandings. Sarup (1993: 146) sees this as 'localised creativity' and Giroux (2005: 49) argues that this offers a promise of a 'cultural politics that focuses on the margins'.

Another term – post-structuralism – is often used synonymously with postmodernism (Brown and Jones, 2001). A key writer associated within this position is Foucault. For Foucault (1977), power is of key importance. Power is not understood as held by people for all time over others; rather, it operates on a far more fluid basis, making it possible for everyone to hold power, be governed by others and also police themselves in given situations. This last form of power – disciplinary power – is especially interesting because it relates to the way particular ideas or 'regimes of truth', which can be likened in part to Lyotard's metanarratives, hold sway at given times. The 'beauty' of disciplinary power is in the way that the ideas embodied in such regimes of truth are seen as so self-evidently 'true' that they are accepted uncritically. From a post-structuralist perspective, therefore, individuals take up such ideas or discourses in such a way that they embody those discourses. In other words, for Foucault, individuals become 'docile bodies' (Holligan, 2000) as these discourses govern their own behaviour and thinking. But more than this, disciplinary power operates in a way that ensures the governability of *groups* of people. This happens through the 'normalizing' of certain practices and concepts to such an extent that surveillance of groups of people for their 'well-being' is largely legitimated (Flax, 1990). I discuss how this applies to early childhood practice in the following section.

Another key aspect of postmodernism is the speed at which ideas, technologies and fashions are embraced, rejected and transformed (Malpas, 2005). This can be seen most clearly in the idea of globalization and the notion of the world as shrinking, not least due to technologies such as the internet, which make access to a wide array of knowledge possible. In returning to the idea of Fordism discussed earlier, one aspect of post-Fordist theorizing is the greater economic demand for a knowledgeable and skilled workforce as well as the development of flexible as opposed to hierarchical management systems (Brown and Lauder, 1992). When applied to education, the perceived need for *ongoing* professional development and the increased emphasis on leadership and management might be positioned within a post-Fordist conceptual framework. However, the *standardization* of curriculum imposed by the English National Curriculum can be linked to Fordist thinking. As noted earlier, we should not suppose that Fordist or modernist thinking has disappeared.

To sum up the postmodernist position discussed so far, it is a theory that embraces diversity, uncertainty and complexity. However, it is a theory (or rather a range of theories) that originated not within the early childhood tradition or the field of education, but within the wider milieu, and can be applied to almost all aspects of social, cultural and economic life. Although in this section I have outlined the key ideas behind modernist and postmodernist theorizing, it would be wrong to see these positions as exclusive and constantly at odds with each other in every detail. An example might be some of the advancements made in the field of medicine that have made a real difference to the life expectancy and quality of life of many people – advances borne from the application of strictly scientific (and modernist) principles. It is the supposed applicability of such thinking to *all* aspects of social, cultural and economic life that many postmodernists question.

The value of postmodern theorizing to early years education

So far in this chapter, I have discussed postmodernism in terms of understanding it in its broadest sense. In this section, I aim to show how such theorizing can be applied to early childhood practice. Like Alloway (1997), who takes the idea of Lyotard's (1979) 'metanarratives' or commonly held 'truths' and applies this to various aspects of early childhood practice in order to show its important contribution to practice, my aim here is to deconstruct a few commonly held 'truths' about early childhood practice.

1. There are universal understandings of 'children' and 'childhood'

One such 'truth' we might deconstruct is that there are universal understandings of 'children' and 'childhood'. Aries (1962) was one of the first writers to view childhood as multiple and perspectival and posit the idea that 'childhood' itself is a recent human construction. Gradually, human beings who are younger have come to be seen as a distinct group that can be categorized differently than older human beings. In the late 19th and 20th centuries, the work of developmental psychology has served to add further weight to this distinction. This can be seen most prominently in the criticisms of Piaget's work, which is seen as confining children to particular stages of development (Burman, 1994).

The understandings derived from developmental psychology about what is 'normal' and 'natural' in young children's behaviour and understanding have resulted in pedagogies designed with such understandings in mind, and thus are complicit in the production of understandings of children that categorize them as developing 'normally' or 'abnormally' (Walkerdine, 1986). We will see some examples of this later in this section. Because of this, Viruru (2001) asserts that young children have been 'colonized' by adults in a similar way that we might describe the colonizing of countries in the majority world by minority world countries. She maintains that: 'Colonised human beings (including those who are younger) are created as subjects who are lacking, not fully advanced and needing intervention' (Viruru, 2001: 141). This has similarities to Qvortrup's (1994) notion of children being viewed as human 'becomings' as opposed to human beings.

Crucially, by employing the idea of colonial power – something outlined earlier in this chapter – to children, we might envisage children, like those territories that were (and are) colonized, in terms of what they might *become* as opposed to what they *are* at present (Gandhi, 1998). Thus, the postmodern/post-colonialist task is for practitioners to 'rethink and reconceptualize what they think they know about the child and childhood' (Cannella and Viruru, 2004: 84).

But whilst *childhood* is viewed as a variable of analysis, a postmodernist perspective does not view children's experiences of their childhoods as homogenous. Variables such as gender, race, ability, class, as well as comparative research looking at childhoods in different parts of the world, show that it is differently experienced. Thus, when Piaget talks about 'the child', he is criticized for representing in the singular the supposed naturalness of *all* children's development (Prout and James, 1997). Postmodernist thinking embraces the idea that individuals can be located within a *range* of discursive positionings (Grieshaber, 2004), which has particular resonance for the way issues of diversity are conceptualized in early childhood practice. For example, in the area of gender, this means that being a male or female does not carry with it *fixed* traits because subjectivities are viewed as changeable (Robinson and Diaz, 2006).

2. Children need to be socialized into 'appropriate' behaviours

Another metanarrative that can be applied to early childhood practice is the way it is seen as important that children are socialized from birth into the gradual control of their emotional and bodily expressions (Leavitt and Power, 1997). Indeed, the distinction of 'child' from 'adult' is often described in terms of dualisms such as: body v. mind;

dependence v. independence; savage v. civilized (Cannella and Viruru, 2004), with control of the body, for example, viewed as an essential part of becoming an adult. For Grosz (1994: 3), children's bodies are often conceptualized as 'unruly' and 'disruptive'. Therefore, managing the child's body – with all the implications of disciplinary power that this suggests – is often regarded as a crucial part of daily practice in early childhood settings (Leavitt and Power, 1997). Moreover, the construction of early childhood practitioners' professional identities is often intertwined with issues of *controlling* children in childcare settings (Phelan, 1997).

In practice, the 'disciplining' of children's bodies can be seen in the use of timetables and mechanistic routines in which time is demarcated to such an extent that the immediate lived needs of young children are subordinated to the imposed timetabling of practitioners. This impacts on the opportunities children have for periods of uninterrupted play (Polakow, 1992). Recent curricula developments such as the Primary Frameworks for Literacy and Mathematics (DCSF, 2009) are further examples of the way that time is demarcated into 'units', with learning compartmentalized and fragmented into segments. This can also be linked to the post-Fordist critique of standardized and bureaucratic Fordist education systems (Brown and Lauder, 1992).

The child who adheres compliantly to the temporal and spatial elements of a particular early childhood programme is viewed as 'normal' and the child who finds this more problematic is viewed as 'abnormal' (Polakow, 1992). Indeed, the categorization, measurement and labelling of children in such a way can be regarded as a further exemplar of Foucault's notion of 'docile bodies' produced discursively through practices deemed 'appropriate' for young children, as we will also see in the next section.

3. There is such a thing as a 'normal child'

The 'normalizing gaze' that Foucault discusses (Holligan, 2000) can also be seen in other areas of practice, such as assessment instruments used in early childhood practice – for instance, the Foundation Stage Profile, as well as a range of assessment instruments used in the identification of children deemed to have 'special educational needs'. As Holligan (2000: 137) notes, 'They [children] have to be kept under close surveillance to see how normal they are becoming'.

As I noted in the previous section, the 'beauty' of such a system is the way it is viewed as neutral and objective and thus goes unquestioned (Holligan, 2000). It is because of this supposed neutrality that discursive practices that result in the identification of the 'normal' and 'abnormal' child have developed. Furthermore, these are taken up regionally or nationally to assume greater uniformity and this uniformity (and the guidance produced to ensure this happens) begins to be accepted as a 'true' measure and is thus taken up by practitioners.

Parents too are caught up in this process, because developmental milestones serve to structure their observations of their children and also act as a seemingly 'neutral' baseline from which to compare their child's development with others (Burman, 1994). Thus, long before schooling even starts, the idea that there are 'norms' from which children can be measured has been taken up by parents; indeed, parents may be subject to a high degree of state intervention and stigmatization should their child's development be deemed to be 'behind' that considered 'normal' for their age, owing to a belief that parents may be to some degree responsible for optimizing their children's development (Burman, 1994).

This also impacts on schools. In schools with low baseline testing scores, the school's performance may be assessed according to the impact they have had in ameliorating the supposed 'defects' of the child's home and accelerating the child's development and learning towards that considered more 'normal' for their age – as measured through testing. The corollary of this is that parents and schools are judged against the 'normalcy' of the children in their care and become engaged in a competition – parent against parent; school against school – to see how 'advanced' the children in their care have become. A postmodern perspective encourages us to challenge the conception of the 'normal child' and the supposedly rational instruments that have been devised to measure this.

4. Play is important in the early childhood curriculum

Another metanarrative in early childhood is the primacy of play as a vehicle for learning (Alloway, 1997) and that the curriculum should be child-centred, based on what is 'known' about how young children develop. The belief in the importance of play cannot be overestimated in early childhood writings and this is further exemplified by much of the writing in this book. Play is commonly viewed as vital in children's 'natural' growth and development and is seen as 'normal' behaviour for young children. This 'truth' has been accepted by many early childhood practitioners and taken up in their classroom pedagogies, with play seen as appropriate in the world of early childhood and work being the preserve of adults.

Yet Cannella and Viruru (2004) point out that many parents do not share this belief in the primacy of play in the early childhood curriculum. Furthermore, the separation of work from play seems to be a minority world construct, with the latter conceptualized as offering the possibility for pleasure and the former characterized by its seriousness. In majority world countries, such a distinction is often non-existent, or, at least, far more blurred than this suggests. It is also another example of the binary distinction made between 'child' and 'adult', with children seemingly confined to the romantic world of play and separated from the adult (and less innocent) world of work.

Further criticisms of child-centred, play-based pedagogies have also come from *within* the minority world. Alloway (1997) encourages us to consider the critique of Lisa Delpit, an African American researcher, who argues that progressivist, child-centred approaches to education may privilege white, middle-class children as opposed to poor or black children. Whilst not advocating an overly didactic curriculum of 'drill and skill' (p. 3), Delpit suggests that pedagogies that make *explicit* the expected codes of behaviour in a setting and involve greater direct teaching, as opposed to a more child-centred, progressivist pedagogy, might serve the needs of poor and black children better.

We can see, then, that postmodern theorizing problematizes many long held 'truths' about early childhood practice and there are many other examples that are worth exploration, but which could not be included in a short chapter such as this. This is further complicated as some of the discourses or 'truths' outlined above may also imply different forms of action (see Stainton-Rogers, 2001). An example might be that claim number 2 suggests that children need to be socialized into 'appropriate' behaviours, whereas claim number 4 suggests that play is key to young children's learning and development. The former 'truth' implies adult control and the latter implies a degree of freedom from adult control.

Limitations with postmodern theories

Whilst in this chapter I have outlined the value postmodern theorizing has had on our thinking about early childhood education and care, it can also be criticized. The critique offered here focuses on three main areas that relate to early childhood practice: the lack of recognition of very young children's vulnerability and dependence on adults and sometimes older children; the lack of recognition of embodiment in early childhood practice; and the reluctance to reconstruct a sense of what practitioners *should* do in providing education and care for young children. I also include a fourth criticism, which asks, more broadly, whether postmodernist theorizing is in danger of becoming yet another metanarrative, one that could be regarded as politically weak.

Critique 1: The young child as vulnerable and competent

In critiquing the positioning of children as dependent, less competent and vulnerable, which has long been the project of developmental psychology, there seems to be a dismissal of very young children's *vulnerability* in postmodern writings. In writing about early childhood research, Lahman (2008: 285) holds a view of the child as both vulnerable and competent at the same time, stating: 'I believe both the notions of competent and vulnerable, worded as *competent yet vulnerable child* may be held simultaneously as a way of considering the unique position of children'.

Babies and very young children are dependent to a great extent on adults or possibly older children for their physical and emotional care (Manning-Morton, 2006). This is a biological fact as opposed to social construction. *How* this care is provided and what is considered *appropriate* in this area is a social construction and this is an important distinction to make. But it is not just babies and very young children who are physically and emotionally dependent – levels of dependency are likely to fluctuate in all of us throughout the course of our lives. Lahman's 'competent but vulnerable child' perspective recognizes that alongside their vulnerability, young children are also able to participate and have a right to be listened to. This, I am sure, is something that postmodernists would agree with and the idea of a fluid and changing self fits in well with a postmodernist perspective. However, much postmodernist writing seems to ignore the dependence babies and young children have on those who care for them and this neglect appears to silence what for many early childhood practitioners are the *realities* of their daily practice.

Critique 2: The importance of an embodied and relational perspective in early childhood

Another criticism that can be levelled at postmodernist theorizing is that there appears to be a downplaying of the importance of the body. Whilst postmodern theorizing is important in encouraging a consideration of multiple and fluid identities, it emphasizes 'reading' the body 'at the expense of attention to the body's material locatedness in history, practice, culture' (Bordo, 2003: 38). Similarly, James et al. (1998: 147) argue that 'embodied action [is] performed not only by texts but by real, living corporeal persons'.

Other theoretical perspectives such as phenomenology see our bodily experiences as the *foundation* upon which we make meaning about the world. This alternative perspective might also elevate the body as a means through which we know the world that may not involve language and discourse – something postmodernists neglect (Burr, 2003). Similarly, Flax (1990) argues that postmodernism fails to recognize that the *self* of a person may not be rooted in socio-historical constructions alone. She maintains that there are other important sources of self-formation, such as early mother–child relations, which are highlighted by psychoanalytical writers especially (see Chapter 2). Further criticism can also be made of the lack of attention postmodernist thinking pays to the desires and fantasies of a person and the role this plays in personal agency, such as why we do what we do (Burr, 2003).

In applying the ideas presented here to early childhood practice, these criticisms are especially appropriate. Much of young children's experience of the world appears to be immediate and physical, and positive, sustained relationships are of central importance to young children's all-round development and learning (see e.g. Elfer et al., 2003; Manning-Morton and Thorp, 2003). In addition, to suggest that young children are purely subject to discourse appears to assign them a passive rather than an active role. For early childhood, this may be a criticism that has particular resonance because the young child has often been conceptualized as a blank slate and passive receiver of knowledge rather than an active co-constructor of knowledge. To sum up critique 2, it would seem that there are some difficult issues relating to our physical and relational selves, which also relate to tensions between agency and structure, for postmodernist thinking to resolve (Burr, 2003).

Critique 3: Beyond deconstruction – what should practitioners actually do?

A key criticism that might be levelled at postmodernism when applied to early childhood practice is that in emphasizing deconstruction and encouraging the disruption to long-held 'truths' about early childhood practice, it rarely offers anything *concrete* in its place. Of course, to offer anything as certain as 'what early childhood practitioners might do to improve the quality of their practice' on a large scale begins to look suspiciously like a metanarrative. Yet, settings *do* need to engage with reconstructing a sense of good practice and how to achieve this on a *micro* level and on an *ongoing* basis in order to reflect diversity as well as changing ideas about young children and how they might be educated and cared for. Lyotard's (1979) notion of micro, or little, narratives is highly relevant here and at least offers the promise of *reconstruction* for practitioners and crucially for children and families. In sharing examples of practice from Reggio, for instance, writers from a postmodernist perspective such as Dahlberg et al. (1999) offer a vision of early childhood education that appears to recoil from proclaiming universal applicability and prides itself on localized 'dissensus' and a distinct lack of rigid, formalized standards to be adhered to by practitioners (Moss, 2001) (see also Chapter 1).

However, the development of localized micro-narratives such as this might be viewed as problematic in terms of monitoring practice. In critiquing the notion of universally held ideas about what constitutes 'good practice', how might we recognize good or poor practice? Are there *some* standards we would want in place on a regional or national scale to act as *safeguards* for young children and families? Is there a basic entitlement that *all* children in a region or nation should have access to? If there is, how prescriptive should it be and how should it be monitored? These are very real questions about early childhood practice. We might also ask, as Sarup (1993) does, why we would want to abandon *all* metanarratives, as writers such as Lyotard seem to ask us to do.

In thinking about this, I and many other practitioners and commentators on early childhood would not want to abandon the idea that play is a prime vehicle in young children's learning and development, for example. There is a wealth of research in this area too numerous to document in this short chapter. The postmodern critique of play and the child-centred curriculum is important in alerting us to alternative thinking and might argue that this wealth of evidence about the primacy of play has served to form its own 'regime of truth', a term noted earlier. However, it rarely offers something *concrete* in its place that is helpful to the majority of practitioners working in early childhood in a given context. Also, implicit in the postmodern critique is a suggestion that many practitioners are simply *subjects* of discourse, unable to stand outside and therefore criticize their everyday practices, unlike the academics that write about them (Burr, 2003).

Critique 4: Isn't postmodernism another metanarrative or set of metanarratives (albeit that it does not want to be)?

Finally here, in offering up a theory or rather a set of theories, postmodernism might also be described as yet another metanarrative or set of metanarratives in the same way that Marxism is a metanarrative (Sarup, 1993). Sarup (1993) draws upon the work of Rorty, who argues that the postmodern positions put forward by writers such as Foucault and Lyotard can be characterized by their 'dryness' and their reluctance to ally themselves to any group long enough to say 'we' or 'our'.

This could be seen as political weakness because the postmodern idea of the shifting nature of subject positions, that may (or may not) be taken up within a given context, makes it difficult for individuals to collectivize their experiences beyond the micro-level in order to struggle against oppression (Henriques et al., 1984). Given that issues of race and social class – to name two 'macro' subject positionings – are still dominant in terms of persistent inequalities in attainment in education, this would seem to be very important. Issues of racism and poverty are *real* and *lived* and surely require *action* at least as much as deconstruction.

Final thoughts

Perhaps postmodernist thinking is most valuable in making all of us concerned with early childhood education and care to 'look again' with a critical eye at how we view young children, how they develop and learn and how the early childhood curriculum and associated pedagogy should be developed. This is vital. At a time of increased government intervention into early childhood practice, for example the introduction of statutory frameworks such as the Early Years Foundation Stage in England (DfES, 2007), it is imperative that practitioners maintain a critical stance – the 'incredulity' Lyotard emphasizes (1979: xxiv, mentioned earlier) – towards what they do and why.

 Summary

- Postmodernist thinking troubles the idea that the world is 'knowable' and that there are 'truths' out there waiting to be discovered which are valid for all time.
- It is a viewpoint that embraces diversity and recognizes that all knowledge is contingent and socially constructed.

(Continued)

(Continued)

- When applied to early childhood practice, postmodern thinking encourages a re-examination of commonly held 'truths', such as what is meant by a 'child' and how children develop and learn, especially criticizing theories developed from developmental psychology and the kinds of curricula and pedagogical arrangements put in place because of these.
- Criticisms that can be made of this theory (or set of theories) are: its reluctance to acknowledge the *vulnerability* as well as the competence of very young children; its seeming neglect of the importance of embodiment in focusing on discourse; and its focus on deconstruction at the expense of putting forward positive ideas about good practice on a large scale.

Questions for discussion

1. Consider your own understandings of what constitutes a 'child' – in particular the capabilities of very young children – and how this informs your practice. Does this confine children to a position of being overly protected and/or not listened to and respected? How does this impact on the curricula and pedagogy in your setting or a setting that you know?
2. How might considering early childhood practice through different lenses deepen your understanding of the experience of children, families and practitioners? Try the following exercise: consider the many ways in which you 'know' a setting and write your thoughts down about how you experience this setting from these different perspectives (maybe you are a key person, a parent, a black woman, a governor, a person with a hearing impairment, a Christian or someone with Early Years Professional Status).
3. Is there a place for standards and the development of quality indicators in early childhood practice to ensure a basic entitlement for all children? If you think there is, should they look like the standards used in the country or region where you live or work? If not, what would you change and why? (*Higher level questions*)

Further reading

Levels 5 and 6

Alloway, N. (1997) 'Early childhood education encounters the postmodern: What do we know? What can we count as true?', *Australian Journal of Early Childhood*, 22(2): 1–5.

The strength of this article is in outlining a few areas in which postmodernist thinking can be applied to early childhood practice in a clear and understandable way. Often, writing about postmodernism can be very dense or seemingly unrelated to day-to-day practice with very young children – this article avoids this.

Holligan, C. (2000) 'Discipline and normalisation in the nursery: the Foucaultian gaze', in H. Penn (ed.) *Early Childhood Services: Theory, Policy and Practice*. Buckingham: Open University Press.
This is a useful look at how the ideas of Foucault can be applied to early childhood practice.

Levels 6 and 7

Dahlberg, G., Moss, P. and Pence, A. (1999) *Beyond Quality in Early Childhood Education and Care: Postmodern Perspectives.* London: Falmer.
This text looks in some depth at postmodern theorizing. Its application to the world of early childhood helps the reader to see the relevance for this area of practice.

Foucault, M. (1977) *Discipline and Punishment: The Birth of the Prison*. London: Penguin
This book is not about early childhood education per se, but it is a text that has been highly influential across a number of fields. In reading at this higher level, I suggest you read a 'classic' post-structuralist text such as this and try to apply some of its ideas to early childhood practice, as writers such as Walkerdine and Cannella have done.

Ryan, S. and Grieshaber, S. 'Shifting from developmental to postmodern practices in early childhood teacher education', *Journal of Teacher Education*, 56(1): 34–45. Available at: www.eprints.qut.edu.au/1094/1/JTEreumanuscript%5B!%5D.pdf (accessed 10 February 2010).
This article looks at postmodernism and the implications for teacher education in an Australian context. Some of the most interesting work in the area of postmodernism and early childhood education emanates from there.

Websites

Levels 5 and 6

Burke, B. 'Postmodernism and postmodernity': www.infed.org/biblio/6-postmd.htm (accessed 10 February 2010).
This article gives a basic overview of postmodernism and considers its educational implications. It also provides useful suggestions for further reading.

Levels 6 and 7

Viruru, R. 'The impact of post colonial theory on early childhood education': www.ukzn.ac.za/joe/JoEPDFs/joe%2035%20viruru.pdf (accessed 2 May 2010).
This article by Viruru looks at the impact of postcolonial theory on early childhood education.

References

Alloway, N. (1997) 'Early childhood education encounters the postmodern: What do we know? What can we count as true?', *Australian Journal of Early Childhood*, 22(2): 1–5.
Aries, P. (1962) *Centuries of Childhood: A Social History of Family Life*. New York: Knopf.

Bauman, Z. (1993) *Postmodern Ethics*. Oxford: Blackwell.

Bordo, S. (2003) *Unbearable Weight: Feminism, Western Culture and the Body*. Berkeley: University of California Press.

Brown, T. and Jones, L. (2001) *Action Research and Postmodernism: Congruence and Critique*. Buckingham: Open University Press.

Brown, P. and Lauder, H. (1992) 'Education, economy and society: an introduction to a new agenda', in P. Brown and H. Lauder (eds) *Education for Economic Survival: From Fordism to Post-Fordism?* London: Routledge.

Burman, E. (1994) *Deconstructing Developmental Psychology*. London: Routledge.

Burr, V. (2003) *Social Constructionism* (2nd edn). London: Routledge.

Cannella, G.S. and Viruru, R. (2004) *Childhood and Postcolonialism*. London: Routledge/Falmer.

Dahlberg, G., Moss, P. and Pence, A. (1999) *Beyond Quality in Early Childhood Education and Care: Postmodern Perspectives*. London: Falmer.

Department of Children, Schools and Families (DCSF) (2009) *Primary Framework*. Available at: http://nationalstrategies.standards.dcsf.gov.uk/primary/ (accessed 5 July 2010).

DfES (2007) *The Early Years Foundation Stage*. Nottingham: DfES.

Elfer, P., Goldschmeid, E. and Selleck, D. (2003) *Key Persons in the Nursery: Building Relationships for Quality Provision*. London: David Fulton.

Flax, J. (1990) *Thinking Fragments: Psychoanalysis, Feminism and Postmodernism in the Contemporary West*. Oxford: University of California Press.

Foucault, M. (1977) *Discipline and Punishment: The Birth of the Prison*. London: Penguin.

Gandhi, M.K. (1998) *Postcolonial Theory: A Critical Introduction*. New York: Columbia University Press.

Giroux, H. (2005) *Border Crossing: Cultural Workers and the Politics of Education* (2nd edn). London: Routledge.

Grieshaber, S. (2004) *Rethinking Parent and Child Conflict*. Abingdon: Routledge/Falmer.

Grosz, E. (1994) *Volatile Bodies: Toward a Corporeal Feminism*. Bloomington: Indiana University Press.

Henriques, J., Hollway, W., Urwin, C., Venn, C. and Walkerdine, V. (1984) 'Theorising subjectivity', in J. Henriques, W. Hollway, C. Urwin, C. Venn and V. Walkerdine (eds) *Changing the Subject: Psychology, Social Regulation and Subjectivity*. London: Methuen.

Holligan, C. (2000) 'Discipline and normalisation in the nursery: the Foucaultian gaze', in H. Penn (ed.) *Early Childhood Services: Theory, Policy and Practice*. Buckingham: Open University Press.

James, A., Jenks, C. and Prout, A. (1998) *Theorising Childhood*. Cambridge: Polity Press.

Lahman, M. (2008) 'Always othered: ethical research with children', *Journal of Early Childhood Research*, 6(3): 281–300.

Leavitt, R.L. and Power, M.B. (1997) 'Civilizing bodies: children in day care', in J. Tobin (ed.) *Making a Place for Pleasure in Early Childhood Education*. New Haven: Yale University Press.

Lyotard, J.F. (1979) *The Postmodern Condition: A Report on Knowledge* (translated by G. Bennington and B. Massumi). Manchester: Manchester University Press.

Malpas, S. (2005) *The Postmodern*. London: Routledge.

Manning-Morton, J. (2006) 'The personal is professional: professionalism and the birth to threes practitioner', *Contemporary Issues in Early Childhood*, 7(1): 42–52.

Manning-Morton, J. and Thorp, M. (2003) *Key Times for Play*. Maidenhead: Open University Press.

Moss, P. (2001) 'The otherness of Reggio', in L. Abbott and C. Nutbrown (eds) *Experiencing Reggio Emilia: Implications for Pre-School Provision*. Buckingham: Open University Press.

Mukherji, P. and Albon, D. (2010) *Research Methods in Early Childhood: An Introductory Guide*. London: Sage.

Phelan, A.M. (1997) 'Classroom management and the erasure of teacher desire', in J. Tobin (ed.) *Making a Place for Pleasure in Early Childhood Education*. New Haven: Yale University Press.

Polakow, V. (1992) *The Erosion of Childhood*. Chicago: University of Chicago Press.

Prout, A. and James, A. (1997) 'A new paradigm for the sociology of childhood? Provenance, promise and problems', in A. James and A. Prout (eds) *Constructing and Reconstructing Childhood*. London: Routledge/Falmer.

Qvortrup, J. (1994) 'Childhood matters: an introduction', in J. Qvortrup, M. Bardy, G. Sgritta and H. Wintersberger (eds) *Childhood Matters: Social Theory, Practice and Politics*. Aldershot: Avebury.

Robinson, K. and Diaz, C.J. (2006) *Diversity and Difference in Early Childhood Education: Issues for Theory and Practice*. Maidenhead: Open University Press.

Sarup, M. (1993) *An Introductory Guide to Post-Structuralism and Postmodernism* (2nd edn). London: Harvester Wheatsheaf.

Stainton-Rogers, W. (2001) 'Constructing childhood: constructing child concern', in P. Foley, J. Roche and S. Tucker (eds) *Children in Society: Contemporary Theory, Policy and Practice*. Houndmills: Palgrave.

Viruru, R. (2001) *Early Childhood Education: Postcolonial Perspectives from India*. New Delhi: Sage.

Walkerdine, V. (1986) 'Post-structuralist theory and everyday social practices: the family and the school', in S. Wilkinson (ed.) *Feminist Social Psychology: Developing Theory and Practice*. Milton Keynes: Open University Press.

PART 2

FOUNDATIONAL THEORIES

CHAPTER 4

FROEBEL TODAY

Tina Bruce

Overview

Froebel's influence is deeply embedded in practice today, but it is no longer made explicit in the training of teachers and other early childhood practitioners. The early Froebelians tried to develop his philosophy and principles, but focused on the tangible Gifts and Occupations. This eventually made practice rigid and uncreative. By 1911, the 'revisionist' Froebelians had successfully addressed the problem, and principled practice meant that a more reflective approach developed. Froebel's innovative ideas include: kindergartens, with outdoor learning as important as indoor; the central importance of play in learning; women as teachers; home learning; the importance of the early years of life; and highly educated and trained practitioners who engage in principled and reflective practice.

Froebel's philosophy and practice

Friedrich Froebel (1782–1852) lived and worked in Germany. His ideas are drawn from European Enlightenment currents (influenced by Immanuel Kant, 1724–1804). It is worth remembering that at the time Froebel was living and writing, women were still regarded as chattels. Poor families were illiterate, and upper-class girls learnt embroidery, drawing, music and to read and write as accomplishments to attract husbands, while the boys were versed in the classics and perhaps enjoyed a 'Grand Tour' of Italy and Greece.

Froebel's ideas have entered mainstream educational practice, but at the time he put them forward, they were revolutionary. Froebel did not set down his ideas with great detail in his main work (*The Education of Man*, translated into English and published in 1887) but his principles for educating young children are made clear in the examples he gives (Bruce, 2009).

Key ideas include the Gifts and the Occupations. The Occupations set out a range of craft-like activities such as paper folding, stick and pea patterns in three dimensions, paper weaving, paper pricking and clay. The Gifts were one of the first sets of wooden blocks to be developed for learning, and were groundbreaking in their educational possibilities.

Froebel wrote about principled practice rather than prescribing lists of what to do. For this reason, his influence is subtle and can be missed. From 1851 his ideas spread, particularly in Europe and the USA. Froebelian practice today (Bruce, 2004) is very different from Froebelian practice in the 1850s. It remains an international movement.

Because of the reflective approach of the revisionist Froebelian women who led the work in the Training Colleges at the turn of the century, Froebelian practice in the UK became less linked to method, which was emphasized by pioneers such as the Ronges (1879) and opened out to link with other influences, such as that of John Dewey and the psychodynamic theories espoused by Froebelians such as Susan Isaacs. The theories of Piaget, Bruner and Vygotsky also helped Froebelians to reflect on their practice together with socio-cultural influences (Kalliala, 2006).

However, the central Froebelian philosophy, embedded in a principled approach and now informed by theory and research, continues to impact on practice, as government documents have successively, albeit unwittingly, drawn upon Froebelian philosophy. Because of the effectiveness of its nursery and infant school practice, especially in the maintained nursery schools and those transformed into integrated children's centres, Froebelianism remains linked with high-quality provision today.

Kindergartens

Froebel was the inventor of the kindergarten. Some words creep into common usage such that their origin becomes forgotten. Examples are 'hoovering' and 'googling' and 'kindergarten'. Everyone knows that hoovering means vacuum cleaning, and googling means finding out information on a computer search engine. The meanings of these two words are clear. But the meaning of 'kindergarten' is not. It is generally understood that a 'kindergarten' is a place where little children are educated, and that a 'kindergarten' education means a good education. In the private sector, the word 'kindergarten' is sometimes used as a designer label to promote what is perceived to be quality education.

Peter Weston (1998: 15) describes Froebel's first kindergarten at Bad Blankenburg in 1839:

> The word cleverly combines the human (kinder) with the natural (garten) and can mean both garden of children, and garden for children. The Bad Blankenburg building originally had a garden at the rear in which each child had a personal patch of land for cultivation and observation. There were nearly 50 children registered in 1839, many of whom had first to be washed in the fountain in the market place before starting school.

Children from about 2 to 7 years were also actively engaged in singing, dancing, storytelling and play with wooden blocks (the Gifts and the Occupations).

Gardens

In Froebel's kindergarten, each child tended a plot of garden, and there was also a community garden (Read, 2009). He pioneered outdoor education, giving it the same status as learning indoors (Milchem, 2010; Tovey, 2007).

Play

Jane Read (1992: 5) outlines Froebel's three strands which ran through the children's play:

- The *forms of life* are the means by which we create and represent what we experience.
- The *forms of beauty* are the way that we see and discover patterns and symmetry.
- The *forms of knowledge* help to make the abstract become tangible.

Froebel realized that a child's play is of central importance in developing and learning, writing at length on the subject in his essays in *The Education of Man* (Froebel, 1887, quoted in Liebschner, 1992: 4, Preface):

> Play is the purest, the most spiritual product of man at this stage, and at the same time, typical of human life as a whole – of the inner hidden natural life in man and all things. It gives, therefore, joy, freedom, contentment, inner and outer rest, peace with the world. It holds the sources of all that is good. A child that plays thoroughly, with self-active determination, persevering until physical fatigue forbids, will surely be a thorough, determined man, capable of self-sacrifice for the promotion of the welfare of himself and others.

Froebel was the first educator to understand that children before the age of 7 years were at an important stage in learning, and that education in the sense of developing and learning begins at birth and does not end until the day we die. He also recognized the power of a child's play in this process, in connecting biological processes with the socio-cultural, although he used the words of his time in saying this. His thinking anticipated current ideas and would also challenge some of the current theories of play.

Froebel's thinking on play is expressed through 12 features of play gathered from current theories and research (Bruce, 1991, 1996, 2001, 2004, 2005b) which are widely subscribed to by academics and play specialists. These provide a navigational tool to guide practitioners in reflective practice. These features of play in the Froebelian sense are:

1. In their play, children make use of the real experiences they have had.
2. Play allows children to express their own ideas, feelings and relationships and to be comfortable in their own bodies, as well as finding ways to challenge themselves in a safe way, as they can move in and out of play according to how adventurous they want to be. Play gives children control. They can make the rules of play. They are not bound by the rules of others.
3. Play encourages children to make props or to mime objects, events or people. Play supports the beginnings of the symbolic life of the child. In play, children represent many experiences, events, objects and people, and find they can create these with increasing sophistication and complexity.
4. Children cannot be made to play. Play is intrinsically motivated. As Froebel put it, play is about making the 'inner' outer and the 'outer' inner.
5. Children often rehearse or reflect on adult roles and life as they play. This is sometimes called fantasy play or role play, but it is based on what is logical and real. Children often explore situations that give them pain and make them sad in their play. Play is not all joy and fun.
6. Children might engage in pretend play, and transform life into unreal phantasies, creating in the secure situation of play, scenarios in which they can explore fear, excess emotion and possible alternative worlds.
7. Children need to play alone, so that they understand themselves and can relate to self, enjoying and feeling comfortable in their own company and building their inner resources. Examples of this would be found in small world play (dolls houses or toy cars) or wooden blockplay.
8. Children also need to play with others, in pairs or in groups. Developing access strategies into group play, and learning to lead, follow and negotiate their play agenda and ideas, in the company of others and collaborating with them, is a powerful aspect of development and learning.
9. Adults can play with children but must be wary of taking over the play. There can be rich play when adult and children play together, respecting each other's ideas, feelings and relationships, and physical possibilities of movement, connecting through words and actions.

10. In a play situation both indoors and outdoors (Tovey, 2007), children focus and concentrate and show deep involvement. They positively wallow in the play. Concentration is an important part of learning to learn.

11. When children are engaged in this kind of play, they show us what they have learnt. Play is not about new learning, or at least not very much. It is much more about what a child has learnt and can do and joyously performs. It shows off technical prowess. In their play, children use skills and show what they know.

12. Play integrates and organizes the development and learning of the child. When Froebel said it is the most spiritual activity of the child, this was because it helps children to know themselves in all their relations. Knowing and understanding self and others, and reaching to do this also in relation to the universe, is the contribution of play. Play brings together in a coherent – and manageable for the child – way all the developing and learning that has been taking place. It is an integrating mechanism.

Home learning

Froebel pioneered the realization that we learn from the time we are born and that the loving home is an important part of this The idea that young children should learn in a homelike environment, with a garden, remains strong in Froebelian education. So too does the view that parents are active participators, and that family life is central to a child's education. This involves children in active learning, with emphasis on first-hand and meaningful experience, rather than book-based learning.

Babies, toddlers and 'Mother Songs'

For babies and toddlers, Froebel developed what he called the 'Mother Songs', which included finger plays and actions, aimed at the emerging symbolic life of the child. 'Pat a cake' is a famous one still used today (Bruce and Spratt, 2008; Spratt, 2007). Froebel valued the mother as an educator. But, in the spirit of the African saying, 'It takes a whole village to educate a child', he did not think that mothers should be left isolated, often lonely and uninformed about the possibilities in bringing up their children.

Women teachers

Froebel pioneered the view that women are capable of teaching. Kindergartens were an important part of the development of educational and professional career possibilities for middle-class women in the late 19th and early 20th centuries. Their strength lay in the fact that they did not challenge the deeply held belief that woman's place was in the home, with her children, performing the duties of a good wife, or caring for parents and being a good aunt or daughter. At the same time as Florence Nightingale was, against all the odds, developing nursing as a respectable profession for women

(Bostridge, 2008), so the early Froebelian kindergarten movement was raising the status of mothers spending time with children, both their own and other people's.

It became possible for middle-class women, tied to their homes and the domestic life, to undertake locally organized Froebel training through the Froebel Society and the National Froebel Union (both founded in 1874), and to study and gain accreditation through a Froebel Certificate (Brehony, 2000). This enabled middle-class Victorian women to start up small, home-based kindergartens.

The development of Froebel's influence

Free Froebelian schools were set up by the voluntary sector in the early 19th century in order to influence practice in the maintained sector, but also to offer a Froebelian education to children living in urban poverty (Brehony, 2000). This was the beginning of the Nursery School Movement.

Famous Froebelian-influenced pioneers in the 1930s were Susan Isaacs (1930) and Margaret McMillan. Both were in the Froebelian tradition of having a school in which to explore practice and to train students. Susan Isaacs went on from the Malting House School in Cambridge to be the founding tutor at the Department of Child Development at the Institute of Education at the University of London, training teachers who predominantly went into the maintained sector. Margaret McMillan established the Rachel McMillan Nursery School in Deptford, which was next to and linked with the teacher training college named after her sister, Rachel.

Revisions

As Brehony (2000: 183) points out, 'Where a movement is established, an orthodox interpretation is created by those who hold power within it'. As the kindergartens began to expand from homes into private schools, they became too rigid in their practice of Froebelian principles. There was a need to revisit the fundamental guiding principles of Froebel, and to be more reflective and less tied to method.

Brehony describes a group of Froebelians as 'revisionists' (Brehony, 2000: 192). They include some famous names:

- Grace Owen (d. 1965), taught Froebelian practice to Susan Isaacs at Manchester College
- Maria Elizabeth Findlay (d. 1912), a tutor at the Froebel Educational Institute
- Elsie Riach Murray, trained and lectured at Maria Grey Training College
- Alice Woods, writing in the 1920s, linked Froebel's work with that of the American educator John Dewey (1859–1952)
- Henrietta Brown Smith became an HMI.

These 'revisionists' saw that the Gifts and Occupations had become rigidly used and were too central to practice. This resulted in a prescriptive rather than a principled approach

(Nawrotzki, 2006), which needed to be re-evaluated. For more details of the rigid use of the Gifts and Occupations, see Liebschner (1992) and Brosterman (1997). The development of the Gifts and Occupations, in more creative, open-ended ways is explored in Gura (1992), Davies (2003), Matthews (2003), Bruce (2005a) and Whinnett (2006).

Principled and reflective practice

Froebelians are not by nature revolutionary in spirit. They are pioneering, and thanks to the example set by the revisionist Froebelians, embrace the need for change when it arises. Through reflective practice, the possibility of change is there, as we shall see in the Froebel Blockplay Research Project (1988–92).

Froebelian philosophy and principles serve as navigational tools to guide practitioners in what they need to think through when relating to official documents and legal requirements, or the implications of theories and research. The starting point is mulling over the practice, to see whether it should continue as it has been, or whether it needs to change, in the light of upholding the integrity of Froebelian philosophy and principles.

This avoids the pitfalls of methods and orthodoxy of practice. It is why Froebel did not wish to see Froebel schools. Instead, there are schools and settings which strive to explore Froebelian principles with diversity, depending on their community and cultural context.

The Froebel Movement is international, and there is a healthy and rich diversity in the way that Froebelianism is practised. The introduction of wooden blocks to a pre-school in Soweto, South Africa (Bruce, 2010), funded by the Incorporated Froebel Educational Institute, will be very different from the Froebel Blockplay Research Project in the UK schools, but the Froebelian principles will be the navigational tools.

Research on Froebelian practice

The Froebel Blockplay Research Project (1988–92)

This was an opportunity to re-examine the Froebelian Gifts and to locate them in current practice. Because of the decision to reduce emphasis on the Gifts and Occupations by the revisionist Froebelians who were successful in breaking the traditionalists' tight stranglehold on practice in the kindergartens and private schools for girls, a need to relocate them into current practice had become urgent by the late 1980s. The Froebel Blockplay Research Project sought to address this. The project was a collaborative research study undertaken with the Senior Researcher Pat Gura in three primary schools – one with a partial hearing unit – and two maintained nursery schools. It demonstrated the need for practitioners to regularly review the basic tenets of their practice, and to see how the principles are located in the context of current practice. It provided an opportunity to gather together recent theory and research and to see how these relate to the Froebelian principles. In the introduction to the book which developed out of the project (edited by Gura, 1992), a quotation from Zimiles (1977: 70) places 'the focus of early childhood education where it belongs, on the study of children in school, and the development of theoretical constructs for explaining the influence of their experience'.

Those involved were a busy group of early childhood teachers, nursery nurses and parents wishing to join in. The aim was to explore practice, and to link this to Froebelian principles, current research and theory. In the book (Gura, 1992), there is agreement with Jonathan Silin (1987: 17) that our increased understanding of psychology and sociology has pushed into the background the philosophical base leading to the articulation of educational principles, which enables early childhood practitioners to tussle with the practical problems of translating these principles into practice. This resonates with the view of the neuroscientist Colwyn Trevarthen (personal communication, June 2009) that over-dependence on an evidence-based approach, to the exclusion of philosophical and principled embeddedness, is not the way forward.

The group met regularly, and Pat Gura also visited the schools. Each school made an audit of blockplay, including looking at timetabling, presentation, availability, pure blockplay and tidying blocks away. Laissez-faire, transmission and interactive approaches to blockplay were explored. This led to consideration of the role of the adult. Adults needed to address gender issues, to introduce some children to blockplay, whilst respecting children and enabling their ideas to develop. Observations highlighted that children might need help in knowing the possibilities of blocks. The adult's first move into conscious play partnering was to join in with what they thought children were doing, but first they needed to observe and be a companion to the child. Children often need to watch others playing with blocks before using them. Children need opportunities to try out their ideas without interference too. Knowing when to join in and when to hold back requires a skilled practitioner – Froebel emphasized the importance of beginning where the learner is, rather than where the practitioner thinks the learner ought to be. Mastery in using the blocks (such as successfully building a bridge) means that children can carry out their ideas unimpeded by practical constraints or lack of skill.

Observations inform practice

Observations revealed children repeating, generalizing, selecting, mixing, matching and varying as their constructions become increasingly complex, sometimes symbolic or narrative in form. 'Stunt building' made it necessary to develop rules with the children to make this safe. The children co-operated with enthusiasm. Strategies were developed to ensure that the use of accessories and a tendency to focus on narrative, storyline and characters did not lead them to neglect the building of complex constructions.

Problems arose when children were asked to verbalize in advance of building with the blocks, as this decontextualized the learning. Children talk more when they are in a real situation. The group agreed with Stephen Krashen (1981) that lack of pressure to speak is important in language development. Real conversations about real things are the way to encourage rich language development. Communication is more than words. All symbol systems are important in human development. Language, dance, music and blockplay are examples. Each provides something unique to a child's education.

We explored the uniqueness of the contribution of blockplay, including three-dimensional space, physical balance, order (you can't put the roof on first!), changing things (making marks on paper cannot be changed so easily), visual harmony and designing sets for play scenarios to develop (castles, shops, houses, roads …).

In 'Reflections' at the end of the book, it says:

> We have, in a modern-day context, used a traditional and time-honoured piece of equipment, Froebel's Gifts, as a starting point through which to explore the curriculum needs of the young and not so young in five schools and more … Froebel helped us to explore the disadvantages of didactic teaching … We have been confronted by historic and continuing debates and arguments, which are important for each generation of educators to explore. (Gura, 1992: 188)

The Froebel Nursery Research Project (1972–77)

In this project, the Froebel Educational Institute realized the vision of a free school attached to the training college. It is a good example of the Froebelian aspiration of interweaving theory with practice. Chris Athey, the Leverhulme Research Fellow who directed the project, writes about this in her book (1990: 17): '[Susan Isaacs] co-ordinated observation of children with psychological theory and subsequently introduced the children to worthwhile curriculum content. This was followed by analyses of the children's responses'. This same approach was taken in the Froebel Project, and continues to exert a major influence on practice, through its emphasis on: observation; supporting children at play; partnership with parents; first-hand experience; developing creativity and an understanding of nature; encouraging symbol use and symbol creation; communicating; and developing languages.

The curriculum offered was in the tradition of the Froebelian Nursery Schools. The focus was not on manual training with prescribed apparatus, or hygiene and carrying out instructions, but instead on participation in cooking, movement, dance and music, constructing, creativity and play, in an atmosphere of community with purpose, with a garden.

One aim, which was in line with the early nursery schools, was to influence the practice in the receiving primary schools at the transition to school stage. The parents in the Froebel Research Nursery School began to make informed choices about which primary schools to select for their children based on those which they considered the most Froebelian in their practice.

Working with parents

Home visiting was part of the practice in the Research School. The spirit was of partnership, with the views of parents respected, and the discussions lively and stimulating for staff and parents alike. Staff and parents worked together with the children, to provide a secure place for them to engage in deep learning. The 20 families with children under five lived on a large housing estate in south-west London and were invited to join the project with the help of the local health visitors.

The challenges of influencing the mainstream

Froebelians continue to influence official documents in a behind-the-scenes way, no matter what the political flavour of successive governments has been, from the Hadow report (1933) onwards, through to Plowden (Central Advisory Council for Education, 1967); *Starting with Quality* (DES, 1990); *Curriculum Guidance for the Foundation Stage* (DfEE, 2000); *Birth to Three Matters* (DfES, 2002); *The Early Years Foundation Stage* (DCSF, 2008). These documents are not statements of Froebelian principles, but they recognize the importance of play, creativity, first-hand experience, families, communication and language, understanding that children are both symbol makers and symbol users, their need for movement, nature and out-of-doors learning environments, seeing the child as an individual who appreciates support in developing self discipline in the context of the importance of the child's feelings, ideas and relationships, and that informed observation is central to working with children. All these principles are embedded in these reports because Froebelians have argued for them.

There is an urgent need for Froebel training which equips teachers and other practitioners to function effectively and with inspiration and vision in a diverse world, and which allows them to explain and analyse the strengths of the Froebelian approach. Given the central control of teacher training, and the move towards this for other practitioners in the early childhood field, the Froebel Certificates have recently been re-established at Roehampton University and are developing in Edinburgh. Both are endorsed by the National Froebel Foundation. The work of the first cohorts is already showing major impact. Froebel's approach still needs the pioneering spirit which will ensure its continuation, but the next generation of Froebelians is emerging, trained, in the practical apprenticeship way, in reflective practice through in-service training. Working with other people's children requires educated, mature and highly trained practitioners.

Principles based on Froebel's philosophy

The following set of principles (Bruce, 1987, 2005b) has endured and still has a useful future. In this chapter, we have explored and examined them through a Froebelian lens. They embrace diversity, not fragmentation, standardization or uniformity. They require regular revisiting and reworking, and they need to be identified in and extracted from reflective practice.

1. Childhood is valid in itself, as part of life. Early childhood education is not simply a preparation for the next stage of education and adulthood. (The terms pre-school and preparatory school are therefore not helpful.)
2. The whole child is important. Children are whole people, with feelings, ideas, thoughts, a sense of embodied self and relationships with others, who need to be physically, mentally, morally and spiritually healthy.
3. Learning is not compartmentalized, because everything links. Areas of learning involving the humanities, arts and sciences cannot be separated: young children learn in an interconnected and integrated way, and not in neat and tidy subject compartments.
4. Children learn best when they are supported in being intrinsically motivated and becoming autonomous learners. This means they need help to be given appropriate responsibility and should be allowed to experiment and make errors, decisions and choices, and are to be respected and valued for their efforts.
5. Self-discipline is emphasized as the only kind of discipline worth having. Reward systems are very short term and do not work in the long term in developing the moral and spiritual aspects of living. Children need to feel appreciated and to learn to value their achievements in their own right, without extrinsic rewards to manipulate what they do.
6. There are times when children are especially able to learn particular things.
7. What children can do, rather than what they cannot do, is the starting point for a child's education.
8. There is an inner symbolic life in the child which emerges under favourable conditions. This takes many forms, but a social and physical environment indoors and outdoors which encourages and supports pretend and role play, imagination, creativity and representations, communicating, literature, writing, mathematics, dance, music, the visual arts, drama and scientific hypothesizing is conducive to making the inner outer and the outer inner.
9. Relationships both between children and between children and adults is of central importance in a child's life, influencing emotional and social well-being and freeing the mind to open up the intellectual life of the child.
10. Education is about the interaction between the child, the context in which development and learning takes place, and the knowledge and understanding which the child is actively part of.

A critique

What criticisms could one make of Froebelian principles and practice?

Clearly, Froebel was a man of his time and society. His work does not express politically correct ideas on, for example, gender and inequality, since these were not current when he was working, and he was writing as a European within the Christian tradition. This does not mean that his overall philosophy is suspect.

Indeed, he was a pioneer in the field of early childhood education. His thinking accorded respect for the child, encouraged the education of women and supported the idea of women working outside the home. He pioneered reflective practice, building a principled approach from this, to mention but a few aspects of his influence.

The ways in which the Gifts and Occupations were taken up and made practice rigid is typical of the way the work of pioneer educators, more often than not, becomes set in stone and misunderstood by those who follow. People yearn for tangible ways forward and simple ways of working with children. But teaching is a subtle and often intangible process and set of skills.

From the 1970s until recently, the Froebelian influence has become less overtly articulated, and therefore more difficult to identify in the mainstream or private sectors. Currently, the way training fosters a narrow focus on goals and outcomes is difficult for Froebelians. Principles are less tangible than apparatus and equipment to be used in prescribed ways, and much more difficult to understand and use. But when this is achieved, through continuing professional development in Froebelian practice, children are educated in the deep and broad sense, rather than merely schooled. The challenge is to bring about reform of training so that Froebelian principles are drawn from practice and applied with informed understanding.

Final thoughts

Froebel's influence lives on in current early childhood practice both in the UK and internationally. He was influenced by the Enlightenment philosopher Kant and the educator Pestalozzi. In turn, his educational principles influenced the McMillan sisters and Susan Isaacs. Froebelian principles continue to influence government documents (from the 1930s onwards, e.g. Halsey, 1972; Plowden; EYFS), with impact on mainstream, private, voluntary and independent settings as well as in home learning environments. He challenged the idea that only men should teach children. Both men and women practitioners are now encouraged to engage in principled and reflective practice arising from training which makes this central. The kindergarten, invented by Froebel, pioneered the community school, and both indoor and outdoor education. Family life and home learning were seen as central to a child's education, with schools being seen as part of the community. Froebel introduced play into the education of young children, as well as giving a central place to the study of nature, mathematics (not just number), music, movement, literature and the visual arts in two and three dimensions. He thought that play took children to the highest levels of their learning, anticipating Vygotsky's theory of play. He thought that relationships between children and between adults and children were an important part of learning. Learning, in his view, begins at birth and continues throughout life.

Summary

- Froebel's influence is deeply embedded in early childhood practice today, but not in explicit ways.
- The principles of his approach are emphasized rather than any specific method.
- The Gifts and Occupations are re-interpreted in current practice with each generation of Froebelians, which avoids narrowly prescribed practice and leads to a flexible approach being adopted by reflective practitioners.
- The kindergarten, with indoor and outdoor learning, was invented by Froebel.
- Froebel pioneered the importance of play in developing learning, and he emphasized home learning and family, learning through and with others, nature, the arts and mathematics, with children involved in real and direct experience (what he called child activity).
- Froebelian education is an international movement, and it advocates the training of practitioners who engage in principled and reflective practice.

Questions for discussion

1. Consider the 10 principles outlined in the chapter and identify in what ways these influence, or not, implicitly or explicitly, the way you relate to children and families.
2. Kindergarten means the garden of children. To what extent does the setting in which you work engage the children in learning about nature? And how are observations gathered? Observe one child and try this out. (Use the books by Chris Athey (1990) and by Susan Isaacs (1930) to help you consider this. They drew on different theories, but used the same Froebelian principles of observation.)
3. Have you ever visited a maintained nursery school or a nursery school that has developed into an integrated Children's Centre? Look at the way that play and creativity are developed, as well as relationships and community. Have you visited a childminder or nanny to see how they work with children up to 3 years? Do they use finger plays? (see Bruce and Spratt, 2008). If you are not in a setting or home learning environment working with other people's children, perhaps you can view a video/DVD showing current practice and reflect on the play, creativity, relationships, community and use of finger play songs. Excellent DVDs are by Siren films.
4. Can you see the modern forms of the Gifts and Occupations in the practice in your setting? Compare the wooden blockplay with the approach of the Froebel Blockplay Research Project and compare the Occupations with the approach in Bruce (2004, 2005a, 2005b), Davies (2003) and Matthews (2003). (*Higher level question*)

Further reading

Levels 5 and 6

Bruce, T. (2005b) *Early Childhood Education* (3rd edn). London: Hodder and Stoughton.
This book explores the commonalities and differences between the educational approaches of Froebel, Montessori and Steiner, incorporating feedback from Barbara Isaacs on Montessori, and Janni Nicoll on Steiner.

Liebschner, J. (1992) *A Child's Work: Freedom and Guidance in Froebel's Educational Theory and Practice.* Cambridge: Lutterworth Press.
The author gives an overview of Froebelian practice and its principles.

Journal article

Bruce, T. (2009) 'Learning through play: Froebelian principles and their practice today', *Early Childhood Practice: The Journal for Multi-Professional Partnerships*, 10(2): 58–72.
This is based on a keynote lecture given at the International Froebel Society Conference in Boston, 2008.

Websites

www.froebel.org.uk

Levels 6 and 7

Brehony, K. (2000) 'English revisionist Froebelians and the schooling of the urban poor', in M. Hilton and P. Hirsch (eds) *Practical Visionaries: Women, Education and Social Progress.* Edinburgh: Pearson Education Ltd.
This gives an excellent analysis of the work of the revisionist Froebelians.

Lilley, I. (1967) *Friedrich Froebel: A Selection from His Writings.* London: Cambridge University Press.
This book is considered one of the classic sources in the early translation from German of Froebel's writing.

Journal articles

Gurland, I. (1960a) 'Play and the growth of intelligence', *National Froebel Foundation Bulletin*, 123(April): 3–12.
Gurland, I. (1960b) 'Play and the growth of intelligence', *National Froebel Foundation Bulletin,* 124(June): 1–6.
Use the Froebel Archive website to find these if necessary.

Websites

www.forestschool@eastwood.wandsworth.sch.uk
www.intfroebelsoc.org
www.sirenfilms.co.uk

References

Athey, C. (1990) *Extending Thought in Young Children: A Parent–Teacher Partnership*. London: Paul Chapman Publishing.

Bostridge, M. (2008) *Florence Nightingale*. London: Penguin.

Brehony, K. (2000) 'English revisionist Froebelians and the schooling of the urban poor', in M. Hilton and P. Hirsch, *Practical Visionaries: Women, Education and Social Progress*. Edinburgh: Pearson Education.

Brosterman, N. (1997) *Inventing Kindergarten*. New York: Harry N. Abrams.

Bruce, T. (1987) *Early Childhood Education*. London: Hodder and Stoughton.

Bruce, T. (1991) *Time to Play in Early Childhood Education*. London: Hodder and Stoughton.

Bruce, T. (1996) *Helping Young Children to Play*. London: Hodder and Stoughton.

Bruce, T. (2001) *Learning through Play: Babies, Toddlers and the Foundation Years*. London: Hodder Arnold.

Bruce, T. (2004) *Developing Learning in Early Childhood*. London: Hodder Arnold.

Bruce, T. (2005a) *Cultivating Creativity: Babies, Toddlers and Young Children*. London: Hodder Arnold.

Bruce, T. (2005b) *Early Childhood Education* (3rd edn). London: Hodder Arnold.

Bruce, T. (2009) 'Learning through play: Froebelian principles and their practice today', *Early Childhood Practice: The Journal for Multi-Professional Partnerships*, 10(2): 59–73.

Bruce, T. (2010) 'Can Asset Based Community Development (ABCD) help to develop a Froebelian approach to early childhood education in Soweto, South Africa?', *Early Childhood Practice: The Journal for Multi-Professional Partnerships*, 11(2).

Bruce, T. and Spratt, J. (2008) *Essentials of Literacy: A Child's Journey*. London: Sage.

Central Advisory Council for Education (England) (1967) *Children and their Primary Schools (The Plowden Report)*. London: Her Majesty's Stationery Office.

Davies, M. (2003) *Movement and Dance in Early Education* (2nd edn). London: Paul Chapman Publishing.

Department for Children, Schools and Families (DCSF) (2008) *The Early Years Foundation Stage*. London: DCSF.

Department for Education and Employment (DfEE) (2000) *Curriculum Guidance for the Foundation Stage*. London: DfEE.

Department for Education and Skills (DfES) (2002) *Birth to Three Matters: A Framework to Support Children in their Earliest Years*. London: DfES.

Department of Education and Science (DES) (1990) *Starting with Quality: The Report of the Committee of Inquiry into the Quality of the Educational Experience Offered to 3- and 4-year-olds*. London: HMSO.

Froebel, F. (1887) *The Education of Man*. New York: Appleton.

Gura, P. (ed.) (1992) *Exploring Learning: Young Children and Blockplay*. London: Paul Chapman Publishing.

Hadow, W. (Chair) (1933) *The Report of the Consultative Committee: Infant and Nursery Schools*. London: HMSO.

Halsey, A.H. (1972) *Educational Priority*, Vol. 1. London: HMSO.

Isaacs, S. (1930) *Intellectual Growth in Young Children*. London: Routledge and Kegan Paul.

Kalliala, M. (2006) *Play Culture in a Changing World*. Maidenhead: Open University Press.

Krashen, S. (1981) *First Language Acquisition and Second Language Learning*. Oxford: Pergamon Press.

Liebschner, J. (1992) *A Child's Work: Freedom and Guidance in Froebel's Educational Theory and Practice*. Cambridge: Lutterworth.

Matthews, J. (2003) *Drawing and Painting: Visual Representation in Young Children* (2nd edn). London: Paul Chapman Publishing.

Milchem, K. (2010) 'The urban forest school: reconnecting with nature through Froebelian pedagogy', *Early Childhood Practice: The Journal for Multi-Professional Partnerships*, 11(1–2): 106–18.

Nawrotzki, K. (2006) 'Froebel is dead! Long live Froebel: The National Froebel Foundation and English education', *History of Education*, 35(2): 209–23.

Read, J. (1992) 'A short history of children's building blocks', in P. Gura (ed.) *Exploring Learning: Young Children and Blockplay*. London: Paul Chapman Publishing.

Read, J. (2009) '"To climb a tree is for the child to discover a new world": danger and adventure, exploration and knowledge in Froebelian pedagogy', Froebel Conference, Gifts for the Future, University of Edinburgh. Also in *Early Childhood Practice: The Journal for Multi-Professional Partnerships*, 11(1).

Ronge, J. and Ronge, B. (1879) *A Practical Guide to the English Kindergarten*. London: A.N. Myers and Co.

Silin, J. (1987) 'The early childhood educator's knowledge: a reconsideration', in L. Katz (ed.) *Current Topics in Early Childhood Education*, Vol. 7. pp. 17–31.

Spratt, J. (2007) 'Finger rhymes: why are they important?', *Early Childhood Practice: The Journal for Multi-Professional partnerships*, 9(1): 43–54.

Tovey, H. (2007) *Playing Outdoors: Spaces and Places, Risk and Challenge*. Maidenhead: Open University Press.

Trevarthen, C. (2009) Personal communication, June, Edinburgh.

Weston, P. (1998) *Friedrich Froebel: His Life, Times and Significance*. London: Roehampton Institute.

Whinnett, J. (2006) 'Froebelian practice today: the search for unity', *Early Childhood Practice: The Journal for Multi-Professional Partnerships*, 8(2): 58–80.

Zimiles, H. (1977) 'A radical progressive solution to the problem of evaluation', in L. Katz (ed.) *Current Topics in early Childhood Education*, Vol. 1. pp. 50–74.

CHAPTER 5

MARIA MONTESSORI IN THE UNITED KINGDOM: 100 YEARS ON

Martin Bradley, Barbara Isaacs, Louise Livingston, Dawn Nasser, Anne Marie True and Margaret Dillane

---

Overview

In this chapter, we offer an overview of Montessori education, which is based on the understanding that children have an innate capacity to learn and to educate themselves when placed in an environment that allows independence and the freedom to work at their own pace. We discuss how Maria Montessori (1870–1952) developed an educational approach from her insights into children's thought processes and how these differ from those of adults. We consider how the resulting educational practices are based on a deep understanding of what children choose to do for themselves. Using specially devised materials in a well-prepared environment, supported by the close observation and guidance of a Montessori-trained teacher, this approach develops strength of character and fosters a lifelong love of learning. We show how current policy initiatives in early education in England and Scotland demonstrate that Montessori thinking is increasingly being recognized as central to good practice.

The development of the Montessori approach to education

Maria Montessori was born in Chiaravalle, Italy in 1870. She entered the University of Rome to study mathematics, physics and natural sciences but changed to study medicine, specializing in paediatrics in her final two years. In 1896 she graduated as one of the first women with a degree in medicine. She was particularly interested in children and studied the work of earlier European practitioners and philosophers. For example, Jean Itard (1775–1838) and Edouard Seguin (1812–1880), both of whom considered that observation was crucial to treatment, regarded 'mental deficiency' as a pedagogical problem rather than a medical one, and used graduated exercises to aid motor development. Montessori also studied Rousseau's (1712–1778) ideas on individualized learning, Pestalozzi's (1746–1827) view of training the senses using increasingly difficult formal exercises and Froebel's (1782–1852) work which emphasized play, using specially developed toys and materials, and who regarded learning as a series of developmental stages leading to self-awareness.

A common thread in the ideas of these practitioners and educationalists is the child's inner potential to develop in their own natural manner, if appropriately guided and supported. Modifying Itard's and Seguin's sensory teaching materials, Montessori reviewed the 'prepared environment' and the structured approach to child development, focusing on what she considered children really need. Montessori observed that children used a particular activity or exercise, then repeated it several times, rather than moving to a new one. It was work for its own sake, not for reward. She found that toys and activities given to children were chosen and rejected. She later replicated her experiments in different cultures and different places around the world, developing a scientifically based and universally applicable educational approach.

In 1900 Montessori was appointed by the 'National League for Retarded Children' as director of a demonstration school. She succeeded in improving children's attainment and some began to gain skills thought to be far beyond their capabilities, including reading and writing. Some passed examinations on a level with children in 'normal' primary schools – which led her to question the quality of the education provided in such establishments. Increasingly, Montessori began to be seen as an educator rather than a medical professional. In her first book, *The Montessori Method* (1909, translated into English in 1919), she wrote 'After I had left the school for deficients … I became convinced that similar methods applied to normal children would develop or set free their personality in a marvellous and surprising way' (Montessori, 1919: 33).

Montessori's school, the Casa dei Bambini (Children's House) for 3–6-year-olds, opened in January 1907 in the San Lorenzo slums of Rome. The owners hoped that the children of working mothers could be kept off the streets and that vandalism could be reduced – a parallel with Rudolf Steiner and the Waldorf Factory owners (see Chapter 6).

Between 1907 and 1914, Montessori's work and influence increased significantly. A second school was established in Milan in 1908 and in 1911 the first American school opened. In England, a Montessori school was set up by the Chief Inspector of Schools, Edmond Holmes, with Bertram Hawker. Holmes had become disillusioned with traditional English education and had visited Montessori schools in Italy. He regarded these as revolutionary, challenging preconceived notions of education. In 1916 the London Borough of Acton began to convert all its schools for young children into Montessori schools, with Montessori-trained teachers and a full range of Montessori equipment.

Montessori's schools attracted visitors from all over the world and led to her first training course in 1909, supported by the first outline of her approach, *The Method of Scientific Pedagogy Applied to the Education of Young Children in the Casa dei Bambini* (*The Montessori Method*, 1919). Montessori described children as having characteristics which would develop naturally when their needs were supported:

- being capable of extended periods of concentration
- enjoying repetition and order
- revelling in freedom of movement and choice
- enjoying purposeful activities (preferring work to play)
- displaying self-motivated behaviour that requires neither punishments nor rewards
- taking delight in silence and harmony of the environment
- possessing personal dignity and spontaneous self-discipline
- being capable of learning to read and write (see Isaacs, 2007: 6).

For the rest of her life, Montessori travelled throughout the world, lecturing and developing her ideas. Private Montessori schools were established in Europe and the United States with some countries adopting the approach for their school systems. In 1913 the first international teacher training classes were held.

Between 1914 and 1935, the Montessori movement flourished in Europe. In 1919 Montessori gave her first training course in London, followed by courses every other year until 1939. In 1929 the Association Montessori Internationale (AMI) was founded to help disseminate and continue her work, with the English courses continuing at its London centre. Hitler and Mussolini were interested in Montessori's method as a means of creating a new social order through the education of young children. Mussolini even became the President of the Montessori Society of Italy. After Montessori disagreed with these interpretations of her work, the Nazis banned the Montessori method in 1935, and by 1936 all the Montessori schools in Italy had closed. Again, a parallel may be drawn with the experiences of Steiner schools.

In 1939 Montessori went to India to establish a training centre and to teach. She established a London centre in 1947, which became the Montessori St Nicholas Centre in 1954. Her son, Mario, continued to work with the London AMI centre. Her final years were spent in Holland where her last home became the headquarters of AMI which Mario led until his death in 1982.

Montessori education today

In 2009 the Montessori Schools' Association (MSA) census, with 329 returns (from a membership of 622 nursery and primary schools), showed that over 31,000 children use Montessori settings in the United Kingdom (UK). The approximate annual turnover nationally is between £20,500,000 and £21,500,000, emphasizing Montessori's significance in private and independent provision. Montessori schools vary in size from six to 225 places, the average being around 38. Most nurseries (60%) operate full time, the remainder open part time – mornings or afternoons – and many are small. The majority provide for 2–5-year-olds (84%), but the number of schools for children aged 6 or over had doubled to 39 from the previous census in 2004. However, many schools only use the Montessori approach with the younger children before following the National Curriculum with the older children. This is due to an emphasis on entry requirements for secondary schools and the lack of Montessori-trained teachers for older children.

Most settings are in south-east England, with others distributed across the UK. Many occupy premises such as private homes, church and village halls and cricket pavilions. Often, materials and equipment have to be taken out and put away each day. Provision for outdoor play is also variable.

In the last decade, three state schools in Manchester, Essex and Lincolnshire have become Montessori Schools, with the support of the St Nicholas Trust, and more are planned. In the mid-1990s, Montessori Education (UK) (MEUK) (2009) set up an accreditation scheme for Montessori Schools which remains in operation. In 2008 the St Nicholas charity also set up an accreditation scheme, accrediting about 70 schools by the end of its first year of operation.

When reviewing *The Advanced Montessori Method – Spontaneous Activity in Education* in 1918, *The Times Educational Supplement* noted that the Montessori method 'has reached a stage when it is an integral part of the new education' (10 January 1918). Criticisms were made of its apparatus and of specific methods for teaching reading and writing. However, the themes of freedom of choice, of observing how children develop and learn, and the use of structured materials were applauded. These themes remain evident today in the principles underlying the Early Years Foundation Stage (EYFS) in England (DCSF, 2008) and the Scottish Curriculum for Excellence (HM Inspectorate of Education, 2007; The Scottish Executive, 2004; The Scottish Government, 2008), as we discuss in more detail later in this chapter.

Montessori's approach to the child and learning

Several *themes* underpin Montessori's view of education:

- the child's independence
- learning through active play
- the ability to think creatively and the ability of children to educate themselves
- developing concentration
- the adult's respect for the child as a unique individual
- the adult's use of observation
- the environment prepared according to individual children's needs.

These themes are also developed through the *three key components* of Montessori's method of education: the child; the favourable environment; and the teacher.

Montessori education aims to provide 'education for life' as well as specific skills, such as reading and writing. Montessori strongly believed in the child as a 'unique individual' with a 'spiritual embryo' that creates its own spiritual characteristics, just as the physical embryo develops physical characteristics – ideas which have parallels in current thinking on neuroscience (Eliot, 1999; Lillard and Quest, 2006). She considered that children develop in relation to their environment. Consequently, education begins at birth with the child following their own timetable rather than an adult-determined curriculum dictating a fixed stock of knowledge to be imparted to the child. The prepared environment in which the child learns should be designed to allow this natural unfolding to occur. In Montessori's view, adults should take their cue from observing the development of the whole child. Freedom is limited by respect for others and the environment, enabling the child to develop self-discipline. Children should make decisions for themselves and be in control of themselves, yet be aware of others' needs. They will also become self-motivated, able to concentrate and persevere. Reggio Emilia has a similar approach, although with a collaborative adult–child relationship rather than Montessori's independent child. To achieve these ends, the school's approach should be reflected in the home environment, hence the need to work closely with parents – again a parallel with Reggio Emilia (see Chapter 1).

Montessori believed that as children develop, they progress through *stages* or *planes*, each with its own characteristics requiring different environments, and slightly different approaches by the adults. She identified *four main developmental stages*:

- From conception to age 6: the child's absorbent mind assimilates information effortlessly, creatively exploring through their senses. It is a phase of self-creation when the child begins to develop their own view of the world within their culture.
- Childhood: from age 6 to 12 is a period of calm expansion of what has been developed previously. The child uses their intellect to learn and is hungry to find out about the world.
- Adolescence: from age 12 to 18 is another creative phase.
- Early adulthood: from age 18 to 24 is a further stage identified as a period of calm expansion of what has been created between 12 and 18 (although this was not discussed as fully).

The concept of developmental stages was a theory of its time, influenced by its Western, and in particular European, background. It sought to explain children's maturing awareness of the world in a philosophical construct rather than one based on direct scientific evidence; the latter was used to support and inform the former, rather than the reverse. However, Montessori was working at a time when scientific approaches were being developed – intelligence testing, for example – and her background enabled her to use such work to support her theories. While others developed notions of stages of development, Montessori used them as a basis for educational planning, defining the nature of the environment for each stage. It is a testimony to her insight that her ideas continue to influence current educational thinking.

Montessori outlined a comprehensive educational plan based on observation of the child's pattern of concentration and work. Montessori's approach identifies the growing child's need to be active, employing all their senses through concrete experiences and manipulation with their hands, and thereby learning. The innate drive is the desire to engage in activities without considering whether these constitute play or work.

The seeming dichotomy between play and schoolwork remains central to many current debates. The English *Independent Review of the Primary Curriculum* (DCSF, 2009) stated that children should start school in the year of their 4th birthday, whilst the Cambridge Primary Review (Alexander, 2010) considered that formal schooling should be delayed until the age of 6. Both regarded play as central to a child's learning, but the context in which this should be provided – school, home or other provision – remains a matter for debate. Similarly, the status of the content of the curriculum – whether it is distinct from the processes of learning – remains an issue. For Montessori, the content and the process are integrated, together leading to the wider goals of autonomy, perseverance and concentration.

According to Montessori, during the stage of the 'absorbent mind' the child's inner drive predisposes them to acquire human characteristics during 'sensitive periods', particularly for:

- coordination of movement
- language
- order
- small detail
- refinement of the senses
- socialization.

In this, the adults should observe the child, looking for signs of these sensitive periods so that the environment, including adult/child interactions, can be best organized to promote learning. She saw the six key sensitive periods as working in conjunction with each other, some running concurrently, although peaking at different times during the stage of the absorbent mind. From the age of 3, the child is more able to organize and classify experiences and concepts.

The Montessori approach identifies six areas of activity:

- practical life (or daily living)
- refinement of the senses
- communication, language and literacy
- mathematics
- cultural aspects of life – understanding of the world
- creative expression.

Practical life activities provide skills to support children's independence – such as pouring, dusting, dressing, clearing away. These active tasks develop manipulative skills and gross and fine motor control, as well as coordination between the mind and the hand and other physical skills. They become routines, offering security within the changing classroom environment and fostering competence and independence outside the classroom. They reflect events which could occur in the home, but in the early years setting they are structured and presented in ways which enable the adults to monitor children's developing skills.

Sensorial work enables the child to organize their environment, such as by sorting objects into size order and exploring two- and three-dimensional forms. This helps them to clarify what they experience around them and enhances their further exploration of the world using their senses – visual, tactile, auditory, olfactory and gustatory – as well as developing understanding of the three-dimensional aspects of objects.

Effective *language and communication skills* lay the foundation for later phonic understanding. Phonics is a significant element, using sandpaper letters to provide a multi-sensory approach to learning. As with other Montessori learning, the emphasis is on small, structured steps enabling the child to work systematically through an organized learning process; in this case, of phonic awareness preceding teaching of letters, and writing as a route to reading. This has close links with the EYFS and the Independent Review of the Primary Curriculum ideas of good practice.

Mathematics emphasizes concrete, practical learning with equipment made of natural materials and which the child can manipulate and experience, starting with pre-mathematical concepts such as sorting, matching and ordering. The experiences will also include using numbers in everyday contexts such as preparing snacks, or using measurement to see which objects are longer than others. This parallels Steiner's approach to mathematical learning in the early years (see Chapter 6).

Cultural aspects cover what the EYFS terms 'knowledge and understanding of the world'. This includes botany and zoology and observation of nature and the seasons, such as using a nature table with fresh flowers, stones, tree bark and other natural materials to extend the children's awareness and their developing understanding of the world. Geography starts with the wider picture of natural aspects of physical geography before looking at continents and countries. History is developed through time lines and other means of appreciating the passage of time.

Self-expression includes dance and drama as well as free access to painting and other art media, often using natural materials, such as sponges for printing and painting. Similarly, musical instruments – mainly tuned and un-tuned percussion – are available for the children's use. Storytelling is a feature of most Montessori classrooms as a spontaneous activity when children ask to hear a story.

The prepared environment

Throughout their development, children's spontaneous learning is affected by the environment. Montessori believed that it should be organized to promote the development of individuals as active learners. The teacher prepares the environment following observation of the child's needs, interpreting behaviour in the context of the individual's developmental stage and sensitive periods. Materials, equipment and activities are set against the child's prior experiences and knowledge, so extending and developing learning.

Montessori saw the favourable environment as being:

- accessible and available to the child
- providing freedom of movement and choice
- enabling the child to take personal responsibility for looking after the environment
- providing real materials and a natural environment
- possessing beauty and harmony.

The ideas of the environment as accessible and available to the child were major innovations in her day, supporting her view that it should respond to the child's developmental needs and thus foster independence. Today, we accept that furniture and equipment should be suited to the child's physical size, with chairs and tables of an appropriate size for the child's height and proportions, and which the children can move to suit their needs. We also now accept that some activities may take place on the floor.

The child's freedom of choice and movement has several implications for organizing the environment. It should be set out to encourage the child to take personal responsibility, thus aiding independence. The space should not be too cluttered, and there should be ease of access to both indoor and outdoor environments wherever possible. Outdoors should not just be a playground, but should be prepared for purposeful work. Both indoors and out, materials and equipment should be set out in sequential order and accessible for the child to choose. Children should be autonomous and able to tidy up after activities or wash cups and plates used for snacks. Consideration for others has implications for social behaviour and for ensuring that the environment remains accessible to others. The practice of putting groups of children of different ages together provides role models for behaviour and the use of materials and equipment.

Montessori considered that the environment should be attractive to the child and invite their interest and curiosity. Decorations should be kept simple so as not to distract the child – echoed in the design of Reggio Emilia provision. The harmony of the classroom is also reflected in the atmosphere; in part this is due to activities being self-directed. Concentration is promoted because the activities respond to the child's developmental needs. The classroom should not be silent; instead there should be a hum of activity with children working as they choose: alone, in pairs or in groups. The equipment provided for the child should be made of natural materials where possible. Montessori argued that three-dimensional objects were far more likely to promote children's development than two-dimensional pictures or images.

To gain the most from this environment, self-directed activities should be followed for as much of the day as possible, according to the child's own rhythm. Children should have sufficient time to explore the full potential of their selected open-ended activity, using this repeatedly for as long as they wish. Many Montessori schools regard a three-hour uninterrupted cycle as the optimum time for work. Ideally, there should be no break for specialist lessons such as music, foreign languages or physical education. Outdoor activities should be accommodated in the free-flow of children between the outdoor and indoor environments. Interruptions break the child's natural rhythm and are counter-productive. Storytelling should be a spontaneous activity when the children ask for this. Set times for stories or snacks interfere with activities in which the children are already independently engaged. Montessori wrote that her schools

> have proved that children need a cycle of work for which they have been mentally prepared; such intelligent work with interest is not fatiguing and they should not be arbitrarily cut off from it by a call to play. Interest is not immediately born, and if when it has been created, the work is withdrawn, it is like depriving a whetted appetite of the food that will satisfy it. (Montessori, 1948: 95–6)

During the work cycle, besides periods of concentration, there are times when the child finds choice more difficult and looks around or begins to wander – such periods of 'false fatigue' are part of what Montessori calls the 'curve of work'. Careful adult observations will note that the curve of work varies for each child and from day to day. Longer-term observations show the child's unique pattern – when they need help, a challenge or the chance to rest. This forms the rhythm of the child's day and the teacher should not intervene to replace the child's decisions with an imposed adult idea of what to do next. As the child develops self-control, some major outcomes of Montessori education emerge – the capacity to concentrate for extended periods, to be autonomous in choosing and sustaining activities and to grow in competence.

The role of the adult

The teacher's role, as the *third element* of Montessori education, is to strike a complex and delicate balance, preparing an environment based on observations of the child's development, needs and interests but without seeking to impose adult ideas or structures on that development. Fundamentally, the adult must trust the child's ability to select and explore the materials, considering ways of using them. Adults should support the children as they move from one activity to another.

Montessori believed that every useless help to a child is an obstacle to development. Adults can constrain the child's natural development by seeking to do things for them rather than letting them do things for themselves. Such intervention destroys the child's concentration and undermines their efforts. As an unobtrusive observer, the adult tailors the child's individual learning plan to their natural learning, allowing them to build confidence and self-esteem. This revision of the traditional adult–child educational relationship enables the child to become active and the adult passive. Montessori commented: 'The greatest triumph of our educational method should always be this: *To bring about the spontaneous progress of the child*' (Montessori, 1919: 230, emphasis in original). This also changes the nature of the curriculum from having an existence separate from the development of the child into being a means by which the broader development of the child can be promoted; clearly this creates tensions where state-defined approaches such as the EYFS specify learning objectives based on things that adults think children need to know – an instructional curriculum rather than Montessori's developmental education.

Using continuous observation of the children, the Montessori teacher develops each child's individual learning plan. Supplemented by samples of work, photographs and other records

> [the] plan shows the Montessori activities, organised by areas of learning and outlines the progressive nature of children's learning, reflected in the organisation of the classroom. The plan is developmentally organised and so charts the child's development and learning by recording when an activity was introduced. It also records the child's continued interest in and repetition of the activity and the child's level of competence, as well as exploration of the activity. (Montessori Schools Association/DCSF, 2008: 18)

Following observations of the children, the teacher then develops her lesson plans or 'Montessori Presentations'. These identify how the learning environment is to be organized, building on each child's prior achievements in small steps, specifying materials and indicating the level of adult support. The Presentations form the Montessori schemes of work. The small steps identified in the Presentations reflect the observations made by the teachers and so the cycle of observation, planning and provision of work continues. Observations made during sessions are often supplemented by longer narrative observations, illustrated by photographs and samples of work, to form the child's learning story which has developed from Montessori's 'Biographical Chart' (Montessori, 1919: 65). These supplement the overall record of achievement and periodic reports to parents and are also often passed on to the child's next school. They are regularly shared with the parents as a means of ensuring that practices at home and in school reflect one another as far as is possible.

Montessori education: the Early Years Foundation Stage in England and the Scottish Curriculum for Excellence

In September 2008, the English EYFS was introduced and applied to all provision for children aged between birth and rising to 6 years old. The EYFS principles share many elements of good Montessori practice. Barbara Isaacs, principal of the Montessori Centre International training college, summarizes the principles as being:

- practitioners should ensure that all children feel included, secure and valued
- no child should be excluded or disadvantaged
- early years experiences should build on what children already know and can do

- parents and practitioners should work together
- the early years curriculum should be carefully structured
- there should be opportunities for children to engage in activities planned by adults and also those that they plan or initiate themselves
- practitioners must be able to observe and respond appropriately to children
- well-planned, purposeful activity and appropriate intervention by practitioners will engage children in the learning process
- the learning environment should be well planned and organized
- care and education must be of high quality (Isaacs, 2007: 45).

Montessori's structured approach to learning is reflected in the EYFS. Common elements include: the need to observe children; the belief that learning is best when undertaken in practical situations; the idea that adults should only make appropriate interventions; an emphasis on high-quality provision; the view of the child as a unique person; and a structured curriculum. There remains the distinction between an instructional curriculum and a developmental curriculum combining curriculum content with pedagogy, for example in the nature of adult interventions. Montessori emphasizes developing the unique child and the work cycle.

Montessori practice easily fulfils the aims and requirements of the EYFS and the government. Support for Montessori work was emphasized when the Department for Children, Schools and Families funded a *Guide to the Early Years Foundation Stage in Montessori Settings* (Montessori Schools Association/DCSF, 2008) jointly written by Barbara Isaacs and Ruth Pimenthal, then Director of the EYFS. This tacitly recognized earlier research, such as that of Chattin-McNichols (1992), who noted that Montessori programmes perform as well as similar programmes in areas such as school readiness and intelligence, and perform better than similar programmes in developing attention and concentration, general intelligence and academic achievement, and especially in maintaining progress. An independent document was also produced by MEUK, *Montessori and the Early Years Foundation Stage: Guidance for Teachers* (2009, www.montessorieducationuk.org).

Montessorians have worked with the Primary National Strategy to inform inspectors from the Office for Standards in Education (Ofsted) and local authority officers about Montessori approaches and to promote these. In 2008, 88% of Montessori nurseries were considered by Ofsted to be 'outstanding' or 'good'. Concerns remain that local authorities have the power to oversee EYFS provision and to monitor its quality when assessing nurseries' eligibility for state funding for 3- and 4-year-olds' places. Interpretations of the EYFS can vary from one local authority to another and, in attempts to establish conformity to a single approach, can easily ignore the particular nature of Montessori education.

Another issue is that the EYFS curriculum is organized differently to the Montessori approach, although both cover similar content. Also, the EYFS is assessed in a Profile to be completed during the child's final year of working within the guidance. Many Montessorians do not wish to assess young children formally, arguing that systems of extrinsic targets and outcomes, potentially promotes conformity to a system based on a fear of failure (see Montessori, 1919: 22). Also, Montessori teachers' qualifications still do not enable them to work as qualified teachers in state schools.

Meanwhile in Scotland, the *Curriculum Framework for Children 3 to 5* (Scottish Consultative Council on the Curriculum, 1999) and subsequent documents have emphasized the need for a coherent curriculum from the age of 3 to 18, aimed at developing four capabilities which closely match Montessori's ideas: 'successful learners, confident individuals, responsible citizens and effective contributors' (The Scottish Government, 2008: 11). These themes develop a view that 'Children are naturally curious and eager to find out about the world around them. We must build on their curiosity and enthusiasm to learn when we develop their learning environments, working outwards from their individual interests and needs' (HM Inspectorate of Education, 2007: 5). Again, this links with Montessori's ideas of engaging the child's interest, and working from their current awareness of the world.

Critique of the Montessori approach to education

Criticisms of Montessori's approach often focus on her views regarding play and imagination. The emphasis on seeing work and play as synonymous and focusing on the real world has suggested to some that the possibilities of imaginative play are undervalued. Maria Montessori's own background, and the nature of the families with whom she worked, undoubtedly influenced her approach. The publication by Montessori Schools Association/DCSF (2008: 6) suggests that criticisms of this aspect are historical: 'The characteristics of the child's work are closely linked with what we consider today to be play'. The authors continue: 'The defining factors are freedom of choice, the exercise of will and deep engagement, which leads to concentration' (2008: 21).

Some early critics noted Montessori's approach to phonics. Susan Isaacs, a contemporary of Montessori, acknowledged that the approach was focused on the individual child and sought to compare Montessori-educated children's interest in reading with that of children in Froebelian kindergartens (see Chapter 4). She commented that 'it is the paucity of other games in Montessori schools which makes the children take to this new occupation' (Smith, 1985: 255). Nonetheless, in the Montessori guide to the EYFS (Montessori Schools Association/DCSF, 2008), the focus on phonics is identified as an appropriate element of an early years curriculum and is strongly supported by the EYFS.

Final thoughts

The continuing relevance of Montessori practice can be attributed to several factors. It was devised scientifically and rigorously developed in diverse cultures, so ensuring its international relevance. The emphasis on training ensured the dissemination of the practice and key elements were rapidly absorbed into mainstream practice. The use of observation of how, and what, children are learning was recognized as good practice. Yet, fundamental elements have not been absorbed into mainstream education and these continue to provide the distinctive Montessori approach. In particular, the change to the adult/child relationship from adult direction to adults observing children; the use of the results of these observations to form assessment, planning and organization; the detailed structuring and use of materials; and the focus on developing confidence, self-discipline and character, are all elements which continue to ensure that Montessori education has a distinctive and comprehensive plan for education. Time spent in Montessori nurseries and primary schools lays the foundations for future learning. As such, it is truly 'learning to live and living to learn'.

 Summary

- Montessori education considers that children have an innate desire to learn which is best promoted when they work at their own pace in an environment prepared to support learning.
- Montessori's scientific and international work ensured that her approach is universally applicable.
- Three elements interact to develop children's character and self-discipline while learning and throughout life: the child, working independently; the environment specifically prepared to meet individual children's learning needs; and the trained adult.
- The adult/child relationship changes from adult domination to observation of children's needs according to their stage of development.
- Much of Montessori's approach has been absorbed into mainstream practice; however, Montessori practice remains a distinctive approach to modern education.

 Questions for discussion

1. Consider how learning is organized in Montessori settings and in your own setting, or one you are familiar with. What are the similarities and differences?
2. How does the relationship between work and play in a Montessori setting relate to your understanding of play?
3. Reflect on the value of Montessori's notion of children's independence in relation to their competence and initiative. How does this compare to your own experiences?
4. In what ways is the role of the Montessori teacher similar or different to that of a teacher from another tradition that you know well? (*Higher level question*)

Further reading

Levels 5 and 6

Kalliala, M. (2006) *Play Culture in a Changing World*. Buckingham: Open University Press.
This text usefully examines real-life activities, free flow and human activity.

Montessori Schools Association/DCSF (2008) *Guide to the Early Years Foundation Stage in Montessori Settings*. London: Montessori St Nicholas/DCSF.
This publication is recommended by the National Primary Strategy as part of its good practice guidance on early years. It considers how the Montessori approach to planning, learning and assessment can meet the EYFS requirements without compromising Montessori principles.

Levels 6 and 7

Laevers, F. (2005) 'The curriculum as means to raise the quality of early childhood education: implications for policy', *European Early Childhood Education Research Journal*, 13(1): 17–29.

Montessori, M. (1988) [1949] *The Absorbent Mind*, Vol. 1. Oxford: ABC-Clio Ltd.
This book discusses the issues of education for life, the periods of growth, teachers' preparation, discipline and obedience.

Yelland, N. (2005) *Critical Issues in Early Childhood Education*. Buckingham: Open University Press.
This is a particularly useful book for considering the issues of freedom, independence, the nature of childhood and children's needs as well as social interaction.

Websites

www.mariamontessori.org
This is the website of the Maria Montessori Institute responsible for Montessori training.

www.montessori.org.uk
This website offers articles and details of conferences, etc. It is aimed at parents and practitioners.

www.montessorieducationuk.org
The focus of this website is national standards for Montessori education in Britain. Again, it offers a great deal of helpful reading and background information.

References

Alexander, R. (ed.) (2010) *Children, their World, their Education: Final Report and Recommendations of the Cambridge Primary Review*. Abingdon: Routledge.
Chattin-McNichols, J. (1992) *The Montessori Controversy*. New York: Delmar Publishers Inc.
Department for Children, Schools and Families (DCSF) (2008) *The Early Years Foundation Stage*. London: DCSF.
Department for Children, Schools and Families (DCSF) (2009) *Independent Review of the Primary Curriculum*. London: DCSF.

Eliot, L. (1999) *Neuroscience – What's Going on in There? How the Brain and Mind Develop in the First Five Years of Life.* New York: Bantam Books.

HM Inspectorate of Education (HMIE) (2007) *The Child at the Centre: Self-evaluation in the Early Years.* Livingston: Livingston HMIE.

Isaacs, B. (2007) *Bringing the Montessori Approach to Your Early Years Practice.* London: Routledge.

Lillard, P. and Quest, E. (2006) 'The early years: evaluating Montessori education', *Science*, 29: 1893–4.

MEUK (2009) *Montessori and the Early Years Foundation Stage: Guidance for Teachers* (www.montessorieducationuk.org).

Montessori, M. (1919) *The Montessori Method: Scientific Pedagogy as Applied to Child Education in 'the Children's House'.* London: Heinemann.

Montessori, M. (1948) *To Educate the Human Potential.* Oxford: ABC-Clio Ltd.

Montessori Schools Association/DCSF (2008) *Guide to the Early Years Foundation Stage in Montessori Settings.* London: Montessori St Nicholas/DCSF.

Scottish Consultative Council on the Curriculum (1999) *Curriculum Framework for Children 3 to 5.* Edinburgh: Scottish Consultative Council on the Curriculum.

Smith, L. (1985) *To Understand and to Help.* London: Associated University Presses.

The Scottish Executive (2004) *A Curriculum for Excellence.* Edinburgh: The Scottish Executive.

The Scottish Government (2008) *Curriculum for Excellence, Building the Curriculum 3: A Framework for Learning and Teaching.* Edinburgh: The Scottish Government.

CHAPTER 6

STEINER WALDORF EARLY CHILDHOOD EDUCATION: OFFERING A CURRICULUM FOR THE 21ST CENTURY

Jill Tina Taplin

Overview

In this chapter, I offer an introduction to the Steiner Waldorf early childhood environment including a brief historical perspective of this well-established approach. I describe the principles that underpin this environment with examples of the practical methodology, covering: imitation and example; purposeful activity and free movement; imagination; rhythm and repetition; and child observation.

A view into the Steiner Waldorf kindergarten

What might you see if you visit a Steiner Waldorf kindergarten? There will be children using furniture and blankets to build dens, others building small-world scenes, not out of Lego, but with logs, pine cones and very simple home-made dolls. There will be no evidence of adults directing this play or leading it towards any pre-planned educational aims. The adults in the setting will be busy with necessary tasks, such as food preparation, housework and washing up, and there will be children helping them. There are no computers or programmable toys.

Outside in the garden, you may well find adults involved in traditional handcrafts, such as spinning or wood carving. These are not tasks that the children can do themselves, but the children are near the adult 'helping' or playing with the off-cuts or materials in their own ways. Later in the morning, all the children gather around an adult who is telling a traditional fairy tale, learnt by heart. No DVDs or story tapes are available and no picture book is in use, although there may be some beautiful picture books in the room for the children to enjoy at other times.

What is happening here? Where are the usual aids to early years education – the bright colours, opportunities for electronic interaction, informative labelled displays and questioning conversations? They are not present in the cosy room decorated in muted colours and furnished and equipped with predominantly natural materials and simple playthings. How does this setting meet the needs of the young child?

The beginnings of Steiner Waldorf education and the education today

Dr Rudolf Steiner was born in 1861 in Austria. He was a philosopher, a great thinker, an artist with a scientist's interest in the natural and the man-made world, and a person with an inner life so rich and deep that he initiated and inspired innovative work in areas ranging from education, medicine and social development, to agriculture and theatre and design. The movement based on his ideas is called Anthroposophy – the study of humanity.

In 1917, during the chaos in Germany at the end of the First World War, Steiner was asked by the Stuttgart industrialist, Emil Molt, the director of the Waldorf Astoria cigarette factory, for help in founding a school for both the children of his workmen and for children of well-off families, employing a new kind of education based on the ideas of the development of the human being that Steiner spoke about. Today, there are about 900 schools and 1,800 kindergartens in more than 60 countries across all five continents. Any school which today calls itself a Steiner or a Waldorf school should be based on the principles of this first school, which aimed to support all pupils to develop their potential for clear thinking, sensitive feeling and motivated doing through teaching the Steiner Waldorf curriculum.

In Britain, there are about 90 individual kindergarten groups for children aged from rising 3 to rising 7. There are also parent and child groups and in some settings daycare is provided. Some kindergartens prepare children for mainstream settings and some are attached to Steiner Waldorf schools, which may be schools for pupils up to the age of 18 or 19, preparing them for university entrance. The Steiner Waldorf curriculum of the 'lower school' (eight classes for children aged 6 through to 14) builds on the foundations that have been laid in kindergarten and which are discussed later in this chapter. Gradually, the interest fostered in the natural world in kindergarten will become scientific study. Well-nourished imaginations will be drawn into the acquiring of sound academic skills and knowledge, with an emphasis remaining on an artistic approach to presenting work. Healthy bodies will continue to be given opportunities for movement, from gymnastics and team games through to circus skills and a special art of movement linked to speech and music known as eurythmy. (This is unique to Steiner schools and may be included once a week in the kindergarten.)

Throughout this lower school period, the children will stay in their own mixed-ability class with their peer group. It is normal for the class teacher who joins them in class one, to stay with that class as long as possible, up to class eight. This class teacher will have the increasing support of subject teachers as the children grow older, but will always carry the main focus for the class's well-being. The intimate understanding of each pupil that this system engenders means that there is less need for testing as the children pass from one academic year to another, although of course assessments and records will be kept throughout the child's time in the school, including the early years, with the emphasis on the whole child and not just academic abilities.

At the age of 14, pupils cross another threshold into the 'upper school'; here they will remain in their class group and meet a variety of subject teachers with specialist backgrounds. These teachers will continue the rich, broad-based curriculum and increase the intellectual demands on the children. ICT will be part of the curriculum and the pupils may take some public examinations. However, they will also continue to balance their academic work with challenging craft skills and have regular opportunities for expressing themselves artistically, musically and dramatically. Many of these young people are still likely to be in the same class as the peer group with whom they were in kindergarten, and the social skills which they learnt when they were aged 4 will have helped them to mature friendships that may last the rest of their lives. It is normal for the early childhood department, the lower school and the upper school to be situated on the same campus and it is an asset to be able to maintain relationships between all the age groups in the school.

The principles and practice underpinning the Steiner Waldorf approach

Imitation and example

According to the Steiner view of self-development, young children learn primarily through imitation, and whatever is happening around the child becomes part of that child as she absorbs not only the outer actions of the adults, but the inner attitudes too.

> Whatever a young child is told to do should not be artificially contrived by adults who are comfortable in our intellectual culture, but should spring from life's ordinary tasks. The whole point of a kindergarten class is to give young children the opportunity to imitate life in a simple and wholesome way. (Steiner, 1988: 81)

As Jaffke said: 'All normally developing children receive their guidance and their impulses for their actions, their play and their behaviour from the adult world' (Jaffke, 2000: 29–30).

The adult stands before the child as an example, modelling to the child ways of managing day-to-day life that will be absorbed by the child. Adults who treat other people and the environment with respect are teaching children to do likewise. Children inherit the accents and habits of those in their surroundings and family traits can be seen not only physically, but also in the way children move, gesture and respond to life's events.

For the Steiner practitioner in an early childhood setting, working through the means of imitation and example allows direct instruction to be avoided. It is imitation that is seen as the key learning method for children under the age of 7. Teaching by example is the preferred Steiner approach up to this age because it does not stimulate the child's intellect, but allows them to spend their time in a mood of unself-conscious participation. In this mood, they learn in the same way that they learnt their mother tongue. For example, if the adult in the kindergarten gets up from the table and care-fully pushes her chair into the table, the children will be inclined to do likewise. If they do not, the adult might make a general comment: 'Now my chair is in the right place, I am ready to leave the table', and then slowly look round at all the other chairs – 'I can see that lots of the chairs are in the right place now'. If this happens every day, then all the children will push their chairs in to the table and a good habit will have been learnt about completing one thing before moving on to the next. The adult will, of course, have to keep repeating the action herself for the habit to be maintained.

If the adult in kindergarten wants the children to learn to sew, this will be brought about using imitation and example. First, the table is prepared with all the equipment necessary both for the adult task (perhaps mending a play cloth) and for the children to explore sewing skills for themselves. Already the sight of this preparation draws some children from their play. The older ones (most of the kindergartens are mixed age from 3 to 6+) may already be enthusiastic sewers and have their own basket with needle-book, pin cushion, etc. in it, and they may be choosing cloth from the scrap basket and setting to work measuring and cutting thread, threading the needle and so on. The adult proceeds with his or her work slowly and carefully. The adult's actions will show the children what to do. Older children in the mixed-age kindergarten can provide models and give help to the younger ones. The youngest children may be happy to 'help' by pulling the needle through the cloth for the adult. Others may want their own piece of work and will be helped to prepare their needle and thread and encouraged to do as much as they can themselves. They may then begin to sew a piece of cloth, pulling the stitches tight until it becomes a ball on a thread, which can be completely satisfying to them. Others may have a particular project in mind such as making a little purse. All the time the adult is there as a model and example of a good sewer, with time to encourage and help as seems necessary, until it is time to put all the equipment away.

Meanwhile, some children in the kindergarten will have gone on playing and not come to the sewing table, but this example of a busy, happily engaged group around an adult supports the mood of their own play. If something begins to go wrong in the play and the children don't seem able to resolve it themselves, then the adult may be able to make a helpful comment without leaving the sewing table, or it may be dealt with by beckoning a child over to help at the sewing table while the issue defuses, thus enabling the potential malefactor to shine as a helper. Observation over time will show which children do not like or feel able to sew and they may be invited to help with a special sewing project one day, or another kind of task that involves fine motor skills, so that the adult can judge their abilities and needs in this area.

Activity and movement

The Steiner Waldorf curriculum focuses on the ability of young children to learn through imitation and through activity.

> Movement facilitates integration of sensory experience … Actions carried out in space help us literally to 'make sense' of what we see. Sight combined with balance, movement, hearing, touch and proprioception … help to integrate sensory experience and can only take place as a result of action and practice. Movement is the medium through which this takes place. (Goddard Blythe, 2008: 140)

The setting will typically provide many opportunities for worthwhile activities. There is a place for craft projects at the table, but even more meaningful to the child are the variety of activities involved in looking after one's 'home' and preparing food. Washing and cleaning, mending and gardening alongside careful adults are domestic arts that give countless opportunities for the child to gain control of his or her body, to learn useful practical skills and to develop the physical and emotional attributes necessary for everyday life. Frank Wilson, in his book *The Hand*, argues that it is our hands that make us truly human, not our brains, and that to learn to use these hands is the worthy precursor to intellectual development (Wilson, 1998).

Steiner Waldorf schools do not teach reading and writing until after the children leave kindergarten for class one, at the age of 6. Extending the play-based curriculum in this way, with plenty of movement opportunity, has recently been supported by the publication of the Cambridge Primary Review (Alexander, 2010: 168–9), which calls on evidence that an early start to formal learning does not translate into later achievement and risks long-term damage. Research from the University of Otago, New Zealand, gives quantitative evidence that teaching children to read from age 5 is not likely to make them any more successful at reading than those learning from age 7 (Suggate, 2009). A later start leaves time for learning through self-initiated play, which Steiner advocates believe provides a vitally important individualized learning tool for all young children. By the time children in Steiner settings reach the end of kindergarten, they will be ready to start 'real' school and forge ahead with learning first to write, and then to read, along with many other exciting new skills that maintain the emphasis on active engagement in learning.

In the Steiner early childhood setting, practitioners see the child's eagerness to move and be active as an asset. Research shows that children learn through movement

(Goddard Blythe, 2008; Wilson, 1998). In the Steiner setting, purposeful movement is given a central place outdoors as well as inside, a priority which is in line with the Play Strategy, and the Big Lottery Fund's Children's Play initiative, which give unprecedented financial assistance to support children's outdoor play (Play England, 2009). But the metal and plastic play structures that populate children's play areas are not to be found in Steiner settings. Instead, and as much as circumstances allow, there is a real garden in which the children may play and work with the adults there. There may be flowers and vegetables growing, trees to climb, earth and sand to dig in and dens to build with brushwood. The children are likely to build their own 'play structures' out of logs, planks, crates and the like, which will change every day giving fresh challenges to growing bodies, impetus to budding engineering skills and avoiding the repetitive movements that some outdoor play equipment encourages. At the same time, the children enjoy all the possibilities to experience the seasonal round of the natural world. Many Steiner settings spend time regularly in, for example, a local woodland or nature reserve. This gives the kind of nature experience that is becoming more widely advocated as the Forest School movement grows (Bennett, 2009), but balances this experience with that of the 'house and garden'.

Another important element of kindergarten work focusing on movement, but adult-led, is the ring or circle time. This is a time when the whole group comes together to be led by the kindergarten practitioner for 15–20 minutes, following a flowing sequence of finger games, action songs and poems, and whole group movement games specifically chosen and linked to provide an enjoyable, imaginative and energetic time for the whole class. This may happen inside or outdoors. This is when polarities of all kinds (loud/quiet, fast/slow, fine movements/whole body movements, etc.) can be explored and the special skills of, for example, anticipation and holding back (essential for later classroom habits) can be honed as part of group games. This 'teaching', like almost everything in the kindergarten, is done by just doing it with the children joining in. They do this because they are natural imitators, because that's what always happens at this time in the morning, and because it is enjoyable. Ringtime provides repetition of the words, music and gestures, seasonal celebration, movement and language play and is also, as a practitioner-led activity, a contrast to self-initiated play.

Imagination

Young children have a capacity for fantasy that allows them to transform endlessly and this provides another tool for the practitioner. Many of the toys in a Steiner Waldorf kindergarten are 'open-ended' – the logs, pine cones and simple puppets that are part of the small-world play allow the child's own imagination to flourish.

> Rationality works with the known, the finite. Imagination, on the other hand, is timeless and engages with the possibility of what might be. Imagination penetrates the veil of the future and trawls the past to supply the human psyche with the multiplicity of meanings it needs; it lends wisdom to the soul. (Jenkinson, 2001: 57)

As the kindergarten child moves the pine cone across the green cloth, she may be picturing a snail moving through a garden. Other children who have stopped their own play to watch are drawn into the same fantasy world. Similarly, as the practitioner tells the well loved fairy tale to the group, with no picture book, so the children are seeing, each uniquely 'in their mind's eye', the story unfolding. In this way, young imaginations are being exercised in a gentle kind of 'mind gym' and are prepared for the creativity that adult life increasingly demands.

> Imagination means creating images that are not present to the senses. All of us exercise this faculty virtually every day and every night … the whole crux of human intelligence hinges on this ability of mind. (Pearce, 1997: 117)

The fully animated film and the intricately detailed plastic model, though they may engage the child, do not call on her initiative in the same way as simple toys do. In the Steiner Waldorf kindergarten, it is seen as vital that children are more than just physically active. When the young child sees adults washing up every day with care and quiet enjoyment, they are learning both that human life is only sustained by our activity and that we can enjoy what we have to do. When entertainment does not arrive ready packaged but requires exercising the imagination, similar skills and lessons are learned so that the independent and free adult will not find the practical side of life to be drudgery, nor will she be in need of a constant stream of entertainment.

Given the time and equipment for self-initiated play, the child can do what she needs to, play out what is most important for her and practise the skills that are on the brink of being grasped. For example, the puppet may do what the child would like to do, but is not yet brave enough to. Six-year-old children devise constructions involving endless knotting of ropes, just as their fingers are ready to make them and their mental capacities are similarly leaping to make connections that they did not notice before. Play is serious work for young children and the practitioner will need to be observant and skilful to keep play time harmonious and to bring it to a close, with a tidy-up time that may be chaotic in its process but that concludes with the room tidy and the children gathered together for the next event of the daily rhythm.

Rhythm and repetition

Steiner practitioners observe that young children are nurtured by the security of rhythm and repetition – within which their inherent skills and abilities can flourish. 'The ordering potential of rhythm gradually guides the child's movements and contains his energy until such time as he himself can be the guide' (Oldfield, 2001: 79).

In the kindergarten, rhythm is an essential tool of the practitioner. Many rhythms and routines fill the kindergarten day, week and year. Within a few days of starting in the group, the child has 'learned', without overt instruction, what comes next and how the whole session fits together. There will be tiny rhythms, such as how we wash our hands or how we begin and end meals. Having well thought through and repeated routines builds habits that are useful (properly washed hands), respectful (creating a peaceful mood at the table) and comforting ('this is how we always do it here'). This requires at first gentle encouragement on the part of the adults, then watchfulness and consistency, so that the habits started at the beginning of the year are still there at the end.

Having a healthy rhythm to the whole session is just as important. Some of the activities that happen in kindergarten draw the children in, for example gathering all the children together for a ring-time, a meal or a story. Some have more of an expanding gesture, for example child-initiated play indoors and out. A healthy rhythm is one that breathes, as the freedom to move vigorously and shout outside may be followed by the quiet and inward mood of story time, or children move in their own time, from a focused table activity to their own unconscious choice of play.

The most challenging parts of any early childhood session are the transitions from one kind of activity to another; having a healthy rhythm where an 'out-breath' is followed by an 'in-breath' is key to this. If the children have had sufficient time to play outside and consistent routines of preparing to come inside, they will be more ready to sit quietly and listen to a story than if the story comes at a random time; for example, if they have had only five minutes to 'let off steam' outdoors and the cloakroom is chaotic and messy. There is the possibility that a routine can stagnate and disengage the observational faculties of the practitioner, but working skilfully with a breathing rhythm retains the flexibility to avoid this danger. Health and well-being and 'the feeling of coherence … [are] strengthened through rhythm and order [which] bear fruit in adulthood in increased resources of resistance and resilience' (Patzlaff et al., 2007: 32).

A song or a rhythmical repeated phrase can move children on in a way that ordinary speech often does not, for example when the tidy-up time begins. The tidy up then needs to proceed in a regular way that the children can learn and understand through repetition. The play-cloths are gathered in a pile and then folded to the accompaniment of a song before being laid in their basket, furniture is put back in place, baskets are filled with their right contents and dolls are put in their beds in the dolls' corner. This is a process making sense to the children and clearing the space, both physically and emotionally, for the next event in the rhythm of the day.

Rhythm and repetition are there when the meal table is set and the chairs are counted. The menu in the Steiner Waldorf setting follows a weekly rhythm, appealing to the child's sense of order – Monday is rice day, Tuesday is soup day, Wednesday is bread day, etc. Normally, the children will have been involved in the preparation of the food and, without the need for any explanation, they learn that our food is the result of worthwhile work and that work is good to do.

The importance of the seasons through the kindergarten year brings in another, larger rhythm that thrills the older child in the mixed-age kindergarten when she recognizes the return of a familiar seasonal song or activity. Rhythm through the year brings in something that is larger than the child, his family or even his community and so connects him to the whole of the kingdom of nature and the diverse cultures of the world. The celebration of festivals through the year adds to the child's feeling of being connected to a much bigger world. These festivals will represent all the cultures and faiths that are present in the kindergarten group and will be an opportunity for the practitioner to work with parents in preparing wonderful 'special days' for the children.

Respect for the child's journey

For most children, the step into nursery, playgroup or kindergarten is their first step outside the home and it can be a very delicate one to achieve without trauma. In a Steiner setting, the transition can be eased by a visit to the child's home and family before she joins the group. Every child has their own journey. 'Children need time to fulfil each of their developmental stages. Let kids be kids. Life isn't a race. They hitch-hike their way with us, asking for conversation as we accompany them on their journey' (Schweizer, 2006: 25). They may be in childcare as babies, or they may come quite late into kindergarten or school, have a big family or a very social community network around them, or a quiet life with only one carer. Kindergarten rhythms need to be flexible enough to meet their needs and early childhood practitioners need to be both interested and observant enough to get to understand each unique child.

It is never possible to solve the riddle of another person but striving to do so is part of the educator's task. Steiner practitioners undertake this by recording observations and meeting regularly to discuss these with colleagues and with individual children's parents. Sometimes this will be supported by a 'child study' on a particular child. In this case, there will be a process over time where first of all adults share the questions that they have about the child, then a detailed sequence of observations is collected, including physical attributes, how the child moves and speaks, how they express their feelings and how their thinking processes manifest. Later reflections and proposals for actions will emerge from this. Child studies like this are undertaken by the early childhood faculty regularly as part of their meeting structure.

Respect for the child is mirrored in all the aspects of the life of Steiner Waldorf settings.

Critique of Steiner Waldorf early childhood provision

The stance taken by Steiner Waldorf education not to introduce literacy in any formal way until the age of 6 is often greeted with incredulity by many British practitioners (and sometimes with envy). The absence in Steiner Waldorf settings of the up-to-date technology found in many other early childhood settings and in most homes is replaced by what is termed '"warm" technology, i.e. hand driven machinery such as grain mills, scales, apple juice press, spinning wheel' (Steiner Waldorf Education, 2009: 29). The question for many people around both literacy and technology is whether Steiner Waldorf education equips children for life in the 21st century.

Attempts have been made to draw links between what is demanded by the English Early Years Foundation Stage (EYFS) (DCSF, 2008) and the approach adopted in Steiner Waldorf schools (Steiner Waldorf Education, 2009). Steiner settings in England may also apply to the Qualifications and Curriculum Development Agency (QCDA) (www.qcda. gov.uk) for exemption from aspects of the EYFS requirements. However, it may be that it is only this approach, with its focus on affective and creative aspects of development (Conroy et al., 2008), which will truly prepare children for adult life in an unknown future. There are many critics of Britain's current system (see e.g. Palmer, 2006) and a great deal of evidence that a later start in, for example, literacy does not disadvantage – and may advantage – children (see e.g. Alexander, 2010; Suggate, 2009).

Final thoughts

As adults, we take on the responsibility for bringing up the next generations and how we work together determines our success. If we have one commonly agreed goal, it would be to live together in harmony with our fellow human beings and the natural world around us. Where else can one learn this more effectively than when we are young in our families, with our peers and in early years provisions and schools (Clouder, 2008: 41)?

The principles of Steiner Waldorf early childhood education emerge from the Steiner picture of child development that sees the child under 7 as needing a protected environment where foundations can be laid for future intellectual learning, but where formal academic learning does not begin. There is current evidence-based research that draws attention to the unhappiness and vulnerability of children today and to society's view of childhood as a dangerous and fearful time. This is to be found reflected in the findings of The Good Childhood Inquiry by The Children's Society (Layard and Dunn, 2009) and the 'toxic childhood' picture painted by Sue Palmer (Palmer, 2006) and Oliver James (James, 2007), as well as in the Cambridge Primary Review (Alexander, 2010) referred to earlier in this chapter.

One response is to look at children's education as an opportunity to apply therapies, to give children a chance of emotional well-being and to manage this with a stream of assessment. This is explored by the contributors to *Childhood, Well-Being and a Therapeutic Ethos* (House and Loewenthal, 2009). An alternative response, and that which Steiner practitioners advocate, is to provide an enabling environment in which children can grow strong and healthy from the very start.

Advocates of the Steiner approach are sometimes accused of over-protecting young children by cocooning them away from the real world. The Steiner answer is that the kindergarten world of 'house and garden' *is* a real world that the child can understand, grow and flourish in, and which will transform them into adults whose early educational foundations have given them resilience, strength of purpose and the inner freedom to see their way forward in the world of the future.

For many years, there has been a tendency for Steiner practitioners to shy away from research into their work; however, this is fortunately now beginning to change. The kind of evidence-based research that is needed is beginning to happen, such as that of Suggate (2009), referred to above, and *Meeting the Child*, a joint report from the University of Plymouth and the Steiner Waldorf Early Years Research Group (Drummond and Jenkinson, 2009).

What Steiner Waldorf early childhood settings endeavour to offer is an education that supports the young child to understand and love herself, other people and the earth. The intention is not to preserve children in an idyllic version of the past, but to prepare them for the future by building secure foundations indicated by the principles and examples outlined in this chapter.

Summary

- Steiner Waldorf early childhood education is part of an international fellowship of settings and schools, some taking pupils up to the age of 19 and developed from the indications given by Dr Rudolf Steiner for the first Waldorf school founded in 1917.
- For the child under 7, it focuses on the ability of young children to learn through imitation and through activity.
- Priority is given to allowing children the time and space for self-initiated play, while the adults focus on activities that show care for the environment, including food preparation, and which the children may join in with.
- The environment, activities and equipment aim to nurture creative imagination while a breathing rhythm provides a sense of security.

Questions for discussion

1. How does the extension of a play-based curriculum until the child's seventh year benefit or disadvantage the child?
2. Do children under 7 learn more easily through their capacities to imitate a clearly modelled and repeated example than through direct verbal instruction?
3. How is the gifted child served by the Steiner curriculum and kindergarten experience?
4. Is this early childhood approach just the product of early 20th-century educational theory or does it have a particular relevance to progressive early childhood education and care today? (*Higher level question*)

Further reading

Levels 5 and 6

Jaffke, F. (2000) *Work and Play in Early Childhood*. Edinburgh: Floris Books.
This is an introduction to the Steiner picture of child development and teaching methodology, enhanced by photographs of Steiner settings in action.

Oldfield, L. (2001) *Free to Learn: Introducing Steiner Waldorf Early Childhood Education*. Stroud: Hawthorn Press.
Written by an experienced Steiner kindergarten practitioner working in Britain but including international examples, this book builds a detailed picture of the environment and the principle of Steiner kindergarten education.

Oldfield, L. (2009) 'The Steiner foundation stage', *Nursery World*, August.

Levels 6 and 7

House, R. (2009) 'Trailing clouds of glory: protecting dream consciousness in young children', *The Mother*, 33: 36–9.
Patzlaff, R. and Sassmannshausen, W. et al. (2007) *Developmental Signatures: Core Values and Practice in Waldorf Education for Children Aged 3–9*. New York: AWSNA Publications.
This publication ties in principles and guidelines for the Steiner approach for children through kindergarten and into school.

Steiner, R. (1988) *The Child's Changing Consciousness and Waldorf Education*. London: Rudolf Steiner Press.
This is one of Rudolf Steiner's series of lectures on education, given in 1923. The first four are of particular relevance to early childhood work.

Websites

www.allianceforchildhood.org.uk
www.allianceforchildhood.org
These websites highlight the work of the Alliance for Childhood in this country and elsewhere in the world. The aim of the organization is to improve children's childhood experiences.

www.iaswece.org (International Association for Steiner Waldorf Education)
www.steinerwaldorf.org.uk
These websites give detailed information, newsletters and DVD footage about Steiner Waldorf education in this country and, as the name implies, internationally. They offer an excellent resource.

References

Alexander, R. (ed.) (2010) *Children, their World, their Education: Final Report and Recommendations of the Cambridge Primary Review*. Abingdon: Routledge.
Bennett, R. (2009) 'Lessons in life at the Forest School', *The Times*, 6 October.
Clouder, C. (ed.) (2008) *Social and Emotional Education: An International Analysis*. Santander (Spain): Fundacion Marcelino Botin.
Conroy, J., Hulme, M. and Menter, I. (2008) *Primary Curriculum Futures: The Primary Review Research Survey3/3*. Cambridge: University of Cambridge.
Department for Children, Schools and Families (DCSF) (2008) *The Early Years Foundation Stage*. London: DCSF.
Drummond, M.J. and Jenkinson, S. (2009) *Meeting the Child – Approaches to Observation and Assessment in Steiner Kindergartens*. Plymouth: University of Plymouth.
Goddard Blythe, S. (2008) *What Babies and Children Really Need*. Stroud: Hawthorn Press.

House, R. and Loewenthal, D. (eds) (2009) *Childhood, Well-Being and a Therapeutic Ethos*. London: Karnac.

Jaffke, F. (2000) *Work and Play in Early Childhood*. Edinburgh: Floris Books.

James, O. (2007) *Affluenza*. London: Vermillion.

Jenkinson, S. (2001) *The Genius of Play*. Stroud: Hawthorn Press.

Layard, R. and Dunn, J. (2009) *A Good Childhood: Searching for Values in a Competitive Age*. Harmondsworth: Penguin.

Oldfield, L. (2001) *Free to Learn: Introducing Steiner Waldorf Early Childhood Education*. Stroud: Hawthorn Press.

Palmer, S. (2006) *Toxic Childhood: How Modern Life is Damaging our Children*. London: Orion Books.

Patzlaff, R. and Sassmannshausen, W. et al. (2007) *Developmental Signatures: Core Values and Practice in Waldorf Education for Children Aged 3–9*. New York: AWSNA Publications.

Pearce, J.C. (1997) *The Magical Child*. New York: Plume.

Play England (2009) *Welcome to Play England*. Available at: http/www.playendland.org.uk

Schweizer, S. (2006) Well, I Wonder: Childhood in the Modern World. Forest Row: Sophia Books.

Steiner, R. (1988) *The Child's Changing Consciousness and Waldorf Education*. London: Rudolf Steiner Press.

Steiner Waldorf Education (2009) *Guide to the Early Years Foundation Stage in Steiner Waldorf Early Childhood Settings*. Forest Row: The Association of Steiner Waldorf Schools.

Suggate, S.P. (2009) 'School entry age and reading achievement in the 2006 Programme for International Student Assessment (PISA)', *International Journal of Educational Research*, 48: 151–61.

Wilson, F. (1998) *The Hand: How its Use Shapes the Brain, Language and Culture*. New York: Vintage Books.

PART 3

CONTEMPORARY THEORIES

CHAPTER 7

THE HIGHSCOPE APPROACH

Ann S. Epstein, Serena Johnson and Pam Lafferty

Overview

This chapter describes the HighScope approach including its philosophy, support-ing research, child development, curriculum content, the practice environment and methodology, assessment instruments and approach to professional develop-ment. We present the rationale (philosophy, theory and research) behind the HighScope approach and consider how to define and apply the ingredients of active participatory learning. We also stress the importance of planning and reflection in young children's development and highlight research demonstrating the effectiveness of the HighScope approach. We discuss how HighScope addresses all areas of early learning, the important and diverse roles practitioners play in the early years, and how assessment and training fit within the approach.
   In the chapter, we address the following:

- HighScope philosophy
- research that supports HighScope

(*Continued*)

(*Continued*)

- HighScope curriculum content
- HighScope practice methodology
- HighScope assessment tools
- the HighScope training model.

Several key concepts about the approach are emphasized throughout the chapter, beginning with the philosophy on which the approach is based.

HighScope philosophy

The HighScope approach is a complete system of early childhood education, based on child development theory, rigorous research (which we discuss below) and proven practitioner strategies to enable children's learning and social-emotional well-being. The approach has four components: a method of practice for adults to implement which can be replicated; comprehensive curriculum content that complements and supports early learning with key developmental indicators for children; assessment tools to measure the standard of practitioners' professional expertise and children's progress; and a training model to help practitioners in using HighScope to support children's development.

How children learn

In the HighScope approach to learning in the early years described in *Essentials of Active Learning in Preschool* (Epstein, 2007a) and *Educating Young Children* (Hohmann et al., 2008), young children build or 'construct' their knowledge of the world. That means learning is not simply a process of adults giving information to children; rather, children participate actively in the learning process.

The philosophy on which the HighScope approach is grounded is based on child development theory and research. It originally drew on the cognitive-developmental work pioneered by Jean Piaget (Piaget and Inhelder, 1969) and the progressive educational philosophy of John Dewey (1938/1963). Since then, the approach has been updated using the results of ongoing research on children's 'learning pathways' or 'developmental trajectories' (Goswami, 2002), brain research (Shore, 1997; Thompson and Nelson, 2001) and specific content learning. For example, new knowledge about early literacy (Snow et al., 1998) and mathematics (National Council for Teachers of Mathematics, 2000) are incorporated, respectively in *Growing Readers Early Literacy Curriculum* (HighScope Educational Research Foundation, 2005) and *Numbers Plus Preschool Mathematics Curriculum* (Epstein, 2009).

The way that HighScope practitioners support children's learning was first derived from the work of developmental psychologist and educator Lev Vygotsky (1934/1962), particularly the notion that development occurs within socio-cultural settings where adults interact with children in their 'zone of proximal development' to advance their thinking to the next level. Subsequently, as Jerome Bruner's idea of 'scaffolding' gained currency – the notion that education is most effective when adults *support* children's reasoning, while simultaneously challenging them to re-examine and *extend* their understanding (Bruner, 1990) – has been increasingly incorporated into HighScope's strategies for practitioners. These educational practices in the HighScope model continue to be updated, based on the theory and research of those who have followed Vygotsky's lead and Bruner's educational applications (Rowe and Wertsch, 2002).

The role of adults

HighScope practitioners are as active and involved as children in the early years setting. They thoughtfully provide materials, plan activities and talk with (not at) children in ways that both support and challenge their explorations, observations, ideas and thoughts. Activities are both child-initiated to capture children's natural curiosity and inherent motivation, and adult-guided so practitioners can build upon children's interests to challenge their reasoning and expand their critical thinking. In this model of 'shared control', both children and adults take responsibility for children's learning.

The notion of *intentional teaching* (Epstein, 2007b), together with ongoing refinement of ideas about *developmentally appropriate practice* (Copple and Bredekamp, 2009), are at the forefront of early childhood education today. The HighScope approach details what such practices look like through the concept of 'active participatory learning' (described below) – a process in which practitioners and children are partners in shaping the learning experience. This interactive model, whereby adults intentionally provide children with the materials, experiences and conversations they need to explore their world, respects the social context of learning that is advocated by Vygotsky, Bruner and the many other educational theorists cited above.

Adaptability in different settings

The HighScope approach promotes independence, curiosity, decision-making, co-operation, persistence, creativity and problem solving in young children. These characteristics are valued worldwide, making HighScope both appealing and applicable in settings around the globe. The transferability of the HighScope approach is clearly demonstrated by its use in over 20 countries in Europe, Asia, Africa and Central and South America. (See the research section below for evidence of the model's effectiveness internationally.) Moreover, the model is adaptable for early years settings serving children and families of different cultures and economic backgrounds within, as well as across, countries. For example, in the United States HighScope is used with low-income and minority populations, immigrants, English-language learners and Native Americans, as well as within urban, suburban and rural settings. Because practitioners daily plan activities that are individualized to children's interests and abilities, HighScope is also adopted by settings serving children with special educational needs

(Dowling and Mitchell, 2007). HighScope in the United Kingdom reflects much of the American experience and is practised across the state, private and voluntary sectors. This includes supporting children in inner cities and schools where multiple languages may be spoken, children who are in home daycare settings, those with a wide range of additional learning difficulties and children who are deemed vulnerable. Additionally, because the HighScope approach requires no special materials, HighScope UK works to support and train early years practitioners in countries such as Tanzania and Kenya, where few material resources are available, enabling them to realize the riches in their natural environment and utilize them to support children's learning.

Active participatory learning

To promote such experiences, the HighScope approach features five ingredients of active participatory learning:

1. *Materials* – Early years settings offer substantial quantities of diverse age-appropriate materials for children to use in a variety of ways. Materials that are open-ended and appeal to all the senses are chosen to expand children's experiences and stimulate their thought. These materials are frequently natural (e.g. shells, stones, pine cones, leaves, clay), which are free or cost little to acquire and are organized in freely accessible storage units.
2. *Manipulation* – Children examine, manipulate, combine and transform materials and ideas. They make discoveries through direct hands-on and 'minds-on' contact with these resources.
3. *Choice* – Children choose materials and play partners, contribute ideas and plan activities. Because experiences build on their personal interests and goals, they are highly engaged in the learning process.
4. *Child language and thought* – Children describe what they are doing and under-standing. They communicate verbally and non-verbally. Children reflect on their actions and modify their thinking to take new learning into account. Language and thought are the basis of literacy and other areas of academic and social growth.
5. *Adult scaffolding* – Adults know and understand how young children reason. They support their current level of thinking and challenge them to advance to the next stage. In this way, adults help children gain knowledge and develop creative problem-solving skills. Peer learning is highly valued and practitioners frequently invite children to share their knowledge and understanding in support of others.

The importance of planning and reflection

Although many early childhood settings, especially those espousing a constructivist approach, use 'active learning' practices, HighScope is unique in emphasizing the importance of 3–5-year-old children planning activities based on their own interests and reflecting with adults and peers about what they learn from carrying them out. This process, known as the plan–do–review sequence, is a hallmark of the HighScope approach. Young children in HighScope settings express their intentions (make 'plans' involving choices about materials, actions and people), carry out their ideas ('do' things to achieve their goals) and reflect on the experience ('review' what they did and what they learned). For example, a group of children talked together, found playdough and made 'cakes' which they decorated with paint, sequins and buttons. They then offered them to adults and other children and eventually brought the remainder to the review group to recall how they planned the cakes, made them and shared them – they followed a plan–do–review sequence. This sequence is rooted in the work of several theorists and is supported by research as described and referenced below.

Planning is both a cognitive and social-emotional process. Cognitively, to make a plan, children must have a mental picture of what they want to do. Developmental psychologists describe these mental tools as 'executive control structures' (Case, 1985) or 'executive function' (Zelazo and Mueller, 2002). From a social-emotional perspective, when children successfully carry out their intentions, they develop a sense of initiative. By encouraging exploration and independent problem solving throughout the day, HighScope practitioners support the development of planning. As children carry out their plans at 'work time' (the 'do' part), they are being purposeful as well as playful. What differentiates HighScope 'work' time from the 'free choice' in other early years curricula is a sense of intentionality or 'forethought' as well as purpose. A choice may be impulsive, based on what is immediately appealing, whereas a plan involves thinking ahead about the how, who, what, and possibly the why, of one's choice. In making a plan, children approach play as a way to accomplish something important to them. They are not merely choosing among options offered by an adult. Many theorists recognize the value of purposeful play in young children's learning. John Dewey (1938/1963) saw playfulness and seriousness as the ideal combination for learning. Educator Michael Ellis (1988) sees play as an important problem-solving strategy in all humans. He says play is how our species adapted in the past and will continue to deal with an unpredictable future.

Recall time is when children make sense of their purposeful play. It involves more than simply remembering what they planned and what they did. During recall, children actually build or construct memory, forming a mental representation of their experience and interpreting it based on their current stage of thinking. When children talk with others about their actions, they are also engaging in the storytelling process. Psychologist Roger Schank (1990: 115) says 'creating the story also creates the memory structure that will contain the gist of the story for the rest of our lives' – 'talking is remembering'. Thus, the memories created when children review their active learning experiences help to bring about permanent changes in their growing understanding of the world. Berry and Sylva (1987: 35) further underscore the importance of recall time as providing 'a rich potential for language use, discussing means-ends relationships, and exploring connections'. In addition to sharing aloud with others what they have learned, the regular practice of reviewing their actions and the lessons learned from them encourages children to engage in an ongoing dialogue with themselves as they carry out their plans. Vygotsky (1934/1962) refers to thought as 'internalized talk' and the plan–do–review sequence encourages children to engage in both internal and external talk as they interact with materials and people, and make sense of their experiences and observations.

Research supporting the HighScope approach

Research by HighScope

The Foundation's best known research is the *HighScope Perry Preschool Study* (Schweinhart et al., 2005), based on the random assignment of 123 children born into poverty and entered into a programme or no-programme group. Ongoing research finds positive effects for the programme group through age 40 on school achievement and literacy, high school graduation, adult earnings, home ownership and lifetime arrest rates. A cost–benefits analysis shows society saves more than US$17 for every dollar invested. Moreover, another longitudinal study comparing three curricula – HighScope, a traditional nursery school model and a directive teaching approach – found those attending the teacher-directed curriculum had significantly more years of special education for emotional impairment and more felony arrests than participants in the other two models (Schweinhart and Weikart, 1997). These findings provide support for the efficacy of developmentally appropriate practices over more didactic approaches to early education.

In 1998 the UK government launched 'Sure Start', an initiative originating with HM Treasury, to bring together childcare, early education and health and family support services. As the cornerstone of the government's drive to tackle child poverty and social exclusion, Sure Start development districts were initially selected according to the levels of deprivation within their areas. The *HighScope Perry Preschool Study* (see above) was quoted extensively to endorse the proven short- and long-term results of early years intervention in improving the life chances of children and their families.

The HighScope training of trainers evaluation (Epstein, 1993) looked at the effects of training on the quality of practitioners' expertise and child outcomes in HighScope and comparison settings. The settings of practitioners who attended HighScope training received significantly higher quality ratings on variables generally agreed to constitute best practices, such as ample provision of diverse materials, a consistent daily routine and supportive adult–child interactions (National Association for the Education of Young Children, 2005). Moreover, children in HighScope compared to non-HighScope settings scored significantly higher on measures of development. The findings especially showcased the importance of the plan–do–review sequence, described above. The more practitioners provided opportunities for children to plan and review activities of their own choice – hallmarks of the HighScope approach – the higher children scored on measures of the academic and social skills needed for school success.

Independent research

Support for the advantages of a developmentally based over a directive teaching model also comes from Portugal. The Three Curricula Comparison Study (Nabuco and Sylva, 1997) compared the learning experiences of 220 children in 15 early years settings comprising three types of curricula: laissez faire (i.e. free play with no formal curriculum or assessment to plan provision); teacher-directed formal skills curriculum; and HighScope's balanced approach. Early years settings were assessed on opportunity for choice, problem solving, pretend play, informal conversation, and effects on reading, writing and anxiety. Subsequent progress in school learning identified better child outcomes in social acceptance, reading and writing as a result of curriculum balance between choice and guidance, 'cultural' play and problem solving in children who had experienced the HighScope approach.

Other independent studies confirm that children in well-run HighScope settings do better than those in other curriculum models. Studies in the United Kingdom (Sylva, 1992) and The Netherlands (Veen et al., 2000) found that when children plan, carry out and review their own learning activities, they play with more purpose and perform better on measures of language and intellectual development. The Head Start Family and Child Experiences Survey (Zill et al., 2003) in the USA showed those attending HighScope settings improved significantly more from autumn to spring on measures of literacy and social development than children in other curricula. HighScope UK research (Wickstead, 2005) gathered information at the end of the first year in 19 primary schools about children who had previously attended HighScope early years settings. Data looked at mathematical abilities, social and emotional development, and communication, language and literacy skills. All areas identified a significant reduction in the difference between girls and boys against the national percentages for achievement in these areas.

HighScope curriculum content

HighScope has developed a comprehensive approach to early years education that addresses all areas of development and uses the dimensions of learning typically found in the standards of early childhood professional organizations and government education agencies (e.g. Head Start Child Outcomes and state standards in the USA and the UK Department for Children, Schools and Families (DCSF) standards for the Foundation Stage). The eight HighScope curriculum content areas are: approaches to learning; language, literacy and communication; social and emotional development; physical development, health and well-being; mathematics; science and technology; social studies; and the arts. In addition to this broad framework, HighScope has in-depth curriculum materials in specific content areas such as literacy, mathematics, conflict resolution, visual arts, and movement and music. New curriculum materials are continually being developed.

Within each of the learning areas, HighScope further identifies key developmental indicators (see Figure 7.1), which are the building blocks of thinking and reasoning. Practitioners use them to guide and support all aspects of practice, including how they organize the setting, what materials they provide and how they plan the day, observe children, support and extend children's thinking and measure children's progress. The key developmental indicators are based on the latest research and are periodically updated as the field discovers more about children's development and how adults best support early learning (for detailed descriptions of the key developmental indicators and supporting research, see Hohmann et al., 2008). In addition to the key developmental indicators identified in Figure 7.1, similarly organized and developmentally appropriate indicators inform the curriculum for children up to 3 years of age (Post et al., 2011), providing continuity for children from 6 months to 5 years in HighScope settings.

Approaches to Learning

- Making and expressing choices, plans and decisions
- Solving problems encountered in play

Language, Literacy and Communication

- Talking with others about personally meaningful experiences
- Describing objects, events and relations
- Having fun with language: listening to stories and poems, making up stories and rhymes
- Writing in various ways: drawing, scribbling, letter-like forms, invented spelling, conventional forms
- Reading in various ways: reading storybooks, signs and symbols, one's own writing
- Dictating stories

Social and Emotional Development

- Taking care of one's own needs
- Expressing feelings in words
- Building relationships with children and adults
- Creating and experiencing collaborative play
- Dealing with social conflict

Physical Development, Health and Well-Being

- Moving in non-locomotor ways (anchored movement: bending, twisting, rocking, swinging one's arms)
- Moving in locomotor ways (non-anchored movement: running, jumping, hopping, skipping, marching, climbing)
- Moving with objects
- Expressing creativity in movement
- Describing movement
- Acting upon movement directions
- Feeling and expressing a steady beat
- Moving in sequences to a common beat

Arts and Sciences

Mathematics

Seriation

- Comparing attributes (longer/shorter, bigger/smaller)
- Arranging several things one after another in a series or pattern and describing the relationships (big/bigger/biggest, red/blue/red/blue)
- Fitting one ordered set of objects to another through trial and error (small cup and small saucer/medium cup and medium saucer/big cup and big saucer)

(Continued)

(Continued)

Number

- Comparing the numbers of things in two sets to determine 'more,' 'fewer', 'same number'
- Arranging two sets of objects in one-to-one correspondence
- Counting objects

Space

- Filling and emptying
- Fitting things together and taking them apart
- Changing the shape and arrangement of objects (wrapping, twisting, stretching, stacking, enclosing)
- Observing people, places and things from different spatial viewpoints
- Experiencing and describing positions, directions and distances in the play space, building and neighbourhood
- Interpreting spatial relations in drawings, pictures and photographs

Science and Technology

Classification

- Recognizing objects by sight, sound, touch, taste and smell
- Exploring and describing similarities, differences and the attributes of things
- Distinguishing and describing shapes
- Sorting and matching
- Using and describing something in several ways
- Holding more than one attribute in mind at a time
- Distinguishing between 'some' and 'all'
- Describing characteristics something does not possess or what class it does not belong to

Time

- Starting and stopping an action on signal
- Experiencing and describing rates of movement
- Experiencing and comparing time intervals
- Anticipating, remembering and describing sequences of events

Social Studies

- Participating in group routines
- Being sensitive to the feelings, interests and needs of others

The Arts

Visual Art

- Relating models, pictures and photographs to real places and things
- Making models out of clay, blocks and other materials
- Drawing and painting

Dramatic Art

- Imitating actions and sounds
- Pretending and role playing

Music

- Moving to music
- Exploring and identifying sounds
- Exploring the singing voice
- Developing melody
- Singing songs
- Playing simple musical instruments

Figure 7.1   HighScope key developmental indicators

The word 'key' emphasizes that these are meaningful ideas. Young children master a wide range of knowledge and skills. Rather than present practitioners with an overwhelming list of learning objectives, key developmental indicators stress areas that lay the foundation for further learning.

'Developmental' means learning is gradual and cumulative, moving from simple to complex. A curriculum must be consistent with what we know about human development. It is inappropriate, not to mention futile, to expect young children to behave and learn like children in later stages of education. Finally, 'indicators' emphasize that educators need evidence that children are developing the knowledge, skills and understanding considered important for school and life. By defining child outcomes in measurable terms, we can develop assessment tools that help us plan around children's needs and abilities in ways that are consistent with HighScope principles.

The key developmental indicators are universal. Research shows that children from different cultures and countries experience and learn similar things. For example, all children take objects apart and put them together, or sort them into containers. The objects and containers may vary across cultures, but the activity and the resulting learning about how the world works is the same. Likewise, cross-cultural research in many countries supports the conclusion that settings which promote exploration of materials and provide rich adult–child language interactions at age 3 are positively and significantly associated with educational outcomes in the primary stages (Montie et al., 2007).

HighScope practice methodology

HighScope practitioners arrange and label setting interest areas and resource them with diverse materials to give children a broad range of experiences and help them understand how the world can be organized. To promote initiative and independence, practitioners make sure the materials are easy for children to get out and put away on their own, thereby promoting a find–use–return cycle. Practitioners also make sure materials reflect children's interests and their home culture, so the children are both comfortable and excited about learning. A clear example of this was a child from a mining area who brought into the setting a traditional 'companion stand' with a brush, fork and shovel to keep the fireplace clean. These are implements unfamiliar to children in an urban setting, but standard cleaning tools in homes in his community. He put it in the House Area, beside the 'fire' and declared excitedly, 'Now it's a proper house!'

The daily routine provides a balanced variety of experiences. Children engage in both individual and social play, participate in small and large groups, assist with tidying up, socialize during meals, develop self-care skills, and practise fine and gross motor skills. Some parts of the routine revolve around children's plans and choices; children are free to choose where to go in the setting indoors and out and what materials and people to work with. Other parts of the routine such as small group times are planned and set in motion by adults. Even in these adult-led activities, however, children contribute their own ideas and choose how to use the materials supplied by the practitioner.

The heart of the daily routine is the *plan–do–review sequence* in which children make choices about what they will do (planning time), carry out their ideas (work time) and reflect on their activities with adults and peers (recall or review time). Children thereby gain confidence as thinkers, problem-solvers and decision-makers. They act with intention and reflect on the consequences of their actions, abilities that serve them well in school and throughout their lives. (For more on plan–do–review, see the discussion of planning and reflection under 'Philosophy' above.)

Underpinning every aspect of the approach is the reciprocal relationship between adults and children which is essential to children's well-being in giving them the confidence to become effective learners. Practitioners in HighScope settings follow children's focus and pace in conversations, accept children's explanations, acknowledge their feelings and problem-solve resolutions to conflict, thus supporting children in developing skills to solve conflict independently. Children in HighScope settings are motivated from within to learn and keep on learning supported by 'encouragement' (defined in dictionaries as 'making sufficiently confident or bold to do a specified action'). HighScope practitioners describe back to children what they have achieved, giving children the opportunity to reflect on their blossoming skills and abilities. They do not offer empty praise – 'Good boy/girl' or 'Well done' – which comes from 'outside' and creates a desire to please the praise-giver rather than creating a desire to learn. In addition, HighScope practitioners empower both families and children by forming authentic relationships with parents and caregivers and sharing what children have achieved on an informal daily basis through written anecdotal observations.

HighScope assessment tools

Assessment of early years practice

Settings maintain quality and improve outcomes by measuring how well practitioners support learning and how much children learn. HighScope has developed and validated two comprehensive observational assessment tools to help settings review and enhance their practice. The UK Programme Implementation Profile (PIP) (Blackwell et al., 1992) both evaluates whether practitioners in settings across the early years workforce are using effective strategies in support of learning, engaging with parents and caregivers, and assesses management practices. The HighScope UK Quality Assurance Scheme (Humphreys et al., 2002) was developed to enable settings that consistently achieve high standards of practice to be registered on the HighScope UK website, as having nationally accredited practice endorsed by the government's quality assurance scheme 'Investors in Children' (subsequently replaced by the National Quality Improvement Network). HighScope Assessors use the age-appropriate instrument (Infant Toddler QA, Foundation Stage QA or Primary QA) to provide in-depth assessment of seven areas of practice, awarding national accreditation if required standards are met.

Child assessment

The HighScope UK Child Observation Record (COR) (Johnson and Underwood, 2002) assesses children's learning in all curriculum content areas using anecdotal observations and was accredited by the Qualifications and Curriculum Authority, England, as an open baseline assessment scheme. It is appropriate for children aged 3–5 years. The PIP and COR embody best early years practice and reflect basic child development principles, as identified by leading early childhood professional organizations and agencies (e.g. in the USA, the National Association for the Education of Young Children, 2005; Copple and Bredekamp, 2009; in the UK, Investors in Children, now the National Quality Improvement Network). As such, these assessment tools can be used in all developmentally based practice settings, not just those using the HighScope approach.

The HighScope training model

An approach to early learning only works if it is used consistently and properly. We know from nearly 50 years of research that HighScope offers significant benefits to young children. However, to obtain those benefits, children must receive the same high-quality, active learning approach that was proven in the research. To guarantee these optimal conditions, HighScope UK (and the HighScope Foundation USA and other international HighScope Institutes) provide an extensive training programme of professional development courses for organization and setting managers and early years practitioners.

Evidence of the effectiveness of the HighScope training model is described above in the research section (e.g. Epstein, 1993). Ongoing studies of effective early years training practices in general also validate a hands-on approach to professional development. For example, training is found to be most effective when it promotes reflective practice as well as honing specific pedagogical skills (Mello, 1984; Smith and Acheson, 1991). Practitioners benefit when they apply the techniques learned during workshops in their own settings, are observed by trainers and then receive feedback on what is working and what needs to be improved (Black et al., 2003). This combination of workshops and onsite support promotes appropriate experimentation and risk taking if practitioners see it as collaborative and non-judgmental (Redell, 2004), an attitude that HighScope training strives to create. Furthermore, studies such as Sparks and Hirsh (2000) link this integrated training approach to higher student achievement offering additional proof of HighScope's potential to not only improve early years practice, but foster child outcomes as well.

(For additional materials to support effective training and implementation, see the 'Further reading' section below.)

Common criticisms of HighScope

There are two main criticisms of HighScope, one related to practice methodology and the other to curriculum content. With regard to its practices, HighScope has been characterized as 'too structured' on the one hand and 'too free' on the other. Early critics said the daily routine does not allow enough free play time. They believe all activities should be child-initiated, whereas HighScope group times are initiated by adults. Later criticism holds the opposite view and says that HighScope does not provide sufficient time for adults to directly teach children specific lessons in a didactic format. These contrasting criticisms often reflect current political views and highlight the fact that HighScope is a 'balanced' approach in which children *and* adults initiate learning activities. As current educational opinion also strives to find a balance, criticism of HighScope's practices has greatly diminished in the face of demonstrated results.

The other criticism is that the curriculum content is too difficult and/or too time-consuming for practitioners to use and understand. Research on the effectiveness of training (summarized above) has shown that adults from a wide variety of backgrounds are able to understand and implement the approach. Nevertheless, HighScope takes this criticism seriously as it wants to make the approach accessible to many populations in different countries and settings. To accomplish this objective, HighScope Endorsed Trainers are trained to adapt materials and courses to meet the backgrounds and capacities of practitioners. Additionally, HighScope recommends visits to Quality Assured settings and publishes simplified versions of its curriculum, including the increased use of audio-visual aids that rely less on use of the printed text.

Final thoughts

In their policy brief *Preschool Curriculum Decision-Making: Dimensions to Consider*, Frede and Ackerman (2007) promote the benefits of using a validated early childhood curriculum. They pose a set of essential features administrators should examine in choosing a curriculum, including the respective roles of practitioners and children, domains of learning addressed, provision for children with special needs, assessment tools, evidence of effectiveness and professional development. With decades of development, training, implementation and ongoing research, the HighScope approach can provide useful information for reflecting upon each of these issues. Preparing young children for the opportunities and risks of today's world presents educators with a daunting but meaningful challenge. Choosing wisely requires broad knowledge about early development and the skills to effectively nurture every child's full potential. The HighScope approach offers a comprehensive set of proven resources to help us meet this challenge.

 Summary

- HighScope is a validated approach to early learning, supported by 50 years of research.
- The curriculum is based on five principles of active participatory learning (materials; choice; manipulation; child language and thought; and adult scaffolding) to encourage children's initiative, independence, creative problem solving and self-confidence.
- A signature feature is the plan–do–review sequence whereby children make plans based on their interests, carry out their intentions and reflect on what they learn.
- The curriculum content (key developmental indicators) is comprehensive, integrated and developmentally sequenced.
- The principles of active learning in children are also used to train practitioners.
- Validated assessment tools monitor the quality of early years practice, guide educational planning and document children's developmental progress.

 Questions for discussion

1. Draw a line down the middle of a piece of paper to create two columns. Fold it so only one column shows. Pick an everyday object such as an apple, book or chair. Read a description of the object in the dictionary or encyclopedia, or ask someone to describe it to you. In the first column, write down what you remember from reading or hearing the description. Unfold the paper so the other column is showing. Explore the same object for at least five minutes using all your senses. Write down what you learned about it in the second column. Open the paper and compare the two lists. Which method of learning produced more knowledge about the object? Why?

2. Observe a setting or a situation with at least one adult and one young child, where there is an opportunity for learning (for example, an early years art or literacy activity; a parent and child cooking or shopping for groceries). Review the list of active learning ingredients: materials, manipulation, choice, child language and thought, and adult scaffolding. Which of these are present in the situation you are observing? How would you change the situation to increase the amount of active learning? *(Continued)*

Further reading

Levels 5 and 6

Epstein, A.S. (2003) 'How planning and reflection develop young children's thinking skills', *Young Children*, 58(5): 28–36.

This article describes the importance of planning (choice with intention) and review (memory with reflection) in developing critical thinking abilities in young children. It presents practical strategies practitioners can use to implement these hallmarks of the HighScope approach.

French, G. and Murphy, P. (2005) *Once in a Lifetime: Early Childhood Care and Education for Children from Birth to Three*. Dublin: Barnardo's National Children's Resource Centre Ireland.

Once in a Lifetime is a very readable practical introduction and overview to HighScope best practice in the birth to 3 phase.

Holt, N. (2007) *Bringing the HighScope Approach to Your Early Years Setting* (2nd edn). Abingdon: Routledge.

This book covers the main points of the approach. The theory underpinning the approach is linked to practice from personal experience of HighScope over many years in a variety of settings.

Levels 6 and 7

Epstein, A.S. and Schweinhart, L.J. (2009) 'The HighScope preschool curriculum and dimensions of preschool curriculum decision-making', *Early Childhood Services*, 3(3): 194–208.

This article explains the constructivist theory behind the HighScope approach, presents an overview of the approach's components and summarizes research demonstrating the approach's effectiveness for children, training methods for practitioners and cost benefits for society.

HighScope Educational Research Foundation (1991) *Supporting Young Learners: Ideas for Child Care Providers and Teachers*, Vol. 1. Ypsilanti, MI: HighScope Press.

HighScope Educational Research Foundation (1996) *Supporting Young Learners: Ideas for Child Care Providers and Teachers*, Vol. 2. Ypsilanti, MI: HighScope Press.

HighScope Educational Research Foundation (2001) *Supporting Young Learners: Ideas for Child Care Providers and Teachers*, Vol. 3. Ypsilanti, MI: HighScope Press.

HighScope Educational Research Foundation (2005) *Supporting Young Learners: Ideas for Child Care Providers and Teachers,* Vol. 4. Ypsilanti, MI: HighScope Press.
This series provides collections of articles from the HighScope US newsletter 'Extensions' covering every aspect of the approach.

Hohmann, M., Weikart, D.P. and Epstein, A.S. (2008) *Educating Young Children* (3rd edn). Ypsilanti, MI: HighScope Press.
This book is a comprehensive description of the HighScope approach written for practitioners, managers and students. The manual can be accessed at different levels according to interest and requirement and details how to make active learning a reality in early childhood settings.

Websites

www.high-scope.org.uk
The HighScope UK website provides a contact list of accredited settings to visit, a short history of the development of the HighScope approach, reviews of useful publications, contact information for the UK Head Office and a description of the range of courses that can be provided across the UK.

www.highscope.org
The HighScope Foundation US homepage describes the approach, assessment tools, research, training options and conferences, and has an online catalogue of publications. People interested in an in-depth view of HighScope will find the features on assessment and research most helpful.

References

Berry, C.F. and Sylva, K. (1987) 'The plan–do–review cycle in HighScope: its effects on children and staff', unpublished manuscript, available from HighScope Educational Research Foundation, Research Division, Ypsilanti, MI.

Black, R., Molseed, T. and Sayler, B. (2003) 'Fresh view from the back of the classroom', in R.H. Anderson and K.J. Snyder (eds) *Clinical Supervision: Coaching for Higher Performance.* Lancaster, PA: Technomic Publishing Co. pp. 113–34.

Blackwell, F., Johnson, S. and Lafferty, P. (eds) (1992) *Programme Implementation Profile.* London: HighScope UK.

Bruner, J.S. (1990) *Acts of Meaning.* Cambridge, MA: Harvard University Press.

Case, R. (1985) *Intellectual Development: Birth to Adulthood.* Orlando, FL: Academic Press.

Copple, C. and Bredekamp, S. (2009) *Developmentally Appropriate Practice in Early Childhood Programs: Serving Children from Birth Through Age 8* (3rd edn). Washington, DC: National Association for the Education of Young Children.

Dewey, J. (1938/1963) *Experience and Education.* New York: Macmillan.

Dowling, J.L. and Mitchell, T.C. (2007) *I Belong: Active Learning for Children with Special Needs.* Ypsilanti, MI: HighScope Press.

Ellis, M.J. (1988) 'Play and the origin of species', in D. Bergen (ed.) *Play as a Medium for Learning and Development.* Portsmouth: Heinemann. pp 23–5.

Epstein, A.S. (1993) *Training for Quality: Improving Early Childhood Programs through Systematic In-service Training.* Ypsilanti, MI: HighScope Press.

Epstein, A.S. (2007a) *Essentials of Active Learning in Preschool: Getting to Know the HighScope Curriculum*. Ypsilanti, MI: HighScope Press.

Epstein, A.S. (2007b) *The Intentional Teacher: Choosing the Best Strategies for Young Children's Learning*. Washington, DC: National Association for the Education of Young Children.

Epstein, A.S. (2009) *Numbers Plus Preschool Mathematics Curriculum*. Ypsilanti, MI: HighScope Press.

Frede, E. and Ackerman, D.J. (2007) *Preschool Curriculum Decision-making: Dimensions to Consider*. Preschool Policy Brief, Issue 12, National Institute for Early Education Research (NIEER). Available at: www.nieer.org.

Goswami, U. (ed.) (2002) *Blackwell Handbook of Child Cognitive Development*. Malden, MA: Blackwell Publishers.

HighScope Educational Research Foundation (2005) *Growing Readers Early Literacy Curriculum*. Ypsilanti, MI: HighScope Press.

Hohmann, M., Weikart, D.P. and Epstein, A.S. (2008) *Educating Young Children* (3rd edn). Ypsilanti, MI: HighScope Press.

Humphreys, J., Johnson, S. and Wiltshire, M. (eds) (2002) *Quality Assurance Scheme*. London: HighScope UK.

Johnson, S. and Underwood, R. (eds) (2002) *Child Observation Record (COR)*. London: HighScope UK.

Mello, L. (1984) *Peer-centered Coaching: Teachers Helping to Improve Classroom Performance*. Idaho Springs, CO: Associates for Human Development.

Montie, J.E., Xiang, Z. and Schweinhart, L.J. (eds) (2007) *Role of Preschool Experience in Children's Development in 10 Countries*. Ypsilanti, MI: HighScope Press.

Nabuco, M. and Sylva, K. (1997) 'A study on the quality of three early childhood curricula in Portugal', paper presented at 7th European Conference on the Quality of Early Childhood Education, Munich, September.

National Association for the Education of Young Children (2005) *Early Childhood Program Standards and Accreditation Performance Criteria*. Washington, DC: National Association for the Education of Young Children.

National Council for Teachers of Mathematics (2000) *Principles and Standards for School Mathematics*. Reston, VA: National Council for Teachers of Mathematics.

Piaget, J. and Inhelder, B. (1969) *The Psychology of the Child*. New York: Basic Books.

Post, J., Hohmann, M. and Epstein, A.S. (2011) *Tender Care and Early Learning: Supporting Infants and Toddlers in Child Care Settings* (2nd edn). Ypsilanti, MI: HighScope Press.

Redell, P. (2004) 'Coaching can benefit children who have a harder hill to climb', *Journal of Staff Development*, 25(2): 20–8.

Rowe, S.M. and Wertsch, J.V. (2002) 'Vygotsky's model of cognitive development', in U. Goswami (ed.) *Blackwell Handbook of Child Cognitive Development*. Malden, MA: Blackwell Publishers. pp. 539–54.

Schank, R.C. (1990) *Tell Me a Story: A New Look at Real and Artificial Memory*. New York: Scribners.

Schweinhart, L.J. and Weikart, D.P. (1997) *Lasting Differences: The HighScope Preschool Curriculum Comparison Study through Age 23*. Ypsilanti, MI: HighScope Press.

Schweinhart, L.J., Montie, J., Xiang, Z., Barnett, W.S., Belfield, C.R. and Nores, M. (2005) *Lifetime Effects: The HighScope Perry Preschool Study through Age 40*. Ypsilanti, MI: HighScope Press.

Shore, R. (1997) *Rethinking the Brain: New Insights into Early Development*. New York: Families and Work Institute.

Smith, N. and Acheson, K. (1991) *Peer Consultation: An Analysis of Several Types of Programs*. Eugene: University of Oregon, Oregon School Study Council, 34(6).

Snow, C.E., Burns, S. and Griffin, P. (eds) (1998) *Preventing Reading Difficulties in Young Children*. Washington, DC: National Academy Press.

Sparks, D. and Hirsh, S. (2000) *A National Plan for Improving Professional Development*. Washington, DC: National Staff Development Council.

Sylva, K. (1992) 'Conversations in the nursery: how they contribute to aspirations and plans', *Language and Education*, 6(2): 141–8.

Thompson, R.A. and Nelson, C.A. (2001) 'Developmental science and media: early brain development', *American Psychologist*, 56 (1): 5–15.

Veen, A., Roeleveld, J. and Leseman, P. (2000) *Evaluatie van Kaleidoscoop en Piramide Eindrapportage*. Amsterdam: SCO Kohnstaff Instituut, Universiteit van Amsterdam.

Vygotsky, L.S. (1934/1962) *Thought and Language*. Cambridge, MA: MIT Press.

Wickstead, C. (2005) *Overcoming the Gender Difference at Foundation Stage*. London: HighScope UK.

Zelazo, P.D. and Mueller, U. (2002) 'Executive function in typical and atypical development', in U. Goswami (ed.) *Blackwell Handbook of Child Cognitive Development*. Malden, MA: Blackwell Publishers. pp. 445–69.

Zill, N., Resnick, G. and Kim, K. et al. (2003). *Head Start FACES (2000): A Whole Child Perspective on Program Performance: Fourth Progress Report*. Administration for Children and Families, US Department of Health and Human Services, Contract HHS-105-96-1912, Washington, DC.

CHAPTER 8

THE WISDOM OF VIVIAN GUSSIN PALEY

Trisha Lee

Overview

Vivian Gussin Paley is a natural and inspirational storyteller who weaves together the threads of everything she sees and hears, making connections and pouring forth wisdom. Whether it is a one-hour 'keynote' speech or a snatched conversation at a book signing, those who come into contact with her cannot help but be inspired. In this chapter, I describe the process involved in Paley's unique story-telling curriculum and explore the impact of her work.

Background

Vivian Gussin Paley was born on 25 January 1929 in Chicago, Illinois. She began teaching in the 1950s. In an honest appraisal of her early career, she admits to knowing something was wrong with the way she was being required to teach, but she didn't quite know how to fix it. She began questioning and analysing everything that went on within her classroom. She became curious about the children in her care, taking seriously the things that they said both in their interactions with adults and more importantly in their interactions with each other. Through her study of these interactions, she began to develop an insight into the role of fantasy play in children's lives.

A continued journey of self-discovery

School is a place where, according to Paley's philosophy, both children and adults come to learn. Her quest for answers is apparent in *White Teacher* (Paley, 2000), which started life after Paley attended a meeting with a group of black parents in 1973. During the meeting, Paley listened in surprise as the parents voiced criticism of the predominantly white teachers at the Chicago Laboratory School and the racism they had witnessed around their children. This led Paley on a journey of self-discovery, watching herself reflectively, to see if she responded differently to children of different races.

As Paley probed deeper into this question, she realized that race is often the 'hidden curriculum' within a classroom. She reflects on her own upbringing, and how whatever she learnt at home about her Jewish background was left behind at the school gate. Paley notes that even at the age of 5, children can become strangers in a world that is shaped for someone else (Paley, 2000: xv).

Through the sincere self-analysis that she shared with the reader, Paley realized that much of her teaching leant towards 'colour blindness'. It was easier to ignore colour completely than to challenge or ask questions when she was unsure of where these would lead.

Paley acknowledged how difficult it was to know how to respond when a child mentioned anything that alluded to colour differences. She created a list of statements she had overheard in her classroom that she was uncertain of how to deal with. She confessed to how tricky she found it to transfer her usual 'matter of fact, non-judgemental descriptions of what was being said when race or colour was involved' (Paley, 2000: 8). 'Anything a child feels is different about himself, which cannot be referred to spontaneously, causally, naturally and uncritically by the teacher can become a cause for anxiety and an obstacle for learning' (Paley, 2000: xix).

It is this continual need for reflection and self-evaluation, coupled with her desire to support each and every child through the pathway of leaning, which shines out of Vivian Gussin Paley. It is present in everything she writes and in every action she performs within her kindergarten classroom, and it is this that makes her the inspirational figure that she is.

Paley's urge to find out more about the children she worked with led to the development of a storytelling curriculum which in her later teaching career she undertook in her kindergarten classroom on a daily basis.

A unique storytelling curriculum

Vivian Gussin Paley's storytelling curriculum is based on two inter-connected classroom activities: part one, *story-telling*; and part two, *story-acting*. In theory, this is a simple approach (Lee, 2002). In part one, the adult sits with the child, listens to their story and writes it down word for word. At the end of the story, the child decides which character they would like to play. The adult continues to take stories from other children.

Part two takes place towards the end of a session. The class gather as audience and actor ready to observe and take a role in acting out the stories of their peers. A simple taped stage is marked on the floor and immediately the classroom is transformed into a theatre. Sitting around the edges, children listen while the stories of their peers are narrated aloud, and take turns from their place in the circle to step onto the stage to act these out.

The simplicity of this approach hides many complexities. The process compels us to listen to children and to value their stories. The inter-connectedness between the two parts is also a vital ingredient. If a story is scribed on one day, it is essential to the fulfilment of the task that it is acted out on the same day, even if that means it needs to happen whilst the children are queuing for the school bus.

Story-telling and story-acting help us to question our interactions with the children we come into contact with, and have the potential to change us; this is the wisdom of Vivian Gussin Paley.

The wisdom of Vivian Gussin Paley

According to Wikipedia, wisdom is having the knowledge of what is true or right coupled with just judgement as to action; it is an intuitive understanding, alongside a capacity to apply this quality well towards finding a solution.

Throughout all of Vivian Gussin Paley's 13 books, a sense of her wisdom and intuition shines through (Paley, 1990, 1993, 2000, 2004). Her ability to take risks, to listen to others, to ask questions and seek out answers is apparent in the dialogues she has with the children she works with. Her search for the truth, as it is for each child, and her intuitive understanding of the role that fantasy play has in helping uncover this truth, is an inspiration. Here is a reflective practitioner who, even in retirement, continues to be enthralled by the role of story in children's lives; understanding its importance to such a degree that she defines it as a child's work (Paley, 2004)

Paley's honesty and self-analytical approach is evident throughout all her books which are filled with insightful observations from a teacher who has never stopped learning. When she stood in her Chicago classroom, she allowed herself to listen to the fantasy play that was taking place around her. By tuning into this world, which many adults overlooked as being of no consequence, Paley began to identify a learning process that for most teachers was invisible.

She started to utilize what she heard in the classroom to develop her practice; paying attention to and reflecting on the narratives that were developed every day by the children she worked with. Through this endeavour, she made connections between the story-making activities a child is naturally engaged in during fantasy play, and the important role this encompasses in intellectual and emotional growth. Paley's perceptive understanding of the important work children are undertaking without guidance on a daily basis, means that the story-telling curriculum she developed all those years ago works as powerfully in the 21st century as it did when she first began to develop it in the 1970s. This is evidenced by the continuing international popularity of her books (Paley, 2010).

The original learning tools

Vivian Gussin Paley labels fantasy play and story-making as the original learning tools that children use to understand and make sense of the world. In a lecture, 'Story and play: the original learning tools', given on 10 March 1997 in Walferdange, Luxembourg, she observed that these tools are akin to what we do as adults when we reflect on our practice: Will this work? What will happen if I try this? How about if I look at it in a different way?

Children at play will try things out, refine them, come back to them, look at them from another angle, bring in other children to support the idea they are exploring, change roles and find reasons and solutions to problems that seem insurmountable.

Paley hypothesizes that if a medical school discovered a software package that could integrate all the teachings that were required to become a doctor, only to decide that they would revert to the old way of teaching, then surely this would be considered questionable?

> Is this not, in effect, what happens to our children when they enter school? For five years, an intuitive program called play has worked so well that the children learn the language, mannerisms, and meaning of all the people with whom they live. They know what every look means, every tone of voice, who their family is, where they come from, what makes them happy or sad, what place they occupy in the world. Then the children enter school and find, strangely enough, that this natural theater they have been performing, this playfully deep fantasy approach to life is no longer acceptable, is no longer valid. Suddenly they begin to hear … 'Do that playing outside, after your work'. (Paley, 1997)

In every classroom, playground and place where children congregate throughout the world, stories are being created, scenarios invented, plots conjured up and dialogues fashioned. Complex narrative structures are produced by children without any teaching and yet the value of story has been ignored by education systems across the world. Paley's work identifies these narrative structures and uses them as the key component to her story-telling curriculum. This enables her to bring into the classroom the fundamental tools for learning that appear to get left at the classroom door. This is despite the fact that the Early Years Foundation Stage (EYFS) supports the role of play in learning (DfES, 2007).

Throughout her work, Paley demonstrates several key qualities which we can learn from today:

- *A curiosity for asking questions and finding answers*: one facet of Paley's inspirational work is her ability to ask complex questions concerning the children in her class and their relationships with each other and the outside world. Her search for answers to questions that many of us would shy away from is what makes her writing so refreshingly honest. One of the major questions she con-stantly returns to concerns fairness (Paley, 2000). She identifies fairness as some-thing for which practitioners must strive (Paley, 1984) and safeguard for children (Paley, 1988).

- A *belief in the wisdom of children* ('By associating with wise people you will become wise yourself', Menander, www.inspirational-quotes.info/words-wisdom. html): Paley's need to contemplate meaning reveals the great respect and under-standing that she has for the wisdom of children. She seeks out their wisdom, recording her interactions so as to be able to look more closely at these at a later date. Her desire to understand the words, thoughts and actions of everyone in her class immersed her in their world. In her books, Paley is not just the teacher but also takes on the role of student, watching as the children's stories anchor fantasy to purpose. She investigates how her class use fantasy play to find the invisible lines of connection between themselves and the communities in which they grow.

- A *non-judgemental approach*: when I first met Paley in 1999, I was amazed to see how truly non-judgemental she was of the children she came into contact with. I observed her working in a kindergarten classroom in Indianapolis. She asked a 4-year-old boy if he wanted to tell her a story. He shook his head. She smiled at him and said: 'That's fine, you can be a story listener'. The boy visibly grew with the announcement of the title that was to be his role. On his next day in school, because he had not been pressurised the day before, he was now ready and his stories began to flow.

The impact of Paley's work

So how well known is Paley's work? Although celebrated in certain areas of early years education, her story-telling curriculum is not mainstreamed. In 2002 Vivian Gussin Paley agreed to become patron to MakeBelieve Arts, a theatre and education company which develops and delivers innovative approaches to engaging pupils with learning. MakeBelieve Arts have embraced Paley's story-telling curriculum into the ethos of the company and disseminate her story-telling and story-acting approach throughout the United Kingdom via in-service training and in-class sessions entitled 'The Helicopter Technique', named after her book *The Boy Who Would Be a Helicopter* (Paley, 1990). The Texas Rice University's Centre for Education is another organization that actively promotes and trains teachers in Vivian Gussin Paley's story-telling and story-acting curriculum. However, education students studying at, for example, Roehampton University and the London Metropolitan University in England, have the opportunity to find out more about Paley's work due to the enthusiasm of individual members of staff. Therefore, knowledge about Paley's approach to story-telling and story-acting tends only to be disseminated by Paley enthusiasts. Cooper (2009) suggests that the reasons for this are that Paley's work is more complex than a simple reading suggests; that her books tend to focus on the single issue with which she is wrestling at the time of writing; and that she does not readily accept mainstream thinking for its own sake. This can be seen in her writing about literacy or about gender.

The potential of story-telling and story-acting

The potential of story-telling and story-acting lies in the following qualities.

Immediately engaging all children regardless of ability

Story-telling and story-acting have an immediacy that set them apart from many other activities within a classroom. As soon as a teacher begins to demonstrate the process of gathering stories, the children understand how to do it. They don't need long descriptions or complicated explanations; they intuitively know how it works. The whole process is so closely connected with what children do already in their fantasy play that it needs no teaching. Children are instantly empowered as the experts, they know what is expected of them and they eagerly embrace this play. In *Mrs. Tully's Room*, Paley (2001: 5) describes 2-year-olds dictating and acting out their stories. She concludes that even at this young age, children demonstrate 'an ability to bring a character to life and reveal something about themselves'.

Demonstrating a child's understanding of narrative structures

Paley's story-telling curriculum enables a teacher to interact with children and to witness first hand the profound comprehension of story that lies intuitively within them. This is the privilege of only those adults who are prepared to listen meticulously to the everyday narratives of the children around them.

Paley observed children reinventing mythology, generating new versions of old tales and acting out legends (Paley, 1990: 4). For example, in one class a group of children recreate the story of Ngali and the hot hippo that was forbidden to eat the fish. The children consider what would happen if Ngali grew angry and commanded the hippo to eat every animal, or if Ngali died and the hippo became the new god? In their ongoing narratives, Paley watched her class spontaneously investigating other possible endings, whilst at the same time examining compelling universal themes.

Creating a way of supporting children in exploring conflicts and emotions

Paley discovered that children often use story as a way of dealing with conflict. This understanding that fantasy play enables us to put every thought and feeling into story form and to use story as a way to resolve the difficulties we face, is a powerful insight into the potential we have when we are allowed to tap into tools we are born with.

In *Mollie is Three* (Paley, 1986: 1–11), Fredrick has problems following some of the classroom rules. He grabs paintbrushes and play dough from other children, he knocks over a ship made from blocks and does a lot of furious yelling. Learning from 3-year-old Libby, who uses story form to engage Fredrick as a father rather than a robber (because robbers can't play in the dolls corner), Paley finds herself using the same approach, asking a frustrated Fredrick who he is pretending to be. It stops his tears immediately. 'Do you want to be a bad guy or a good guy?' Paley repeats (1986: 10). Fredrick wants to be a good guy and sits contentedly watching as the rest of the children continue to play. Later at the snack table, Christopher asks if Paley is still mad with Fredrick and when she says 'no', he questions further. Mollie steps in:

> 'Because now Fredrick is nice.'
>
> 'And before?' I ask.
>
> 'That's because he was a robber.'

Fredrick, she knows, plays many different roles. She can better explain his behaviour as a character portrayal than in terms of classroom rules (1986: 11).

In *White Teacher* (Paley, 2000), it is a girl named Sylvia who sometimes has problems conforming to the rules of play. One day she takes on the role of 'bad baby' and begins to pull out all the dishes and pots from the dolls corner cabinet and throws them over the floor. Rena tries shouting at her in role as the mother, but Sylvia screams back. Ayana steps in, threatening Sylvia with not playing together if she doesn't pick up the dishes. Sylvia wants to play and begins reluctantly to pick them up. Ruthie saves the day, turning Sylvia's actions into a game:

> 'Pretend we just move in … the moving man dropped all the boxes and now we have to put everything away on the shelf.'
>
> … Rena dials the telephone. 'Mr Moving Boss, we won't pay you because it was a bad job.'
>
> Everyone was laughing as she hung up. The equilibrium was re-established. (Paley, 2000: 81)

Promoting inclusivity and turn taking

In *You Can't Say You Can't Play*, Paley (1993) investigated inclusivity within her classroom and interviewed older children throughout the school to uncover memories of rejection by classmates. She solicited the opinions of all ages about the wisdom of introducing a rule of 'you can't say you can't play'. Throughout the book, Paley demonstrates her unerring faith in the wisdom of the children she talks to. She is also honest and open about her own uncertainties. Is she right in this exploration? Is it possible to legislate for fairness and still allow children to be creative and free in their fantasy play?

You Can't Say You Can't Play was a radical book for Paley as it changed her thinking as to how she engaged with her story-telling curriculum. Prior to this investigation, children had chosen who acted in their stories with them. But following on from this, she began inviting children to participate in stories from their place around the stage. This turn-taking activity eliminated friendship group cliques and resulted in all children having the chance to be involved in acting out the stories. An added bonus of this changed approach was that gender barriers were broken down; for example, boys became princesses and girls became 'baddies' and random chance dictated the story they acted in and the roles they played.

As children waited to get onto the stage, they learned to understand the process of turn taking. If they didn't get to play the character that inspired them in someone else's story, this motivated them to tell a story next time with this new character, adding their own 'take' to the plot. Paley considers it vital that children have the choice of which character to play in their own stories as they might not have this option in their own lives; but in fantasy play even the shyest child can be a superhero.

Breaking down the inequalities of narrative language

We know there are inequalities between the personal experiences of children. Some children are read to every night, or taken on amazing holidays, or visit galleries or museums. Some children have very little in the way of these experiences; their initial stories might involve a journey on the no. 47 bus. But in story-telling and story-acting, all children get to hear the stories of others. For example, if one child tells a story about a magic star that you have to touch to enter into another realm, their images and imagination are shared with the whole class. It may then be that suddenly all the children's stories begin with a magic star that leads into another realm. The possibilities for this re-wording of 'Once upon a time' can be endless. As the class develops its narrative language so they learn from each other, creating similes and metaphors together as they grow through a shared narrative experience.

So story dictation is a shared experience and a creative process and Paley recognizes that in order to maximize its full potential, story-telling needs to be an activity that takes place in situations where children can drop in and out as they choose. One person's story inspires thoughts and images in another and this opens all the children's eyes, allowing them to see the hidden potential for their own version of events. As each child dictates, they add on their own 'supposings' and 'what ifs'. They twist and turn over the stories of each other, examining them from all sides as they strive to find their own story, their own invisible connection to the narrative that is unfolding within their classroom. As Paley says:

> Our kind of story-telling is a social phenomenon, intended to flow through all other activities and provide the widest opportunity for a communal response. Stories are not private affairs; the individual imagination plays host to all the stimulation in the environment and causes ripples of ideas to encircle the listeners. (Paley, 1990: 21)

Developing an understanding of the properties of a story

In her story-telling curriculum, Paley allows the children to teach her new ideas about the properties of stories. Fredrick wants to tell a story; it is his first story. He has been listening to the older boys telling stories for a while now, and today is his day. He turns to Paley and says the word 'Fredrick'. Paley tries to elicit more from the story – what does Fredrick do? She suggests he could go to school, but Fredrick isn't interested – the story is Fredrick, no more, no less. Paley talks to the children around her, and tells them that she wonders about a one-word story.

> John, nearly five, responds quickly, 'It's not one word. It's one person'.
>
> Paley responds. Of course. A person is a story. (Paley, 1986: 12)

Paley's openness in accepting the ideas and solutions suggested to her by the children is the strength that runs through all her enquiries. She sees that Frederick needs a justification for his presence in the story and helps to provide one. She appreciates how easily children accept ideas that she might find challenging, and how things that don't make sense to her adult world often do make sense to the children.

Hidden complexities

There is a profound subject matter at work during story-telling and story-acting. The potential that is opened up in a classroom that is following a story-based curriculum is multifaceted, allowing children to learn from each other, deal with conflict and develop personal, social and emotional skills. The story-telling and story-acting approach may appear simple, but in fact it provides a sophisticated structure, giving adults access to copious information about the interests and preoccupations facing the children they teach. Furthermore, it gives children an experience of being listened to. In story-telling they have their words accurately scribed by an adult who listens intensely to every word they say. How often does this happen in many of our children's lives? How often do we hear the joyful cries of a 3-year-old echo with all the excitement of new discovery, only to be silenced by an adult too tired or too involved in their own story to share in the adventure?

However, currently there is growing political and professional interest in improving the skills and confidence of parents in listening to children (Clark, 2001; National Strategies Early Years, 2008). Listening to children is hard. When they first start learning to speak, the frustration of all the things they can't say can get in the way of all the wonderful words they can. As speech begins to flow, how frustrating it must be for a child to realize that they have all these stories they long to share and maybe the adults around them don't really understand or perhaps know how important it is to listen.

During story-telling and story-acting, all children are listened to. The process helps to develop not only their creative imagination, but also their vocabulary, listening and auditory skills and, more significantly, belief in the importance of their own thoughts and fantasies. Once the story is told, the fact that it is then represented to the child in a physical dimension increases the sense of ownership that they feel. Going through this process enhances a child's confidence and self-esteem. Each classroom develops their own narratives, rich with the shared imagery and a common language that is clear to all of them.

Through her books, Paley demonstrates her intuitive understanding of the significance of fantasy play. She makes connections between the daily events she witnesses as children dictate their stories, and the greater lessons they are learning through this invaluable process. In *All Our Futures*, Raymond Williams is quoted as stating: 'To communicate through arts is to convey an experience to others in such a form that the experience is actively recreated, actively lived through by those to whom it is offered' (NACCCE, 1999: 70). This sentiment is at the heart of Paley's work. In her view, there is nothing more interesting to any of us than the stories of our peers. Paley's wisdom is contained within her solemn appreciation of this.

Vivian Gussin Paley saw the essential role that fantasy play had, not only in the development of a child, but in the evolution of the community within the classroom. This conviction enabled her to undergo an act of astonishing bravery, taking the risk of believing in the role of story sufficiently to ensure it became the central part of her curriculum.

Vivian Gussin Paley: a critique

Paley's work can be dismissed as not being 'academic'. Her books are based on observation and anecdote and Paley scribes stories exactly as the children dictate them. The strength of her work lies in her insightful descriptions of her interactions within a classroom, but this does not fall into the category of documented, evidenced-based research.

As someone who regularly uses her technique, I have been challenged as to whether this approach enables children to meet the requirements of the formal English curriculum. My answer has always been that story-telling and story-acting are a creative process and that challenging each section of a child's story as it is being scribed is demotivating. The stories that emerge when a child is free to dictate as she chooses are rich in metaphor and often poetically phrased in a way that standard English may hamper.

Below is an example from a school where grammar is at the forefront of the English curriculum and where children's grammar is corrected, during each stage of the scribing process. The adult's focus on the secretarial elements of the narrative hinders the child's expressive attempts to tell his story:

Teacher	Have you got a story for me?
Child	Yes, A gingerbread man run
Teacher	I'm sorry was that run or ran?

Child	Run A … Cross
Teacher	No, Across is one word
Child	The street and the gingerbread man saw a cow, and the cow said
Teacher	Quotation marks, the cows going to talk!
Child	'Can you stop running' said the cow? Then he saw a police
Teacher	A police or the police
Child	A police and the police said 'I'm getting hungry'. He want
Teacher	Want or wanted?
Child	Wanted to eat the gingerbread man and he saw a fox and then She saw a river That's the end
Teacher	That's the end? But we've got lots more room. What happened next?
Child	And the fox said 'climb on his'
Teacher	Climb on his, or climb on my?
Child	Climb on my tail. It getting…
Teacher	It or it's?
Child	It's getting closer to the bottom.
Teacher	He said that or the fox said that?
Child	The gingerbread man said that. So the gingerbread man climb
Teacher	Climb or climbed
Child	Climb onto the fox back
Teacher	Fox or fox's
Child	Fox's back and then it was getting closer and closer
Teacher	I like the way you said that with the expression
Child	So the fox say
Teacher	Say or said
Child	Said 'climb on my nose' The end.
Teacher	And then? Did he eat it? You want to end it right there?
Child	Yes (adamantly)

Another aspect of Paley's work that may give rise to criticism is the predisposition to violence that predominately appears in the stories of boys, for example: superheroes or monsters, battles and fighting, guns and bombs. In Penny Holland's book, *We Don't Play with Guns Here: War, Weapons and Superhero Play in the Early Years* (Holland, 2003), she explores the damage a predominately female early years sector can do to boys' engagement with learning. A culture of zero tolerance of violent play does not address the underlying issues in this type of play, and tends to result in pushing them underground. According to Holland, it teaches boys to lie as the gun made out of Lego becomes a hairdryer when the teacher is around and, like the emphasis on grammar, may demotivate and cause disaffection. Rough and tumble play is broken up by the teacher, only to appear again in a corner of the classroom where the teacher is not present.

Paley meets such criticisms by allowing fighting in the acting-out stage, but when it appears she reminds the class that they need to do this without any touching so that no one is hurt. Having used this approach with numerous children, I have learnt that it gives all pupils a tool to explore violent play in a safe environment.

I have seen boys performing the most amazing dance-choreographed fight scenes, without any contact. Other teachers have witnessed pupils recreating these moves in their own free-play activities, experimenting with no contact and experiencing the joy of expressing extreme emotions in a stylized manner.

Story-telling and story-acting place the true thoughts and feelings, fears, hopes and experiences of the child on the stage, where the teacher can 'see' these and later discuss, examine and question them in a safe and secure way.

Final thoughts

Vivian Gussin Paley's work is inspirational and needs to be more widely known and used within the Early Years Foundation Stage. It so accurately recreates in the classroom what children are engaged in during fantasy play, and it enables the early years practitioner to connect with the feelings and needs of the children in a way that no other approach can duplicate. Having used this method with countless children, I am still amazed at how instantly even a 2- or 3-year-old understands and engages with it. Whenever I work in this way, it feels like I have access to a little piece of magic that is so easy for all of us to recreate with the children we come into contact with. All it takes is a roll of masking tape, a pen and paper and a listening ear.

 Summary

The benefits of Vivian Gussin Paley's approach are that it:

- engages all children regardless of language or other ability
- emphasizes play and narrative and so is immediately accessible to all children
- develops speaking and listening skills and the conceptual understanding of all children, creating a community of storytellers.

 Questions for discussion

1. In what ways do you think this approach supports inclusivity?
2. How does narrative help to create communities of learners?
3. What is the role of narrative in exploring ideas and feelings?
4. What is your view about the use of standard English when scribing children's stories? (*Higher level question*)

Further reading

Levels 5 and 6

Cooper, P. (2002) 'Literacy learning and pedagogical purpose in Vivian Paley's "storytelling curriculum"', *Journal of Early Childhood Literacy*, 5(3): 229–51.
This article further details the story-telling/story-acting aspects of Paley's work, with a focus on its implications for early literacy.

Duckworth, E. (2001) 'Inventing density', in E. Duckworth (ed.) *'Tell Me More': Listening to Learners Explain*. New York: Teachers College Press.
Duckworth has the same easy quality of writing as Paley. She describes this chapter as 'a story about the collective creation of knowledge', and in it she outlines the process of conceptualization. She focuses not simply on young children but on the role that family and friends play in that process, even as children grow older and more experienced.

Paley, V.G. (1981) *Wally's Stories*. Cambridge, MA: Harvard University Press. See section entitled 'Pulleys', pp. 95–100.
It would be no hardship to read the whole book but this reading, exploring the way in which children's conceptual development requires a great deal of careful nurturing, fits well with Duckworth (above).

Levels 6 and 7

Cooper, P. (2009) *The Classroom All Young Children Need: Lessons in Teaching from Vivian Gussin Paley*. Chicago: University of Chicago Press.
Cooper sets out to explain the apparent anomaly (alluded to in this chapter) that Paley is highly regarded by academics and practitioners as an early childhood expert and yet is not widely used on training courses.

Lieberoth, A. (2008) 'Are you the daddy? Comparing fantasy play in children and adults through Vivian Gussin Paley's *A Child's Work*', in M. Montola and J. Stenros (eds) *Playground Worlds: Creating and Evaluating Experiences of Role-playing Games*. Helsingfors, Finland: Solmukohta.
This chapter examines the continuing importance of narrative in thinking and understanding, focusing on the insights provided by Paley's observations.

McNamee, G. (2005) '"The one who gathers children": the work of Vivian Gussin Paley and current debates about how we educate young children', *Journal of Early Childhood Teacher Education*, 25(3): 275–96.
This article challenges the current schoolification of early education and suggests that Paley's approach is likely to increase the likelihood of promoting morally responsible citizens of the future.

Websites

www.kendallhaven.com
Kendall Haven is the author of *Story Proof*. His website describes some of his work and the training that he organizes around using story as a tool for teaching and learning.

www.makebelievearts.co.uk
Vivian Gussin Paley is the patron of MakeBelieve Arts. The Helicopter Resource Pack described explains Paley's story-telling/story-acting approach in full. The title of the pack is drawn from one of Paley's books, *The Boy Who Would Be a Helicopter*.

References

Clark, A. (2001) *Listening to Young Children: The Mosaic Approach*. London: National Children's Bureau.

Cooper, P. (2009) *The Classroom All Young Children Need: Lessons in Teaching from Vivian Gussin Paley*. Chicago: University of Chicago Press.

Department for Education and Skills (DfES) (2007) *Early Years Foundation Stage Profile Handbook*. Annesley: DfES Publications.

Holland, P. (2003) *We Don't Play with Guns Here: War, Weapons and Superhero Play in the Early Years*. Maidenhead: Open University Press.

Lee, T. (2002) *Helicopter Resource Pack*. London: MakeBelieve Arts. Available from: www.make believearts.co.uk

National Strategies Early Years (2008) *Every Child a Talker: Guidance for Consultants*. Nottingham: DCSF.

NACCCE (1999) *All Our Futures: Creativity, Culture and Education*. Sudbury: DfEE Publications.

Paley, V.G. (1984) *Boys and Girls: Superheroes in the Doll Corner*. Chicago: University of Chicago Press.

Paley, V.G. (1986) *Mollie is Three: Growing Up in School*. Chicago: University of Chicago Press.

Paley, V.G. (1988) *Bad Guys Don't Have Birthdays*. Chicago: University of Chicago Press.

Paley, V.G. (1990) *The Boy Who Would Be a Helicopter*. Cambridge, MA: Harvard University Press.

Paley, V.G. (1993) *You Can't Say You Can't Play*. Cambridge, MA: Harvard University Press.

Paley, V.G. (1997) 'Story and play: the original learning tools', lecture, 10 March, Walferdange, Luxembourg. Available at: www.script.lu/documentation/archiv/decoprim/paley.htm

Paley, V.G. (2000) *White Teacher*. Cambridge, MA: Harvard University Press.

Paley, V.G. (2001) *In Mrs. Tully's Room*. Cambridge, MA: Harvard University Press.

Paley, V.G. (2004) *A Child's Work: The Importance of Fantasy Play*. Chicago: University of Chicago Press.

Paley, V.G. (2010) *The Boy on the Beach: Building Community Through Play*. Chicago: University of Chicago Press.

CHAPTER 9

FOREST SCHOOLS IN THE EARLY YEARS

Sarah Blackwell and Linda Pound

Overview

This chapter provides an historical overview of the development of outdoor provision, and the place of Forest Schools within that development. We describe the work of Forest Schools, the organization's ethos and the outcomes for which it is striving. We explore the benefits of working in this way, as well as the issues that surround the approach.

Over recent years, Forest Schools have been increasingly documented in the press and sector-specific journals and magazines. The concept is gaining more momentum since its inception in the United Kingdom in the mid-1990s. Schools, Children's Centres and other early years settings in England are becoming increasingly involved in this movement which aims to 'encourage and inspire individuals of any age through positive outdoor experiences' (www.forestschools.com). Although there are no clear figures for how many Forest School programmes are operating in schools and settings across the country, the growth is evidenced by the number of training courses being demanded and the number of programmes in place. The training organization, Archimedes, ran less than a handful of courses in 2003 but has 25 courses planned for 2010.

What is a Forest School?

Lysa Bromley (2009), who is the area co-ordinator for Children's Centres in South Warrington, has reported on the development of Forest Schools in her area. Incorporating the Forest School approach into an early years setting has proved seamless in the way it contributes to the six key areas of learning through the Early Years Foundation Stage (EYFS) Framework (DCSF, 2008). Practitioners have been able to plan, assess and evidence the impact of Forest Schools as part of the overall holistic development of an individual child within the setting. Forest Schools are typically first introduced within the setting through discussion and sharing of information. The children are assessed by the practitioner with reference to their overall well-being and their development and learning prior to the programme beginning. Parents have usually undertaken a separate 'taster' session so they are making fully informed choices about their child's learning and are able to support the discussion at home around the experiences the child has each week. Whilst key workers and practitioners may be aware of the child's overall traits within the setting, the forest environment offers new challenges and opportunities, therefore the first week is crucial for individual observations. If a child is to be open to the learning opportunities around them, then supporting that process is fundamental.

Week one would therefore begin to explore the senses, such as sight, sound and touch. Age-appropriate opportunities will be made available to introduce these – such as looking and listening stops and feeling textures within the forest. At this stage, children as young as 3 can begin to take part in the assessment of risks, identifying trip hazards. This is especially useful as it is usual for normally confident and steady walkers to stumble and fall on the new uneven terrain. Interestingly, observations show that by week three, the uneven terrain is no longer a threat to their balance as they move swiftly in and out of the trees. The new environment offers an opportunity for exploration and this is encouraged by practitioners; it is usually at this stage that individual interests begin to emerge. An example of this may be where a child bangs fallen sticks/branches onto different trees and also other sticks so that they can observe the difference. Planning would take such an experience into account and build on opportunities for that child to explore deeper learning of that interest and develop it over the following weeks. Small successes for a child each week build up their confidence and self-esteem. Their knowledge of the environment increases weekly, as they're introduced to the names of trees and types of flora and fauna. Children's problem-solving techniques are challenged and developed when building dens and locating resources. Practitioners offer positive role modelling and the continued use of aspirational language transfers to the child and is often shown through the child's own development of altruistic tendencies within the group. Whilst the Forest School programme has elements of planning, it is and must always be child led. The programmes therefore, whilst having an outline for the 12 weeks, will always be different with each group. The only element that is standardized is the general approach and the ethos of overall outcomes. The approach offers a continued inspirational dimension to learning outside, an insight into the world around a child, and a sound base on which to build self-awareness, self-esteem and intrinsic motivation to achieve their potential. Parents have reported the positive impact of the programme on their child and the children have shown great improvement in social and emotional skills.

Forest Schools are run by Qualified Forest Schools practitioners in a woodland setting over a long period of time, ideally throughout the year, and aim to provide opportunities for children to develop self-awareness, self-regulation or management of their emotions, self-motivation, empathy and social skills through the medium of the natural world. Forest Schools are usually, as their name suggests, set in a woodland environment. However, in some cases nursery settings and schools have limited or no access to woodland. This may be because distances are too great, timetabling is too difficult or costs are too high. These difficulties are rarely insurmountable. Some urban schools and settings have created woodland settings in tiny patches of land – and children have the added benefit of seeing these areas burgeon. Woodlands provide infinite opportunities for learning that traditional school grounds, or early years settings, are not able to provide, such as uneven surfaces and a wide variety of natural resources to encourage play opportunities ranging from explorative and mastery play, to imaginative, symbolic play and recapitulative and social play (Hughes, 2002).

Some children (and some adults) find the indoor environment limiting. However, if the same resources and equipment are provided in the outdoor space, then the potential to explore is increased and the learning potential of each individual increases. A new physical dimension is also introduced into the learning mix. This is the impact of natural elements such as sun, wind, rain, warmth, chill, movement, sounds and smells. As soon as a learning opportunity or experience is offered in a woodland, the dynamics alter and the depth of the experience increases exponentially. The natural resources of a woodland are available to the child and can be used in a variety of ways. The ethos of Forest Schools supports the practitioner in encouraging flexible use of resources, self-discovery, problem solving and increased knowledge and understanding of the world. Forest Schools use the concepts of well-being and challenge (Laevers, 2002) as essential starting points in providing opportunities for the child to learn and develop. Direct teaching may take away the potential of deep-level learning experiences for the child, as observed by Forest School practitioners around the country. Deep-level intrinsic learning, and the ability to transform a new discovery into new knowledge or new skills, can all emerge from Forest School experiences.

Evaluation of Forest Schools

The criteria used in an evaluation of Forest Schools in England and Wales (Murray and O'Brien, 2005) were firstly that the provision should be in a woodland context and, secondly, that there should be favourable adult:child ratios. In addition, regular and consistent periods within the woodland must be provided and a reliance on strong sensory input at all levels is involved. A further criterion for being included in the study was that the objectives of EYFS (DfES, 2007) and the priorities outlined in Every Child Matters (http://www.dcsf.gov.uk/everychildmatters/) should be addressed within Forest School provision.

Although commonly mentioned by lay people as key characteristics of Forest Schools, tools and fires are *not* the most important features. They are used as a stepping stone to a number of outcomes, including: knowledge and understanding of the world; critical and creative thinking; historical and cultural understanding; communication and literacy; as well as developing a physical appreciation of systems and resources. Tools are used simply as tools. However, they also serve as a way of introducing the management of risk, self-regulation and understanding of social boundaries, the development of self-worth and self-satisfaction at the outcome of achievement and successful application of learning, understanding and co-operation. Learning occurs through *using* tools rather than focusing on *how* to use them.

New developments in any field need to be underpinned by a fundamental understanding of the intended aims, outcomes and associated processes in order to maintain consistency of approach by all the practitioners involved. This is especially important when indications are that the new development may have a major impact. Any dilution of aims and processes may mean that claims about outcomes are compromised. Sometimes, without genuine understanding of what is involved, misleading claims may be made by practitioners who are inadequately qualified or inexperienced in the Forest School ethos. This can sometimes occur when practitioners try to mould the experience into a 'lesson plan' model rather than trusting that the process will provide better opportunities for deeper learning when child led. Attempts at pre-planning may lose the flexibility which is required to really build on what has been observed about children's learning.

History of Forest Schools

The Forest Schools movement originated as a way of building children's independence and self-esteem. The movement's website (www.forestschools.com) shows that such schools originated in Sweden in the 1950s as a way of teaching children about the natural world. In 1995 a team from Bridgwater College in Somerset went to Denmark, where the concept of Forest Schools in the early years was well established, on an exchange visit. They visited Forest Schools and observed 5–7-year-olds exploring a challenging and exciting outdoor environment. So enthusiastic were they about what they had seen, that they established the first Forest School within a Children's Centre in England.

Forest Schools, as an initiative, has a relatively short history but outdoor provision in the education of young children has a very long history. In the 18th and early 19th centuries, the writings and experimental schemes of Rousseau (Wokler, 2001) and Pestalozzi (Curtis, 1963; de Guimps, 2009) emphasized the importance of nature and the outdoor environment. In the early part of the 19th century, albeit in different countries, Robert Owen and Friedrich Froebel (Selleck, 1972; Whitbread, 1972) established nurseries based on Pestalozzi's ideas. Both were to go on to have an immense impact on the development of early childhood provision throughout the United Kingdom.

Owen believed so strongly in contact with gardens, fields and woods that he sent two of his own sons to Pestalozzi's school in Yverdun, in Switzerland, where they were to be engaged in what was termed 'spade husbandry' (Donnachie, 2000). At New Lanark, the site of his mill, he ensured that the young children of his employees spent many hours each day in the open air. By his instruction, there were to be no toys since 'thirty or fifty infants when left to themselves, will always amuse each other'. Moreover, they were not 'to be annoyed with books' (Donnachie, 2000: 166).

Froebel is credited with devising the term 'kindergarten' (see Chapter 4). For him, nursery education provided a children's garden – both in terms of a garden for children and as an environment where children would be nourished and nurtured like young plants. He was a trained forester and believed that the beauty and freedom, space and light offered by the outdoors supported children's all-round development, including their spirituality (Selleck, 1972).

Early in the 20th century, the McMillan sisters set up the first nursery school in London in response to the poor health of children in Deptford. Their first initiative in the area was an outdoor night camp to improve the health of those at risk of contracting tuberculosis. The nursery school, set up shortly after the introduction of the night camp, had a large garden and classrooms were described as shelters – designed simply to shelter children in bad weather. The expectation was that children would normally live, work and play outdoors. Margaret McMillan also set up an outdoor residential camp in Kent so that children from Deptford could experience the countryside (Lowndes, 1960).

These developments were occurring at about the same time as the Order of Woodcraft Chivalry was being established in 1916. Ernest Westlake, the founder of the order, believed that humans were in danger of losing an understanding of the natural world and of being corrupted by technological and cultural developments. In an effort to bring about a return to a simpler life, he set up the order which, rather like scouting, had its own 'uniforms, badges, rituals and laws' (Selleck, 1972: 39). It catered for all ages including adults, but the youngest, from 4 to 8 years of age, were known as 'elves'. In 1928 the first Forest School was set up in the New Forest. Westlake himself had planned the school, described by Selleck (1972: 31) as 'a romantic, nature-centred establishment', but had been killed in a car accident in 1922. Six years later, his son took on the project but it closed in 1940, with the onset of war.

Westlake's Forest School had many of the characteristics of a number of other progressive schools set up in the inter-war period. The curriculum was relatively informal;

there was a focus on crafts, self-discipline was emphasized and outdoor learning was given a strong focus. In 1924, for example, Susan Isaacs set up her celebrated nursery which encouraged exploration and enquiry, particularly in the garden. This included 'grass, fruit trees, a climbing frame, slides, movable ladders, trees for climbing, flowers and vegetable gardens with individual plots for each child and a range of animals, including chickens, guinea pigs, as well as snakes and salamanders' (Tovey, 2007: 47). In 1924 Chelsea Open-Air Nursery School was set up in London. Its founder described it (in the language of the time) as designed to cater for the 'cripples of Chelsea' (Pound, 1987) – children so cosseted that they needed to learn independence, self-reliance and perseverance. Although now a maintained nursery school, Chelsea Open-Air Nursery School maintains its emphasis on 'risk and challenge as a strong ethic for children's learning and play' (www.playengland.org.uk).

The period following the Second World War saw a rapid rise in the birth rate throughout the UK and a narrowing of nursery education. Many nursery places disappeared as the expectation grew that mothers (who had often been in full-time employment during the war) would be at home with their young children. In order to meet some of this growing demand, places which had previously been offered on a full-time basis were frequently offered as part-time places (Riley, 1983). By the 1960s, changing regulations and the rise of playgroups and nursery classes, meant that many early years settings generally had much less outside space than had previously been considered necessary. More recently, major concerns have been voiced about the further reduction in outdoor play space which has occurred as a result of the sale of schools' playing fields.

What do Forest Schools offer?

A Forest School has, like any other educational setting, broad aims. It seeks to provide each child with the opportunities and experiences that will enable them to learn and develop in order to reach their potential as a human being. What separates Forest Schools is that this happens in a woodland environment. The Forest School seeks, through engagement with a woodland environment, to support the growth of confidence and emotional well-being and develop all aspects of self-esteem including a sense of self. There is a belief by its advocates that the experiences offered in this challenging context build on children's innate motivation, support a positive attitude to learning and offer opportunities to take risks, make choices and initiate learning (www.neweconomics.org/gen/z_sys_PublicationDetail.aspx?PID=179).

The benefits of the woodland environment are numerous and wide ranging. Woodland is considered to be an important and fundamental resource in the holistic development of children. Woodland areas are chosen because they meet the specific needs of a group, providing them with the freedom to explore, to become self-led learners, to establish a close relationship with the natural environment, and to understand their sense of place and their impact on the eco system. Woodlands provide children with opportunities to run and jump and scramble, to fall over and to understand the topography of the ground. This will impact on their abilities to move around efficiently and to manage risk safely. Children can begin to understand the physical laws of the world, develop interests and enthusiasms (such as schema) and use the environment to help them make sense of their world – including the development of creative and critical thinking and problem-solving strategies. Perhaps most importantly, they can play in a fashion that suits the way in which they roam the environment as 'nomads' and 'manipulators' (Tovey, 2007), shaping the context to their needs. In addition, they can seek out props, devised from what Tovey vividly describes as 'loose parts', such as seeds, twigs, petals, stones, planks and blankets.

Archimedes, a company training practitioners to work in and lead forest schools, has considered the questions 'what are the core competences of adulthood?' and 'what do we need to be able to do in adulthood that will enable us to survive, be successful and be happy?' The sections that follow explore some of the benefits identified.

The development of social and emotional competence

In the development of forest schools, the importance of emotional intelligence (Goleman, 1996) has been highlighted. Being aware of selves and others, able to negotiate and understand social boundaries and motivate ourselves to work towards our goal within these boundaries are vital aspects of personal development which the curriculum set in a Forest School can address.

The opportunities to develop social and emotional development in young children are inherent in the woodland environment, remembering that self-discovery, self-mastery, self-motivation will all develop when the child is given the freedom to learn those things. Creating a shelter with a friend, crossing a gap over a log, digging in mud, cooking over a fire and using a range of tools because firewood is needed, all offer invaluable potential for the child to explore their own relationships to their peers, to the significant adults and to the natural world around them. Reflection is a key part of Forest Schools, and through a range of methods the learning that has happened in the child can be seen, observed and discussed in order to maximize the learning opportunities for the child.

Tovey (2007) comments on the importance which woodland activity offers for children to be able to play out of adults' sight. This vital aspect of gaining competence, confidence and independence has all but been lost to children – whether living in town or country. Helen Penn (cited by Tovey, 2007) has suggested that children, like the skylark, have disappeared from our landscapes. Cars, a fear of abduction, smaller gardens and an earlier start to school have all contributed to what has been described as the incarceration of children.

Well-being, health and risk-taking

Being outdoors has of itself an immense contribution to make to mental health and overall well-being. Risk-taking, or rather its absence from many children's lives, has become a major issue in the development of young children. Many writers (see e.g. Furedi, 2001; Lindon, 2003; Palmer, 2006) have drawn attention to the damage that over-protection can do to children's learning. Rogoff (1990) reminds us that learning involves taking risks at the edge of competence. Even The Royal Society for the Prevention of Accidents (ROSPA) has set up the Child Safety Education Coalition to encourage children to be supported in learning to take and manage risks (www.rospa. com/SaftetyEducation/Default.aspx). Contact with nature brings respect for our natural world but also respect for the inherent dangers. Climbing trees, using knives and proximity to fire bring dangers but they also can give young children an enhanced sense of agency, responsibility and resourcefulness. Allowing children to experience the challenges of the natural environment can also give adults greater respect for children and their learning.

In many cultures, children are encouraged to take risks. Rogoff (1990: 130) describes Fore infants in New Guinea as having 'access to all aspects of the environment … Adults intervene infrequently in their activities, to the point that children handle knives and fire by the time they are able to walk'. Daniel Walsh (2004), describing his own child's experience of nursery education in Japan, points out that there, supervision of outdoor play takes a different view of risk from that prevalent in our society. He comments on what initially seemed to him like a lack of care. He describes some tree-climbing:

> In one kindergarten the kids liked to climb a tall tree behind one of the buildings. The tree was made for climbing with large evenly spaced branches. The older kids sometimes climbed quite high, at times making me nervous. The teacher paid little attention and seldom came into this area. I asked the teachers about the tree and how high the kids were climbing. By this time I knew that the teachers cultivated an apparent inattention while almost clairvoyantly aware of every little thing happening on the playground and off. They had talked about the tree climbing at length in their daily meetings. They decided to ignore it because they didn't want to inhibit the children's explorations and because they were concerned that if they supervised the climbing in any way, the kids would become dependent on them and would, in this dependence, become less careful. (2004: 105)

An improved disposition to learn

The approach rests on a basic belief that the natural woodland environment provides so much that is different to the indoor environment. Research (see e.g. Louv, 2005) suggests that access to green spaces reduces stress, promotes well-being, increases mobility, physical coordination and balance, builds both fine and gross motor skills, encourages communication and promotes health. In the woodland, social boundaries are different; physical boundaries are larger; resources are in context – bigger, smaller, softer, harder, colder, rougher smoother; communication can become informal and social dialogue becomes easier, supporting the development of empathy and an understanding that everyone perceives things differently. Learning skills – making, doing and creating – build a sense of agency and self-worth. Self-image becomes more realistic and self-esteem improves. No individual has the right answers and problem solving is a key aspect to developing these positive attributes as children collectively create understanding of the world around them.

Gardner's (1999) work on multiple intelligences has suggested that naturalistic intelligence is of great importance. This view is echoed by Richard Louv (2005) who suggests that children today need to be protected from 'nature-deficit disorder'. He highlights the wide range of learning and understanding that comes from being in a naturalistic environment. Outdoors, children can engage with the natural world and begin to understand their place within it. Nature for the child is sheer sensory experience. It is ever-changing and yet it is predictable. The outdoor world provides challenges which cannot be replicated elsewhere and these promote resilience and resourcefulness. Louv (2005: 185) highlights the report of an American parent teaching his daughter to assess ice. The parent states:

> Crossing the ice, I teach her to read cracks, the ways of figuring out ice thickness and texture, to see the places where there is current – this is where ice is thick; this is where it is thin. I teach her how you must spread out when you have to cross really thin ice, to carry a stick with you, all of these intentional ways of assessing risk and being prepared.

Although not an account of learning resourcefulness in a forest setting, Louv (2005: 185) believes that this experience underlines the power of natural settings, writing that 'the kinaesthetic original experience of risk-taking in the natural world is closer to the natural organic way we've learned for millennia, and that the other experiences don't reach as deeply'.

The development of creativity

The role of creativity and imagination is increasingly acknowledged amongst educationalists (Rose, 2009). Space and time with open-ended materials support imagination. The value of the transformations that occur as a stick becomes a sword, a pencil or a wooden spoon is a fundamental aspect of Vygotskian thinking. This imaginative use of materials contributes to children being able to take a creative view of their role in practical and functional tasks which require problem-solving skills (Sylva et al., 1976).

Tovey (2007: 18) suggests that materials found outdoors 'offer considerable scope for children to act on their environment and transform it'. She further suggests that the rich range of 'loose parts' found outdoors support 'possibility thinking' (Cremin et al., 2006) and the transformations necessary for creative thought. In the process of transforming an object from one thing to another, children make new and exciting connections between one idea and another – an important element of thinking and creativity.

The development of physicality

Tobin (2004) has written of the dangers of what he terms 'disembodied' education – an approach to education prevalent in the USA and the UK, in which literacy and numeracy are privileged over the physical aspects of learning and development. Tobin reminds us that this is despite the fact that brain research has led to increased understanding of the role of motor activity in brain development in infancy. The continuing importance of motor activity in cognitive development may be supported through the emphasis placed by Forest Schools on learning through doing and through the challenging physical environment presented by woodland settings.

The importance of physical activity is also vital in considering children's health. Television and electronic, screen-based games have been criticized as potentially delaying language development (Zimmerman and Christakis, 2005) and limiting thinking (Greenfield, 2006). Even if the jury is still out on these two aspects of development, there can be no doubt that the lack of exercise which results from too much sedentary activity is having an effect on children's health. In the UK, around 27% of children are now overweight and research suggests the main problem is a continual reduction in the amount of exercise children take (www.bbc.co.uk/health/conditions/obesity2.shtml). Donnelly (2009) reports that during the five years up to 2009, increases in hospitalization of children affected by obesity rose by more than a third.

This generation of children and young people is being heralded as the first to die before its parents due to diabetes and chronic heart disease. Research (Cleland et al., 2008) suggests that playing outdoors is an effective strategy for preventing obesity and encouraging increased levels of activity amongst children.

Increased parental involvement

One very interesting facet of Forest Schools is the way in which, despite a climate of anxiety about risk-taking and an apparent desire to push academic achievement at the expense of a more holistic view of development, parents seem ready to accept or even welcome opportunities for children to take risks and focus on physical and social activity. This is something which early years settings in general could learn from. Being clear about objectives and about non-negotiable aspects of provision helps parents to understand the value of what is on offer. The benefit of being part of a national organization also gives parents confidence in the provision, as does the training provided for Forest School workers, enabling them to address parents' concerns with authority and confidence. Evaluation studies (Murray and O'Brien, 2005) indicate a ripple effect, with parents responding to children's interest and taking them out to forests and other outdoor settings at weekends.

Practitioner training and development

Too often in schools and other early years settings, being outdoors can be limited to playtimes where there are few resources. Time available to be outdoors is very restricted and activities may be unplanned and unchallenging. Adult engagement may be limited to supervision, rather than actually engaging and closely observing what children are doing, in order to extend and develop children's play, exploration and learning. The training provided by Archimedes can give practitioners renewed interest in outdoor provision, additional strategies for engaging children in challenging and exciting activities, as well as a means of understanding and articulating the rationale for an approach which differs so markedly from much practice in classrooms and early years settings.

A critique of Forest Schools

Forest Schools in this country are a relatively new concept. The interface between a number of different organizations interested in developing forest schools is charged with strong political overtones. For example, the Forest Education Initiative (FEI) 'aims to increase the understanding and appreciation, particularly among young people, of the environmental, social, and economic potential of trees, woodlands and forests and of the link between the tree and everyday wood products' (www.forest education.org). The FEI has therefore a broad remit. Forest Schools, on the other hand, have a fundamentally different ethos. Their aim is related to the personal, emotional and social well-being of the individual, in tandem with learning to understand the inextricable connection between each individual and nature. Forest Schools seek to develop forests in order to connect or reconnect the child with nature, to enhance experience, encourage confidence and inspire a love of life.

Research in Norway has demonstrated significant benefits for children attending Forest Schools (see Tovey, 2007). It is important, however, to remember that provision there is well established and frequently entails day-long engagement in a forest setting. The benefits found included more complex and creative play, better social interaction with fewer conflicts, as well as improved levels of health and fitness. In relation to the latter, children engaged in forest education were found to be stronger and more agile as well as having better balance and co-ordination. Moreover, the unpredictability of natural climbing materials was linked to children's improved motor skills. The uniformity of commercial climbing apparatus does not make the same demands or challenges as the uneven surfaces and varying distances involved in dealing with natural materials such as trees, logs or rocks.

There is relatively little research on the impact of Forest Schools in England. An evaluation undertaken by Murray and O'Brien (2005) highlighted a rise in confidence, collaboration, awareness of the consequences of choices and actions, improved stamina and concentration as well as heightened respect for the environment. These findings are common sense, but it must be remembered that the sample group (while mostly made up of 3–5-year-olds) was small, at only 24 in number. It does, however, highlight the positive responses of everyone concerned. A later study by the same authors (O'Brien and Murray, 2006) focused on older children. Both evaluation studies were in part funded by an organization called Forest Research and used what might be termed 'soft' methodologies. Neither of these factors renders the research invalid but both mean that results must be carefully scrutinized and interpreted.

Many writers (see e.g. Palmer, 2006; Tobin, 2004) have lamented the apparently widespread view that 'childhood has no place in modern society' (Gullov, 2003, cited by Tovey, 2007: 87). There is a feeling that children are regarded as though they should be hidden away – rendered invisible in restaurants and galleries, for example. Gullov argues that in creating Forest Schools, there is a danger of marginalizing children even further from society – sending them to out of the way places and teaching them skills no longer useful in the 21st century. Tovey (2007) takes up and extends this by asking whether, by separating Forest Schools from everyday life, educators may fail to help children appreciate the built environment. She also comments on the very different cultural expectations which exist in Scandinavia. This is embodied in the very terms used. In Nordic countries, these settings are regarded as 'kindergartens' with an emphasis on imagination, creativity and collaboration, while in this country the term 'school' is used, suggesting a rather different ethos.

Final thoughts

The tradition of outdoor play in early childhood education was historically a strong one. Over many years, it has become buried in what might almost be called heightened levels of concern about health and safety (Palmer, 2006), pressures to get young children engaged in formal learning at an earlier age (Paley, 2004; Tobin, 2004) and blindness to the benefits of living and learning outdoors (Louv, 2005).

Physical activity from an early age which is fun, creative, engaging and motivational will (it is reassuring to believe) have a lasting impact on those individuals given the opportunities to participate. Louv (2005) claims that the more alienated children are becoming from the natural environment and the wonders it contains, the higher the increase in behavioural disorders. Woodlands provide oxygen and a vast ecological diversity. They are essential not only to promote emotional well-being and social skills, but also in developing in children a sense of awe and wonder, which provides a spiritual dimension to the educational process.

Those involved in Forest Schools have witnessed first hand the impact that they have on both children's and adults' lives. Access to the outdoors, together with the approach that Forest Schools employ in meeting individual learning needs and creating a positive lifelong relationship to the woodland environment, should, they believe, be seen as a fundamental right. The benefits of this would be:

- enhanced self-confidence and well-being
- positive learning opportunities
- collaborative learning opportunities
- a basic physical competence
- a sense of ecology and social responsibility for the outdoor spaces which our society is dependent upon for the future.

Tovey (2007: 96), mindful of the heritage of the nursery garden, favours an integration of the ideals of early childhood education and the approach advocated by Forest Schools. She concludes that: 'the forest … should be encouraged to grow and encroach on some of the garden so that the wilder, more challenging and riskier aspects of the forest become an integral part of the philosophy'.

 Summary

In this chapter:

- Forest Schools as an initiative has been defined.
- An overview of outdoor provision prior to the introduction of Forest Schools in England has been provided.
- Some benefits of Forest School education to children and adults have been identified.
- Two criticisms of Forest School provision have been highlighted – one focuses on the nature and validity of the research undertaken, while the other is more esoteric as it relates to the marginalization of children and childhood within British society, and questions whether Forest Schools contribute to this.

 Questions for discussion

1. Do you agree that learning outdoors is an essential element of children's development? What specific part do Forest Schools have to play in this?
2. What is your view about whether Forest Schools should be seen as a separate entity or whether they should be integrated into the long-held traditional view of the nursery garden?
3. Can integrated approaches occur when, or if, the two settings of Forest School and pre-school/school are at a distance from one another?
4. Could the approach offered by Forest Schools, in your view, be described as 'anachronistic'? (*Higher level question*)

Further reading

Levels 5 and 6

Knight, S. (2009) *Forest Schools and Outdoor Learning in the Early Years.* London: Sage.
This provides a comprehensive guide to the theory and practice of Forest Schools in the early years.

O'Brien, L. and Murray, R. (2007) 'Forest School and its impact on young children: case studies in Britain', *Urban Forestry and Urban Greening*, 6: 249–65.
This study highlights the physical and personal benefits of Forest School experience. The authors conclude that Forest School experience is compatible with constructivist theories of learning.

White, J. (2008) *Playing and Learning Outdoors*. London: Routledge/Nursery World. See Chapter 2.
In the suggested chapter, this practical book considers the importance of interactions with the natural world and natural materials.

Levels 6 and 7

Little, H. (2006) 'Children's risk-taking behaviour: implications for early childhood policy and practice', *International Journal of Early Years Education*, 14(2): 141–54.
This paper critically reviews policies on risk-taking and concludes that in general they fail to take account of the personal components of risk-taking such as sensation seeking, temperament and child-rearing practices.

Louv, R. (2005) *Last Child in the Woods*. New York: Algonquin Books. See Part Two.
Part Two is entitled 'Why the young (and the rest of us) need nature'. It focuses on Louv's construct of a nature-deficit disorder and provides some helpful antidotes to the schoolification of ECEC.

Tovey, H. (2007) *Playing Outdoors*. Maidenhead: Open University Press. See Chapters 5 and 6.
These two chapters deal with the controversial debate outlined in the critique section above about the marginalization of children within our society. The second of these two chapters deals with risk-taking.

Websites

There is a plethora of websites associated with Forest Schools and this reflects the political jostling that is still at the heart of a new initiative. Like so much of ECEC, the movement is full of enthusiasts who have not developed a single voice. Here are our recommendations:

www.foresteducation.org
The Forest Education Initiative aims to support increased understanding and appreciation of forest environments.

www.forestresearch.gov.uk
The focus of this group is research and development into sustainable forestry and tree-related research.

www.forestschools.com
This group aims to inspire learners through positive outdoor experiences. It offers training for forest school leaders through Archimedes Training.

www.outdoor-learning.org/membership/forest_schools_sig.htm
The organization to which this website belongs is the Institute for Outdoor Learning. Its aim is to promote good practice amongst all involved in outdoor learning.

www.playengland.org.uk
Play England works towards gaining accessible play space for all children and young people. They were responsible for the launch of the Manifesto for Children's Play.

References

Bromley, L. (2009) 'Forest schools', *In Stop Press*, 27. Warrington: Warrington Partnership Children and Young People.

Cleland, V., Crawford, D., Baur, L.A., Hume, C., Timperio, A. and Salmon, J. (2008) 'A prospective examination of children's time spent outdoors, objectively measured physical activity and over-weight', *International Journal of Obesity*, 32: 1685–93.

Cremin, T., Burnard, P. and Craft, A. (2006) 'Pedagogy and thinking in the early years', *International Journal of Thinking Skills and Creativity*, 1(2): 108–19.

Curtis, S. (1963) *History of Education in Great Britain*. London: University Tutorial Press Ltd.

de Guimps, R. (2009) *Pestalozzi, His Life and Work*. Charleston, SC: BiblioBazaar.

Department for Children, Schools and Families (DCSF) (2008) *The Early Years Foundation Stage*. London: DCSF.

Department for Education and Skills (DfES) (2007) *Practice Guidance for the Early Years Foundation Stage: Non-statutory Guidance*. Nottingham: DfES Publications.

Donnachie, I. (2000) *Robert Owen: Owen of New Lanark and New Harmony*. East Lothian: Tuckwell Press.

Donnelly, L. (2009) 'Record numbers in hospital for obesity', *Daily Telegraph*, 22 August. Available at: www.telegraph.co.uk (accessed 30 June 2010).

Furedi, F. (2001) *Paranoid Parenting*. London: Penguin.

Gardner, H. (1999) *Intelligence Reframed*. New York: Basic Books.

Goleman, D. (1996) *Emotional Intelligence*. London: Fontana.

Greenfield, S. (2006) 'Dumbing down minds?', *Times Educational Supplement*, 24 November. Available at: www.tes.co.uk/article.aspx?storycode=2316539

Gullov, E. (2003) 'Creating a natural place for children: an ethnographic study of Danish kindergartens', in K. Olwig and E. Gullov (eds) *Children's Places: Cross-cultural Perspectives*. London: Routledge.

Hughes, R. (2002) *A Playworker's Taxonomy of Play Types* (2nd edn). London: Playlink.

Laevers, F. (2002) *Research on Experiential Education: A Selection of Articles*. Leuven: Centre for Experiential Education.

Lindon, J. (2003) *Too Safe for their Own Good?* London: National Children's Bureau.

Louv, R. (2005) *Last Child in the Woods*. Chapel Hill, NC: Algonquin Books.

Lowndes, G. (1960) *Margaret McMillan: The Children's Champion*. London: Museum Press.

Murray, R. and O'Brien, E. (2005) *'Such Enthusiasm – a Joy to See': An Evaluation of Forest Schools in England*. Report for the Forestry Commission. Farnham, Surrey: Forest Research.

O'Brien, E. and Murray, R. (2006) *A Marvellous Opportunity for Children to Learn: A Participatory Evaluation of Forest School in England and Wales*. Farnham, Surrey: Forest Research.

Paley, V.G. (2004) *A Child's Work*. Chicago: Chicago University Press.

Palmer, S. (2006) *Toxic Childhood*. London: Orion.

Pound, L. (1987) 'The nursery tradition', *Early Child Development and Care*, 20(1): 79–88.

Riley, D. (1983) *War in the Nursery*. London: Virago Press.

Rogoff, B. (1990) *Apprenticeship in Thinking*. Oxford: Oxford University Press.

Rose, J. (2009) *Independent Review of The Primary Curriculum*. Nottingham: DCSF.

Selleck, R. (1972) *English Primary Education and the Progressives 1914–1939*. London: Routledge and Kegan Paul.

Sylva, K., Bruner, J. and Genova, P. (1976) 'The role of play in the problem-solving of children 3–5 years old', in J. Bruner, A. Jolly and K. Sylva (eds) *Play: Its Role in Development and Evolution.* Harmondsworth, Middlesex: Penguin Books.

Tobin, J. (2004) 'Disappearance of the body on early childhood education', in L. Bresler (ed.) *Knowing Bodies, Moving Minds.* Dordrecht, The Netherlands: Kluwer Academic Publishers.

Tovey, H. (2007) *Playing Outdoors – Spaces and Places, Risk and Challenge.* Maidenhead: Open University Press.

Walsh, D. (2004) 'Frog boy and the American monkey: the body in Japanese early schooling', in L. Bresler (ed.) *Knowing Bodies, Moving Minds.* Dordrecht, The Netherlands: Kluwer Academic Publishers.

Whitbread, N. (1972) *The Evolution of the Nursery-Infant School.* London: Routledge and Kegan Paul.

Wokler, R. (2001) *Rousseau: A Very Short Introduction.* Oxford: Oxford University Press.

Zimmerman, F. and Christakis, D. (2005) 'Children's television and cognitive outcomes', *Archive of Pediatrics and Adolescent Medicine*, 159: 619–25.

CHAPTER 10

RELATIONSHIPS WITH PEOPLE, PLACES AND THINGS — TE WHĀRIKI

Anne B. Smith

Overview

The administrative integration of early childhood education and care in 1986 was a key event, helping set the scene for the introduction of New Zealand's early childhood curriculum, Te Whāriki. The writers, including both Māori and Pākeha partners, consulted widely with the early childhood community to develop the document, which was finally introduced in 1996. The four broad principles of the document are: empowerment; holistic development; family and community; and relationships, while its five strands are: well-being; belonging; contribution; communication; and exploration. The curriculum is based on socio-cultural theory emphasizing the role of socially and culturally mediated learning, and children's participation in shared meaningful activities. A narrative assessment tool, Learning Stories, has been a key ingredient in the successful implementation of Te Whāriki, and has helped to bridge theory and practice for teachers.

(Continued)

(*Continued*)

Te Whāriki, New Zealand's early childhood curriculum, reflects a holistic, bicultural vision for childhood, viewing children's learning 'as a series of increasingly intricate patterns of linked experience and meaning, centred on cultural and individual purpose' (Carr and May, 1996: 102). The Māori term, Te Whāriki, means a woven mat for all to stand on, a metaphor for the possibility of creating many patterns of ideas and philosophy; catering for children of different ages, interests and cultural background; and being suitable for the range of types of early childhood service in Aotearoa/New Zealand. Te Whāriki makes a political statement about the uniqueness, culture and rights of children in New Zealand society (Smith and May, 2006).

This chapter will discuss how Te Whāriki came into being, its philosophical and theoretical underpinning, its main components, how it has been implemented and accepted by the early childhood sector, and both praised and criticized.

Early childhood education in New Zealand

First, it is important to provide a brief context for early childhood education in Aotearoa/New Zealand, and outline some key events which preceded the introduction of Te Whāriki in 1996. Children start school at 5 years of age in New Zealand so the term early childhood services covers a diverse array of provisions for under-5-year-olds. These include kindergartens, play centres, childcare centres (officially known as education and care centres), kohanga reo (Māori immersion centres), Montessori or Steiner-based centres, Pacific Island language nests, playgroups and home-based care. One of the most important events in the history of early childhood education in New Zealand was the integration of all services responsible for the care and education of young children into one government department, the Education Department (now the Ministry of Education), in 1986. New Zealand was the first country in the world to integrate responsibility for all early childhood services in the education system (Moss, 2000). The structural change from separate administrative structures for pre-school and childcare, reflected the belief that care and education are not separate, and that quality early childhood services should incorporate both. Integration was also a policy in response to the unequal resourcing of the early childhood sector, and heralded a series of other fundamental changes, such as the introduction of three-year training for early childhood teachers, and changes to funding and regulation in the sector (see May, 2009 for a detailed account). These reforms, which were the result of almost two decades of activism and persuasion by women (Smith and May, 2006), were slowed down in 1990 when there was a change of government. The new government favoured a shift towards deregulation, small government and market forces.

The new government, as part of its belief in using education to orchestrate economic success, had an agenda of introducing an early childhood curriculum parallel to the school curriculum, which was the reason that Te Whāriki came into being. The idea of a curriculum for early childhood was not popular with the sector, who feared that it would restrict independence and diversity, and that it would focus too much on academic goals to prepare children for school. Two academics, Helen May and Margaret Carr, won the contract to develop an early childhood curriculum in 1991. Both had had first-hand experience as early childhood teachers and had worked in the policy arena. They were conscious of the necessity to develop a bottom-up rather than top-down curriculum, and for the document to reflect the Treaty of Waitangi[1] partnership between Māori and Pākeha (Smith and May, 2006). Dr Tamati Reedy and Tilly Reedy, who had developed a curriculum for Māori immersion centres, worked in parallel and collaboration with Helen May and Margaret Carr, to ensure that Te Whāriki was genuinely bicultural.

The authors of the curriculum were opposed to a subject-based or stage-based approach and wanted to incorporate aspects of New Zealand's child-centred and play-oriented philosophies of early childhood education, from a socio-cultural angle. Different types of early childhood services (such as childcare and home-based care which had earlier on been regarded as second best options) were to be given equal respect in the new curriculum.

The early childhood curriculum within New Zealand is probably unique, because its development, over an extended period between 1991 and its introduction in 1996, involved extensive consultation with a diverse group of practitioners, with Māori perspectives being a separate but integrally related framework. The Ministry of Education funded several projects to develop appropriate assessment aligned to the goals of Te Whāriki (Carr, 1998a, 1998b, 2001; Mara, 1998; Podmore et al., 1998). It focused on protecting diversity, involving families, connecting with people of different cultures, play and the natural environment, an inclusive curriculum and commitment to a bicultural society with the language, culture and values of Māori and Pākeha being incorporated into the principles. Te Whāriki avoids the traditional domains of children's development – physical, intellectual, social and emotional – and instead focuses on a holistic approach of providing a safe and trustworthy environment, meaningful and interesting problems, avoidance of competition and risk of failure, opportunities for collaborative problem-solving and the availability of assistance from teachers.

In 1993 a draft of Te Whāriki was released and a copy sent to every centre in New Zealand, which allowed for revisions and feedback before the final document became the official curriculum in 1996. It was anticipated that: 'With the introduction of Te Whāriki many early childhood practitioners are going to be thrown headlong into a major learning curve' (Nuttall and Mulheron, 1993: 4). While the document was well accepted, initially there was a very large gap between theory and practice to bridge for many early childhood teachers, which necessitated an unprecedented number of professional development and in-service courses (Gaffney and Smith, 1997; Te One, 2003). It was all too easy for centres and teachers to say that Te Whāriki confirmed their existing practice (Te One, 2003). Rather than providing recipes for what to do, Te Whāriki makes bigger demands on teachers and challenges them to apply theoretical knowledge to their practice. Effective implementation of Te Whāriki demands interpretation, reflection, dialogue, careful planning, observation and consultation with parents/whanau and children.

In combination with the government's Statement of Desirable Objectives and Practices (DOPs), the framework of principles, strands and goals in Te Whāriki, is mandatory for all government-funded early childhood programmes in New Zealand.

Principles, strands and goals

There are four broad principles which provide the framework for Te Whāriki. (The Māori concepts are not identical but comparable.)

- **Empowerment – Whakamana**: The early childhood curriculum empowers the child to learn and grow.
- **Holistic Development – Kotahitanga**: The early childhood curriculum reflects the holistic way children learn and grow.
- **Family and Community – Whānau/Tangata**: The wider world of family and community is an integral part of the early childhood curriculum.
- **Relationships – Ngā Hononga**: Children learn through responsive and reciprocal relationships with people, places and things.

The five strands and associated goals (in brackets) of the curriculum which lead to children's behaviours, are as follows:

1. **Well-being – Mana Atua** (the health and well-being of the child are protected and nurtured).
2. **Belonging – Mana Whenua** (children and their families feel a sense of belonging).
3. **Contribution – Mana Tangata** (opportunities for learning are equitable, and each child's contribution is valued).
4. **Communication – Mana Reo** (the language and symbols of their own and other cultures are promoted and protected).
5. **Exploration – Mana Aotūroa** (the child learns through active exploration of the environment).

All licenced early childhood and care services must implement the principles and strands of the curriculum (either the English or Māori versions), in accordance with section 314 of the Education Act 1989 (Ministry of Education, 2008).

Theoretical framework

The curriculum emphasises the critical role of socially and culturally mediated learning and of reciprocal and responsive relationships for children with people, places, and things. Children learn through collaboration with adults and peers, through guided participation and observation of others, as well as through individual exploration and reflection. (Ministry of Education, 1996: 9)

Te Whāriki is based on socio-cultural theory (Rogoff, 1995; Vygotsky, 1978; Wertsch, 1995), which views learning as arising out of the children's activities in the context of social interactions and relationships. Hence, other people, culture and the tools of culture (especially language), institutions and history have a powerful influence on children's learning. Rather than one path for development, there are a variety of potential developmental pathways. Children's learning emerges from cultural goals with the guidance of community practice and expertise.

Children gradually come to know and understand the world through their own activities in communication with others. The greater the richness of the activities and interactions that children participate in, the greater will be their understanding and knowledge. Learning involves a reciprocal partnership where adults and children jointly construct understanding and knowledge. Children participate in cultural activities with skilled partners and come to internalize the tools for thinking they have practised in social situations. Hence, relationships and interactions are of central importance. Children, even very young children, are active co-constructors of their own knowledge and understanding, rather than passive recipients of experiences. Everyday activities in different settings reflect social and cultural practices and are the vehicle for acquiring meanings.

In a Vygotskian model, teachers take an active role and engage in joint activities with children. Development is seen as culturally determined rather than determined by nature. When children co-operate with adults or other children, they are more competent than when they work alone. Teachers within a Vygotskian framework do not just follow the development of children, but adopt socially valued goals. Children learn according to the opportunities they are given to participate, taking an active and inventive role, and co-constructing meaning with teachers (and peers). Such an approach is supported by the findings of the United Kingdom Effective Provision of Pre-School Education study:

> The qualitative (case studies) and quantitative (observational rating scales of quality) approaches came together in revealing the importance of joint involvement and 'sustained shared thinking' in everyday activities. (Sylva and Taylor, 2006: 172)

Te Whāriki focuses on motivational aspects of learning rather than on fragmented skills and knowledge It encourages teachers to support children's ongoing learning dispositions – for example to persevere with difficulties rather than giving up and avoiding failure, difficulty or negative judgements from others. Dispositions to learn are 'habits of mind that dispose the learner to interpret, edit, and respond to experiences in characteristic ways' (Carr, 1997: 2). Dispositions are shaped by and shape children's social interactions and allow them to recognize, select, edit, respond to, resist, search for, construct and modify learning opportunities (Carr, 2001; Carr, Smith, et al., 2009; Smith, 2009). Te Whāriki seeks to support children's autonomy, exploration, commitment and aspirations.

This view of children as agents connects well with other theories, in particular childhood studies and children's rights theory. Childhood studies theorists (James and Prout, 1997; Mayall, 2002) suggest that childhood is a social construction, which is understood differently at different points of history and in different cultural contexts. What we expect of children influences how we interact with them. Childhood studies views children as independent social actors rather than as lesser persons progressing towards adulthood through the process of socialization or education. It criticizes the predominant psychological discourse on childhood, which focuses on the individual and describes 'the universal decontextualised child' (Mayall, 1994: 2). Childhood studies is concerned with children's experience and perspectives in everyday contexts, which fits well with the philosophy of Te Whāriki. Children's capabilities are assumed to be influenced by the expectations and opportunities for shared participation offered by their culture, and the amount of support they receive in acquiring competence. The opportunity offered by the early childhood curriculum for children to participate and make a contribution, has a major effect on their ongoing disposition to learn.

The United Nations Convention on the Rights of the Child (UNCRC) was acknowledged by Margaret Carr as one of the documents which influenced the development of Te Whāriki (Carr, 1991, cited by Te One, 2003). The participation rights in UNCRC suggest that children have the right to be given an active role. Article 12 says that children have the right to be consulted on matters which affect them, and have their opinions taken into account. Article 13 says that children have the right to express their views, and have access to information. Te Whāriki provides a model of children's participation rights being embedded in a curriculum.

> Children are valued as active learners who choose, plan, and challenge. This stimulates a climate of reciprocity, 'listening' to children (even if they cannot speak), observing how their feelings, curiosity, interest, and knowledge are engaged in their early childhood environments, and encouraging them to make a contribution to their own learning. (Smith, 2007: 155)

Learning stories

One of the major challenges for Te Whāriki has been how to assess its impact on learning, given its holistic goals (OECD, 2004). In order to meet that challenge, Carr (2001) developed a holistic, transactional, formative assessment procedure, entitled 'Learning Stories'. Learning Stories describe 'significant learning moments in a child's day-to-day experiences' (Carr et al., 2005: 192), with a focus on children's progress towards becoming confident and competent learners and communicators, and on learning strategies and dispositions. Learning Stories avoids assessing specific skills and the use of checklists or isolated observations. Teachers look at five areas related to dispositions – finding something of interest, being involved, engaging with challenge, persisting when there are difficulties, expressing a point of view and taking responsibility (which align to the strands and goals of the curriculum).

Documentation is a key aspect of Learning Stories, including hand written stories, word processing, scanned photographs, digital photographs and videos. The Stories include short-term reviews which describe and interpret children's learning in relation to the strands and goals, and look at the longer-term question of 'What next?' Parents (and other family members) and children are asked to comment on the Learning Stories and their voices are incorporated into them. The inclusion of children's voice in Learning Stories, and the continuing ownership over their Stories, allows children to share meaning and power with adults (teachers and family members), and for teachers to gain windows into their world views and assumptions (Carr et al., 2004, 2007 and 2009). This assessment approach orients children and teachers to learning goals involving mastery, persistence and striving towards increased competence, rather than performance goals, which are oriented towards avoiding failure.

No curriculum can be effective without the provision of additional resources. The Ministry of Education has provided an excellent series of books of exemplars to provide teachers with examples of assessments based on Te Whāriki (Carr et al., 2004, 2007 and 2009).[2] The authors were contracted by the Ministry to capture exemplars in early childhood centres and produce illustrated books, which are an invaluable resource for teachers. They are not prescriptive but instead illustrate a variety of ways in which the curriculum can be implemented.

The exemplars illustrate how assessment can assist the learning community to develop ongoing and diverse learning pathways. Assessment sits inside the curriculum, and assessments do not merely describe learning, they also construct and foster it. (Carr et al., 2004, Book 1: 3)

Each exemplar is followed by annotations which tell the reader what was happening, what the exemplar showed, how it relates to the area chosen, and how it might be used to support learning and development. The exemplars take place in everyday contexts such as having a nappy changed. In the 'Blinking and clicking on the changing mat' learning story (Carr et al., 2004, Book 1: 11), a teacher, Sue, was changing Jace on a changing mat, and blowing kisses. Jace imitated and did the same action with his mouth. Sue then winked at the baby and made a clicking action with her mouth. Jace imitated her actions again.

Another exemplar portrays Lauren's (4 years) screen printing (Carr et al., 2004, Book 4: 8).

In an exemplar titled 'Oh, no! That's not right!', Lauren tries to print a picture of a basket over [a] screen-printed picture she has made of a cat. She is not at first happy with it and self regulates her way through fixing it. For example she changes the orientation of the image of the cat in relation to the image of the basket so that the cat sits in the basket. She takes control of her own learning, of which mistakes are a normal part. Lauren's strategies for responding to a perceived mistake, are noticed and recognised by the teacher. Teachers provided the scaffolding for helping her to get this right, but in response to the child's initiative rather than imposed. (Smith, 2007: 156)

Using Learning Stories helps to give teachers a positive construction of children's competence, encourages them to involve families in assessment, and gives teachers confidence in their own learning goals together with increasing willingness to try out new and uncertain things, and to consult with others (Carr et al., 2005). Teachers feel positive towards Learning Stories because they are helpful to them in their work, and they do not feel as if they are being imposed externally. As well as exciting and energizing teachers, Learning Stories can strengthen the bonds between parents and other family members and teachers. Parents treasure the learning achievements of their children in their centres, and report showing other people (such as work colleagues and family members) their children's learning stories. Children also have a sense of pride and ownership in their portfolios. As one teacher, Karen Ramsey said: 'Everyone wait[s] with bated breath as they hear stories they have heard so many times before, but never lose interest in hearing again' (Carr et al., 2005: 193).

> The first time we introduced the children to their stories being on tapes, it was an exciting day. Once the video was playing and children saw themselves they automatically went and got their files and began to look through them as they watched the footage. The videos sparked children's conversation as they revisited and talked through their learning experiences. I thought this was amazing; children had made very clear links with their files to their videotapes. (Karen's story in Carr et al., 2005: 204)

Learning Stories and the exemplars demonstrate some of the many possibilities for learning that Te Whāriki offers. Their use helps turn Te Whāriki into a reality in many early childhood classrooms in New Zealand. They preserve the holistic nature of children's learning, are sensitive to context and acknowledge the complexity of children's learning. Assessment measures have a powerful effect on children's learning experiences, but the use of learning stories avoids external evaluative pressure and promotes a vision and expectation that children are resourceful and competent, and that rich learning contexts enhance their knowledge. The exemplars show how learning is intricately connected to experience, and suggest many ideas to try in practice.

Critique of Te Whāriki

While Te Whāriki has been praised by international researchers (Nutbrown, 1996; OECD, 2004; Pramling Samuelsson et al., 2006) and by early childhood practitioners in New Zealand, it is important that informed critique occurs to prevent stagnation and encourage improvement. An early critic, Joy Cullen, was concerned that 'it had taken on a gospel-like status' (Cullen, 1996: 113). This comment was no exaggeration as is illustrated by the comments of New Zealand teachers to a Norwegian researcher (Alvestad and Duncan, 2006). All of the teachers Alvestadt spoke to saw Te Whāriki as a document of great significance and importance, as illustrated in this comment. 'Teacher G: [Te Whāriki] that's basically our bible. We always look at Te Whāriki to make sure we have done it correctly' (Alvestad and Duncan, 2006: 36).

Te Whāriki is generally well accepted in New Zealand and 'appears as a familiar and accepted part of the provision of early childhood education in this country' (Nuttall, 2003: 7). Most teachers clearly have a sense of ownership over it and believe that it gives them a shared language, enhances their professionalism and makes what they do with children more visible (Alvestad and Duncan, 2006; May, 2009; Murrow, 1995). There are some dangers though in this widespread acceptance, especially when teachers use Te Whāriki in a very limited way. Cullen was one of the first to express concern at the large gap between practice and the ideals of Te Whāriki (Cullen, 1996). She believed that unless teachers had comprehensive training with strong theoretical foundations, which enabled them to critically reflect on practice, Te Whāriki could be a conservative force, affirming what was currently being practised. Early childhood practitioners, according to Cullen, tended to be self-congratulatory about how they were implementing Te Whāriki, and used it to justify such practices as using work-sheets and teaching numbers.

Perhaps one of the signs that Te Whāriki has come of age, is that there now exists a huge critical literature on it. A recent Google scholar search on Te Whāriki elicited 692 hits, which included many critical and reflective publications. Te Whāriki has been analysed, admired, praised, criticized, deconstructed and debunked, but it has cer-tainly not been a dead document lying on a shelf. Concerns at 'the absence of schol-arly critique' encouraged Joce Nuttall (2003: 8) to edit a book, *Weaving Te Whāriki*, which along with other work now provides a substantial body of critical literature. This has been a positive force in encouraging more efforts to improve the quality of teacher education and professional development, and support a more professional and informed implementation of Te Whāriki.

One of the main criticisms of Te Whāriki has been its lack of attention to subject-based knowledge. The Education Review Office (1998, cited by Garbett and Yourn, 2002) was critical of the lack of early childhood programmes linking Te Whāriki to the primary school curriculum, and its failure to make explicit the content knowledge required to ensure children's readiness for school. Broström (2003) also argued that it is important for a curriculum to have a long-term perspective and 'a vision of the future person in a future society' (2003: 221), that Te Whāriki was too diffuse and 'that it lacks reflection on *what* children should explore, communicate, think, and so on' (Broström, 2003: 226). Since children are going to live in a future world, he argues that they need to be given the tools to solve global problems, and to be made aware of these problems.

The avoidance of subject knowledge in Te Whāriki was due to concerns that this would result in a trickle down of the primary school curriculum. It was also a reflec-tion of the authors' original focus on the motivational aspects of learning, learning *how* to learn rather than *what* to learn, and that there is not one authentic learning pathway but many. A study by Hedges and Cullen (2005) of the beliefs and practices of early childhood teachers, parents and children, suggests that subject knowledge is not necessarily incompatible with a socio-culturally based curriculum. When children ask questions, it is important for teachers to know enough to answer them – for example, why sand and water are insufficient to make concrete, or questions about car mechan-ics or astronomy. Hedges and Cullen's study found that early childhood teachers missed subject enquiry cues, and rarely used subject knowledge in their teaching or their documentation. Hedges and Cullen argue that 'the lack of emphasis on subject content may limit learning and teaching opportunities and children's inquiry-based learning' (2005: 75). They view depth of subject knowledge as necessary for teachers to be able to respond meaningfully to children's interests and enquiries, and for children to learn about their communities. The study suggested that subject content knowledge is an essential component of early childhood teacher education, which can enhance teachers' capacity to implement Te Whāriki.

The exemplars, however, contain many examples of the use of subject knowledge to implement Te Whāriki, together with an elaboration of the theoretical and research base of Te Whāriki. For example, Connor learns about harvest line haulers (machinery used by his Dad in his work in the bush) and how they work (Carr et al., 2004, Book 14), while Ezra (Carr, Lee and Jones, 2009, Book 18) learns about height, balance, measurement and number when he moves the saw horse around under the tree house in the playground. Subject knowledge is, therefore, embedded in meaningful culturally and locally based shared knowledge and the child's interests. There are multiple pathways to acquiring relevant generic knowledge implicit in Te Whāriki.

Final thoughts

Te Whāriki was introduced by a conservative government. It could have resulted in making the early childhood sector more like the primary sector, but this was avoided. Instead it has exerted an upward influence on school, through, for example, the introduction of Key Competencies (similar to dispositions) in the new primary school curriculum. The document itself is only a small part of the story of its success. Successive governments have invested in professional development, advancement of early childhood training and resourcing (such as videos, handbooks and exemplars), which have influenced the thinking and practice of many early childhood centres. Nevertheless, resources for early childhood education are not strong in New Zealand, according to the OECD (2004), and this remains a challenge for Te Whāriki. Implementation depends on well trained and qualified teachers who have regular opportunities for professional development, appropriate group size and adequate staff:child ratios. The new government has already cut back budgets for early childhood professional development and trained staff, so the political battle continues, not only to improve but to retain the gains which have been made.

Summary

- Te Whāriki, introduced in 1996, is a holistic, bicultural and socio-culturally based curriculum including four broad principles (empowerment, holistic development, family and community and relationships) and five strands (well-being, belonging, contribution, communication and exploration).

(Continued)

(Continued)

- Te Whāriki has influenced New Zealand education through its vision of the child as an active, competent learner, and a partner in meaningful learning activities.
- Te Whāriki focuses on learning dispositions (ongoing habits of mind which dispose the learner in particular ways) rather than on fragmented skills.
- Learning Stories have been used to document significant learning moments, and assess how the goals of Te Whāriki are being met.

 Questions for discussion

1. In what ways does Te Whāriki reflect a holistic, bicultural, socio-culturally framed vision for early childhood education, and what do these terms mean?
2. What relevance does the United Nations Convention on the Rights of the Child have for early childhood education, and how does Te Whāriki reflect its principles.
3. What is the rationale for Te Whāriki's emphasis on learning dispositions and how can the emphasis be translated into practice?
4. Do you believe that Te Whāriki should focus more on preparation for school? What is the basis for your view? (*Higher level question*)

Notes

1. This was a treaty between Māori and the Crown signed in 1840 intended to protect tino rangatiratānga (governance), tāonga (treasured sites, food sources and objects) and land for Māori, in return for British rule of Pākeha settlers.
2. See www.educate.ece.govt.nz/learning/curriculumAndLearning/Assessmentforlearning/KeiTuaotePae/

Further reading

Levels 5 and 6

Smith, A.B. (2007) 'Children and young people's participation rights in education', *International Journal of Children's Rights*, 15: 147–64.
Childhood studies highlights the importance of participation rights, and supports a construction of children as active and involved citizens. This article gives examples of early childhood, primary and secondary education supporting children's participation rights.

Soler, J. and Miller, L. (2003) 'The struggle for early childhood curricula: a comparison of the English Foundation Stage curriculum, Te Whāriki and Reggio Emilia', *International Journal of Early Years Education*, 11(1): 57–67.

This article compares how visions for early childhood are expressed in three different early childhood curricula – in England, New Zealand and Italy. Differing contexts of local and national control give rise to different conceptualizations of learning.

Levels 6 and 7

Carr, M. and Claxton, G. (2002) 'Tracking the development of learning dispositions', *Assessment in Education*, 9(1): 9–37.
Confidence to engage in lifelong learning is more important than particular knowledge and skills. This article explains learning dispositions, and their theoretical rationale, identifying resilience, playfulness and reciprocity as three key learning dispositions.

Smith, A.B. (2009) 'A case study of learning architecture and reciprocity', *International Journal of Early Childhood*, 41(1): 33–49.
This is an ethnographic case study following the trajectory of Lisa's learning disposition, reciprocity, which examines the kind of self that was being created for Lisa, within the discourses and practices of her early childhood centres and school.

Websites

www.educate.ece.govt.nz/learning/curriculumAndLearning/Assessmentforlearning/KeiTuaotePae/
This is the website of the Ministry of Education, New Zealand. The Māori name for exemplars is Kei tua o te pae and this website allows these to be downloaded.

www.ohchr.org/english/bodies/crc/docs/discussion/earlychildhood.pdf
This website presents the conclusions of the UN Committee on the Rights of the Child after a day of discussion about early childhood. It suggests some important aspects of rights for young children and a vision of the nature of early childhood.

References

Alvestad, M. and Duncan, J. (2006) '"The value is enormous – it's priceless I think!" New Zealand preschool teachers' understanding of the early childhood curriculum in New Zealand – a comparative perspective', *International Journal of Early Childhood*, 38(1): 31–45.
Broström, S. (2003) 'Understanding Te Whāriki from a Danish perspective', in J. Nuttall (ed.) *Weaving 'Te Whāriki': Aotearoa New Zealand's Early Childhood Curriculum Document in Theory and Practice*. Palmerston North: Dunmore Press. pp. 215–42.
Carr, M. (1991) 'Developing a curriculum for early childhood: establishing a framework', paper presented at the NZARE conference, Dunedin, November.
Carr, M. (1997) *Learning Stories*. Position Paper 5. Project for Assessing Children's Experiences. Department of Early Childhood Studies, University of Waikato.
Carr, M. (1998a) (ed.) *Assessing Children's Experiences in Early Childhood: Final Report to the Ministry of Education. Part Two: Case Studies*. Wellington: Ministry of Education.
Carr, M. (1998b) 'Technological practice in early childhood as a dispositional milieu', PhD thesis, University of Waikato.
Carr, M. (2001) *Assessment in Early Childhood Settings: Learning Stories*. London: Paul Chapman.

Carr, M. and May, H. (1996) 'Te Whāriki, making a difference for the under-fives? The new national early childhood curriculum', *Delta*, 48(1): 101–12.

Carr, M., Lee, W. and Jones, C. (2004, 2007 and 2009) *Kei tua o te pae. Assessment for Learning: Early Childhood Exemplars.* Books 1–20. A resource prepared for the Ministry of Education. Wellington: Learning Media.

Carr, M., Hatherly, A., Lee, W. and Ramsey, K. (2005) 'Te Whāriki and assessment: a case study of teacher change', in J. Nuttall (ed.) *Weaving 'Te Whāriki': Aotearoa New Zealand's Early Childhood Curriculum Document in Theory and Practice.* Palmerston North: Dunmore Press. pp. 187–214.

Carr, M., Smith, A.B., Duncan, J., Jones, C., Lee, W. and Marshall, K. (2009) *Learning in the Making: Disposition and Design in Early Education.* Rotterdam and New York: Sense Publishers.

Cullen, J. (1996) 'The challenge of Te Whāriki for future developments in early childhood education', *Delta*, 48(1): 113–26.

Education Review Office (1998) *The Use of Te Whāriki.* Wellington: Education Review Office.

Gaffney, M. and Smith, A.B. (1997) *An Evaluation of Pilot Early Childhood Professional Development Programs to Support Curriculum Implementation.* Dunedin: Children's Issues Centre.

Garbett, D. and Yourn, B.R. (2002) 'Student teacher knowledge and understanding subject matter in the New Zealand context', *Australian Journal of Early Childhood*, 27(3): 1–6.

Hedges, H. and Cullen, J. (2005) 'Subject knowledge in early childhood curriculum and pedagogy: belief and practices', *Contemporary Issues in Early Childhood*, 6(1): 66–79.

James, A. and Prout, A. (eds) (1997) *Constructing and Reconstructing Childhood: Contemporary Issues in the Sociological Study of Childhood* (2nd edn). London: The Falmer Press.

Mara, D. (1998) *Implemention of Te Whāriki in Pacific Island Centres.* Final report to the Ministry of Education. Wellington: New Zealand Council of Educational Research.

May, H. (2009) *Politics in the Playground: The World of Early Childhood in New Zealand* (2nd edn). Dunedin: Otago University Press.

Mayall, B. (1994) *Children's Childhoods: Observed and Experienced.* London: The Falmer Press.

Mayall, B. (2002) *Towards a Sociology for Childhood: Thinking from Children's Lives.* Buckingham: Open University Press.

Ministry of Education (1996) *Te Whāriki: Early Childhood Curriculum.* Wellington: Learning Media.

Ministry of Education (2008) Education (Early Childhood Education Curriculum Framework) Notice 2008. Internal document for Early Childhood Centres.

Moss, P. (2000) *Training and Education of Early Childhood Education and Care Staff.* Report prepared for the OECD, Thomas Coram Research Unit, Institute of Education, University of London.

Murrow, K. (1995) *Early Childhood Workers' Opinions on the Draft Document 'Te Whariki'.* Wellington: Ministry of Education.

Nutbrown, C. (1996) *Respectful Educators – Capable Learners: Children's Rights and Early Education.* London: Paul Chapman.

Nuttall, J. (2003) 'Weaving Te Whāriki', in J. Nuttall (ed.) *Weaving Te Whāriki: Aotearoa New Zealand's Early Childhood Curriculum Document in Theory and Practice.* Wellington: New Zealand Council for Educational Research. pp. 7–15.

Nuttall, J. and Mulheron, S. (1993) 'What's for pudding? Curriculum and change for staff of childcare centres in Aotearoa/New Zealand', paper presented at CECUA Early Childhood Curriculum Conference, Christchurch, October.

OECD (2004) *Starting Strong: Curricula and Pedagogies in Early Childhood Education and Care. Five Curriculum Outlines.* Paris: OECD Directorate for Education, March.

Podmore, V., May, H. and Mara, D. (1998) *Evaluating Early Childhood Programmes Using the Strands and Goals of Te Whāriki, the National Early Childhood Curriculum.* Wellington: New Zealand Council of Educational Research.

Pramling Samuelsson, I., Sheridan, S. and Williams, P. (2006) 'Five preschool curricula – comparative perspective', *International Journal of Early Childhood*, 38(1): 11–29.

Rogoff, B. (1995) 'Observing socio-cultural activity on three planes: participatory appropriation, guided participation, and apprenticeship', in J. Wertsch, P. del Rio and A. Alvarez (eds) *Socio-cultural Studies of Mind*. Cambridge: Cambridge University Press. pp. 139–64.

Smith, A.B. (2007) 'Children and young people's participation rights in education', *International Journal of Children's Rights*, 15: 147–64.

Smith, A.B. (2009) 'A case study of learning architecture and reciprocity', *International Journal of Early Childhood*, 41(1): 33–49.

Smith, A.B. and May, H. (2006) 'Early childhood care and education in Aotearoa – New Zealand', in E. Melhuish and K. Petrogiannis (eds) *Early Childhood Care and Education: International Perspectives*. London: Routledge. pp. 95–114.

Sylva, K. and Taylor, H. (2006) 'Effective settings: evidence from research', in G. Pugh and B. Duffy (eds) *Contemporary Issues in the Early Years* (4th edn). London: Sage. pp. 165–80.

Te One, S. (2003) 'The context of Te Whāriki: contemporary issues of influence', in J. Nuttall (ed.) *Weaving Te Whāriki: Aotearoa New Zealand's Early Childhood Curriculum Document in Theory and Practice*. Wellington: New Zealand Council for Educational Research. pp. 17–49.

Vygotsky, L.S. (1978) *Mind in Society: The Development of Higher Psychological Processes*. London: Harvard University Press.

Wertsch, J.V. (1995) 'The need for action in sociocultural research', in J. Wertsch, P. Del Rio and A. Alvarez (eds) *Sociocultural Studies of the Mind*. New York: Cambridge University Press.

CHAPTER 11

CRITICAL ISSUES

Linda Pound and Linda Miller

Overview

In this book, we have looked back at the past in an attempt to understand some of the pioneering work in the history of Early Childhood Education and Care (ECEC) and have also considered more contemporary perspectives. In looking back to the 'roots' of ECEC, we can be made aware of the influences that are brought to bear on the present, and how some important issues – such as the place and role of play and the best environments for learning and development, continue to be debated in the present day. A key aim of this book has been to encourage readers to view ECEC through different lenses, using the book as a tool or resource for thinking about how the themes and issues relate to your own professional working lives. In this final chapter, we consider and reflect upon what might have been learnt from reading this book. In doing this, we have identified what we see as overarching critical issues in the chapters which spill over and cross chapter boundaries.

(Continued)

> (*Continued*)
>
> In Chapter 1, we identified some key themes and threads in the book which are inevitably linked to the issues which we explore in this chapter. We have identified these as:
>
> - the nature of early childhood education
> - the politicization of early childhood
> - enabling environments
> - working in communities of practice.

The nature of early childhood education

Discussion continues over what early childhood education (ECE), and in fact all education, actually is or is for. This is probably *the* overarching critical issue in this book, and most certainly will have been a central question for the educational pioneers and for those developing the more recent innovations featured in the preceding chapters. This debate is evident in the tension between those who view early childhood primarily as a preparation for later schooling and those who support the views of Dewey, that education is about the present and what is needed now to support children's learning and development. Even the Plowden Report (CACE, 1967), which has long been seen as voicing strongly liberal views, identified early education primarily as being about getting children ready for school. In Chapter 7, we see that HighScope arose out of a similar set of values at around the same time as the Plowden Report.

Those who regard early education as being primarily about the needs of the child have tended to favour a developmental curriculum (Bredekamp, 1997). With the rise of sociocultural theories (Rogoff, 1990) and the development of sociological views of childhood (James et al., 1998), the need for education to reflect the cultural aspects of home and community have become more evident. This is reflected in Te Whāriki and in the work of Vivian Gussin Paley; but for Paley the cultural influences explicitly include story and fantasy. Few current theories of ECE would advocate an instructional curriculum and yet in many education systems there is an emphasis on such an approach (OECD, 2006).

These two views of the nature of education appropriate to young children can be presented as distinct and separate, but we take the view, as we noted in Chapter 1, that it is impossible to care without educating children, nor to truly educate without considering children's emotional well-being.

Play, children and curricula

As we discussed in Chapter 1, play has long been seen as an essential component of ECEC (Smith, 2010) but what is regarded as play and its purpose is widely contested. Even amongst well-known and respected current theorists, there are significant differences in what they think play is and is for (see Pound, 2009). Also, as the chapters in this book have shown, play is not necessarily seen as a 'leading activity' in all approaches. The New Zealand early childhood curriculum (Chapter 10), a culturally appropriate curriculum underpinned by socio-cultural perspectives and play-oriented philosophies, places emphasis on other features, such as empowerment, relationships, health and well-being, a sense of belonging and exploration as being of equal importance.

Those involved in the development of Te Whāriki believed that a curriculum should take a holistic view of children, recognizing that most children belong to more than one culture. Paley, on the other hand, who also takes a strong position on socio-cultural issues (Paley, 2010), regards play as fundamental to learning and development. As we have seen in preceding chapters, for foundational theorists such as Steiner and Froebel, imaginative play was vital to children's development. Montessori, however, took a different view of work and play; working as she was with poor and needy families her instinct was that play should not be 'idle' but linked to work. Froebel's rhetoric may be seen as similarly linking work and play – but in putting the theory into practice wide variations can be seen. For HighScope practitioners, work may have playful characteristics but can be differentiated from play by a sense of seriousness.

Smith (2010) reminds us that all children play but that there is much cultural variation (see also Olusoga, 2009). We should also be reminded that current work on creativity and neuroscience indicates that all adults need to play (Brown, 2009; Elkind, 2008; Pellis and Pellis, 2009). Smith (2010: 80) suggests that: 'Play can be seen as an effect of culture, as adult culture influences the play that is seen; but it is also a cause of culture, as children's play reproduces but also changes culture over time'.

Central to most views of teaching and learning in early childhood is the view that knowledge is contingent and is socially constructed (Rogoff, 2003). Most practitioners believe in a holistic view of teaching and learning and that fostering a disposition to learn, rather than teaching fragmented skills and knowledge, are what is needed; although this is not always reflected in practice. External pressures from government guidance or a management hierarchy can lead practitioners to focus on curriculum 'delivery' or 'coverage' as the main focus of their practice. Such a view would have been anathema to the foundational theorists featured in this book, but in England it has become a feature of the Early Years Foundation Stage (EYFS) (DfES, 2008) and the National Curriculum in primary schools, causing uncertainty for many practitioners. The more contemporary theories and approaches featured in Part 3 of this book also advocate an holistic approach to teaching and learning. For example, in Forest Schools the curriculum focuses on the links between nature and the child's all-round development, in particular social and emotional development or well-being.

A recurring theme in this book is the vision or images of a child that practitioners hold which may be derived from a culture, or may become part of the culture, and are central to the way children are treated. Brooks (2006) highlights the very different experiences of nine children in Britain and argues for greater respect for children's rights as a central component of ECEC; a view in which all those who have contributed to this book are united. Although progress has been made in this important aspect of children's lives, much still needs to be done. Brooks (2006) highlights the changes that are necessary if we are to create respect for children. These changes would include recognizing children's competence, challenging the notion of children as cultural capital, and tackling inequalities and the right to an appropriate early childhood education from birth (see Woodhead and Moss, 2007).

The politicization of early childhood

The view of Early Childhood Education (ECE) as a public good is not new. The first Steiner school was established in 1919 because of Steiner's concerns with 'social renewal'. Maria Montessori opened her first 'children's house' in a poor area of Rome in 1907 and Loris Malaguzzi founded the Reggio Emilia system of early childhood education after his experiences in the Second World War. He believed that a new society should nurture a vision of children who could think and act for themselves. Te Whāriki was designed to incorporate equitable educational opportunities in a bicultural society (Miller et al., 2010) and HighScope is an early intervention programme aimed at enhancing children's life chances (see Chapter 7).

This view of ECE as a public good is therefore well established on the grounds that it contributes to the health and well-being of a nation's children, future educational achievement, the labour market and social cohesion (OECD, 2006). The OECD report, based on 30 member countries, confirms that the greater part of ECE is publicly funded and regulated by government. This investment in 'human capital' by countries and governments, is underpinned by the principle that good foundations in early childhood increase the productivity of the next stage (the premise on which the HighScope approach is based, see Chapter 7) – and that investment at this stage in life promises 'high returns'. This principle also underpins the public investment in early years provision in countries such as England, where a National Childcare Strategy (McAuliffe et al., 2006) aimed to reduce child poverty and social exclusion and improve affordable provision for children and families.

However, increased investment in public services brings with it greater monitoring and regulation of both people and services which, it has been argued, reduces the professional autonomy of teachers, early childhood practitioners, schools and early years settings. In such a scenario, children's progress is measured as 'outcomes' against externally prescribed standards and benchmarks to ensure that education is worth the investment. This has prompted criticism of the dominance of government discourses, which Dahlberg and Moss (2005) argue focuses on 'what works'; they make a case for alternative discourses and more ethical and democratic practices.

In some economies (e.g. Australia and, to a lesser extent, England), there has also been a trend towards encouraging an independent 'market' in early childhood provision which critics such as Duhn (2010) and Woodrow (2010) say lead to the 'corporatization' of early childhood education; with education seen as a commodity and early childhood teachers and practitioners accountable for effective delivery. Woodrow (2010) discusses the inherent dangers of this model in Australia, where a 'market-based' approach to childcare provision came to dominate the Australian policy landscape. The collapse of the company responsible exposed problems with such a policy, such as: Who makes decisions about the professional practices of educators? How does an expected return on profits affect the relationship between the owners and shareholders, staff, children and parents? And what types of curricula, practices and resources might be either privileged or frowned upon in a corporate culture? Urban (2008) questions the legitimacy of talking about *services for children* when the driving factors for investing in such services are economic.

Yet, as Dahlberg and Moss (2005: vi) concede, 'Institutionalization of childhood can be a force for good', but in the face of such developments it is imperative that practitioners are informed and vigilant and can maintain a critical stance in relation to both policy and practice.

A further aspect of political interest in ECE is what writers have called the 'schoolification' of early childhood (see Woodhead and Moss, 2007) involving an overemphasis on 'academic' provision for young children; a view that is far from new. It emphasizes the academic over the intellectual (Katz, 1989), demonstrating greater concern for the needs of the institution and society than for the development of the child. Katz (1989) reminds us that curriculum is essentially about what should be learnt. This concern is implicit in Chapter 2 which highlights the importance of emotional aspects of development. Concern about the schoolification of early childhood is a key element of the Steiner Waldorf philosophy, which has strong beliefs about the 'when' and the 'how' of early education. Paley's view about an emphasis on academic pursuits is that it takes away vital time for 'good play' and 'deep thought' (2004: 22) from fantasy play, which is 'the glue that binds together all other pursuits, including the early teaching of reading and writing skills' (2004: 8).

Linked concerns about 'disembodied' education (Tobin, 2004) are also highlighted by the Forest School philosophy, which in common with many ECEC theories and approaches, places a strong emphasis on physical action in learning and development. Tobin suggests that a number of factors have come together favouring 'the brain over the body and skill acquisition over feelings and more complex thinking' (2004: 123). In theory, all of the theoretical stances represented in this book would recognize the prime importance of the physical, emotional and intellectual aspects of development. However, political factors can influence both practitioners and parents so that what is appropriate for young children becomes less clear in public debates.

Enabling environments

The Early Years Foundation Stage (EYFS) (DCSF, 2008) in England identifies enabling environments as a key principle in effective early years provision. The learning environment is identified as not simply being indoors and out but as the emotional context which enables (or sometimes disables) children.

In Chapter 2, Julia Manning-Morton explored the importance of a range of emotional interactions. The phrase 'emotional labour' was probably first used by Hochschild (1983) and is highly pertinent to all early childhood services where everyone working in a teaching and caring role needs to establish warm and loving relationships with children and their families (Nieto, 1999). Practitioners have a dual and inseparable role of both caring and teaching so that warmth and love become even more vital in contributing to children's well-being. At the same time, emotions have to be managed, in the ways that Julia Manning-Morton has described, since the emotional aspects of an enabling environment are undoubtedly paramount.

As we have discussed above, the view that adults hold of children impact on the extent to which an environment may be thought of as enabling. The notion of respect for children is a key factor and will be reflected in adults' relationships with children. Research describing Steiner Waldorf practice talks of adults as being 'present' (Drummond and Jenkinson, 2009), a description which is probably akin to the current emphases on listening to children and engaging in sustained, shared thinking (Clark et al., 2005). Spiritual aspects of development may be seen as an element of an enabling environment and is particularly explicit in Steiner Waldorf Education and fundamental to Froebelian theory. However, more recent theories place a less explicit emphasis on spirituality.

Enabling environments place an emphasis on physical as well as personal development. There are parallels between a willingness to take both physical and emotional risks, as we see in Chapters 2 and 9. In these chapters, the authors discuss the lack of opportunity for young children to embrace risk and uncertainty and adults' unwillingness to help children to learn to manage risk. Forest Schools, as we saw in Chapter 9, have been successful in encouraging both parents and practitioners to take on this crucial aspect of development and well-being. Chapter 9 also reflects the developing interest in nature as an important component of an enabling environment. The theories of Pestalozzi and Rousseau, from which Froebel's theory emerged, placed a firm emphasis on nature and its importance as an integral part of the environment (and curriculum) and is re-emerging, as evidenced by the growth of Forest Schools. However, the way in which the outside area is used in different settings remains diverse.

ECEC environments may appear very similar to untrained eyes – for example, book areas, sand and water and role-play provision are likely to be found in most settings. However, there are factors which make those environments more or less enabling. Everyone would agree that adults have a vital role to play – yet views about what adults actually should do in order to enable learning are often very different. Issues as diverse as risk-taking, the teaching of phonics or the use of outdoor space give rise to wide-ranging views. Similarly, the role of parents and community as part of an enabling environment is viewed differently within different approaches. Such differences are most likely to be visible in practice, as rhetoric is often different to reality.

Communities of practice

Any community of practice will be shaped by the underpinning beliefs, knowledge and values of that particular community – whether these are derived from policy initiatives, such as in national curricular frameworks; by a combination of community, stakeholder and government initiatives, as in Te Whāriki; by a particular philosophy, as in Montessori, Froebelian, Steiner-Waldorf settings or Forest Schools; stemming from a research-based approach, as in HighScope; or inspired by the vision of a particular individual, as in the work of Vivian Gussin Paley and Loris Malaguzzi, the founder of the Reggio Emilia nurseries.

Wenger's notion of a community of practice embraces three main elements: *the domain*; *the community*; and *the practice*. A shared *domain* or area of interest – such as a particular theoretical or historical perspective – is critical to the way practitioners view themselves and their practice with children, families and the community (Wenger, 2006). A shared domain of knowledge, understandings, values and beliefs will impact on the practice and the ethos of individual settings and the people who work there. For example:

- contrasting views of curricula as co-constructed or as defined by regulation and standards
- play or 'work' as a leading activity
- the role of the adult as nurturer, director or learning partner
- the role of resources as cultural or 'natural' artefacts or as pre-prepared materials to be used in particular ways (Miller et al., 2010).

Wenger's (2006: 2) notion of a *community* is one in which, 'Members engage in joint activities and discussions, help each other, and share information. They build relationships that help them to learn from each other'. Of *practice*, he says, '[Members] develop a shared repertoire of resources: experiences, stories, tools, ways of addressing recurring problems – in short a shared practice'; thus promoting learning through professional dialogue.

Such a sense of community may be challenged by new ideas. It may be challenged through revised interpretations of teaching and learning. As discussed in Chapter 2, it may be challenged by a psychoanalytic viewpoint that requires practitioners to focus on their own inner emotional lives before they can work successfully with children. Or it may be challenged by ideas relating to postmodernist thinking, as outlined in Chapter 3. It may also be challenged by enabling and encouraging practitioners to question commonly held 'truths' about our understandings of curricula and pedagogical approaches. This in turn may cause practitioners to confront or question existing practice in their setting.

Wenger (2009) also talks about the notion of professional learning taking place in a '*landscape of practice*'; an example being the territory of a particular work setting and role within which different groups and individuals interact. Persons in a setting (or landscape) will be 'carriers' of different practices. In a recent workshop led by Wenger (2009) and attended by one of the authors of this chapter (Linda Miller), landscapes were represented by a matrix of paper lily pads spread across the floor. In the workshop, participants explored how 'boundary crossing' into new landscapes can be difficult, as familiar practices are left behind and new ideas are encountered which may challenge accepted beliefs. It was also argued that boundaries are where learning happens as you begin to step outside of accepted thinking and practice. Exploring new landscapes containing new ideas or theoretical frameworks offers the opportunity for thinking, reflection and discussion to take place. There is, however, no need to 'throw out the baby with the bath water' as we can bring resources and ideas from the past to bear on the present – reinterpreting and transforming these and thus developing reflexive practice.

Final thoughts

Those of us involved in ECEC are privileged in working with or for young children. But we also have an incalculable responsibility to the children, who as well as being amongst the most vulnerable members of society, are also its future, to parents and to the communities within which we work. The theories and approaches which inform our practice are far too important to be viewed uncritically or unreflectively. Therefore, we have a professional responsibility to ensure that we adopt a reflective approach to the critical issues which surround the theories and beliefs underpinning ECEC. At the same time, we would argue for adopting a 'playful' and 'researchful' approach to this important work. This will involve hard work, curiosity and creative insight into our own beliefs, understandings and practice.

 Summary

In this chapter, we have argued that the roots of ECE can be brought to bear on the present and that:

- foundational theories offer insights into those pioneers who first had the vision to identify and strive to meet the needs of young learners
- contemporary perspectives such as postmodern and psychoanalytic theories offer a framework for reflecting on and questioning practice
- theories and approaches continue to develop but, without deep, reflective and shared thinking about children and curricula, they may fail to address the needs of children or society.

 Questions for discussion

1. What practices and perspectives in this book do you feel closest to – and why?
2. What practices and perspectives in this book do you feel furthest away from – and why?
3. Why do you know what you know about ECE, and why do you do what you do? (*Higher level question*)

Further reading

Levels 5 and 6

MacNaughton, G. (2003) *Shaping Early Childhood*. Maidenhead: Open University Press.
This book has three parts focusing on learners, curricula and curricular contexts. MacNaughton suggests three views of learners and curricula – conforming, reforming and transforming.

Pound, L. (2005) *How Children Learn: From Montessori to Vygotsky – Educational Approaches and Theories Made Easy*. London: Step Forward Publishing.
This book offers a short introduction to a range of theories with which you may be unfamiliar. It will introduce you to key facts and ideas, making further, deeper reading more accessible.

Levels 6 and 7

Hatch, A., Bowman, B., Jordan, J., Morgan, C., Hart, C., Diaz Soto, L., Lubeck, S. and Hyson, M. (2002) 'Developmentally appropriate practice: continuing the dialogue', *Contemporary Issues in Early Childhood*, 3(3): 439–57 (available online).
This article relates to a symposium and consists of a series of short accounts of different views of developmentally appropriate practice. The final account by Hyson is of particular interest.

Nutbrown, C., Clough, P. and Selbie, P. (2008) *Early Childhood Education: History, Philosophy and Experience*. London: Sage.
This book explores important ideas behind the policies and practices in early childhood education illustrated through an informative history of the field.

Tobin, J. (2004) 'The disappearance of the body in early childhood education', in L. Bresler (ed.) *Knowing Bodies, Moving Minds: Towards Embodied Teaching and Learning*. Dordrecht, The Netherlands: Kluwer Academic Publishers.
This chapter explores the way in which physical activity has been marginalized in schools and suggests that this is unhelpful to children's development and well-being.

Websites

http://pzweb.harvard.edu/mlv/index.cfm
This website relates to Making Learning Visible – a project developed as part of Project Zero by Howard Gardner working in collaboration with Reggio Children to understand, document and support individual and group learning, initially in the early years.

www.ewenger.com/theory
This website offers an explanation of 'communities of practice' and provides links to further reading and information.

References

Bredekamp, S. (1997) *Developmentally Appropriate Practice in Early Childhood Programs*. New York: NAEYC.
Brooks, L. (2006) *The Story of Childhood*. London: Bloomsbury Publishing.

Brown, S. (2009) *Play*. London: Avery.

CACE (England) (1967) *Children and their Primary Schools* (the Plowden Report). London: HMSO.

Clark, A., Kjorholt, A. and Moss, P. (eds) (2005) *Beyond Listening*. Bristol: Policy Press.

Dahlberg, G. and Moss, P. (2005) *Ethics and Politics in Early Childhood Education*. London: Routledge Falmer.

Department for Children, Schools and Families (DCSF) (2008) *The Early Years Foundation Stage*. London: DCSF.

Department for Education and Skills (DfES) (2008) *Statutory Framework for the Early Years Foundation Stage*. Nottingham: DfES Publications.

Drummond, M.J. and Jenkinson, S. (2009) *Meeting the Child – Approaches to Observation and Assessment in Steiner Kindergartens*. Plymouth: University of Plymouth.

Duhn, I. (2010) 'Towards professionalism/s', in L. Miller and C. Cable (eds) *Professionalization, Leadership and Management in the Early Years*. London: Sage.

Elkind, D. (2008) *The Power of Play*. Cambridge, MA: De Capo Lifelong.

Hochschild, A. (1983) *The Managed Heart: Commercialization of Human Feeling*. London and Los Angeles: University of California Press.

James, A., Jenks, C. and Prout, A. (1998) *Theorizing Childhood*. Cambridge: Polity Press.

Katz, L. (1989) 'Pedagogical issues in early childhood education', ERIC database ref. ED321840 (www.eric.ed.gov).

McAuliffe A., Linsey A. and Fowler J. (2006) *Childcare Act 2006: The Essential Guide*. London: National Children's Bureau.

Miller, L., Devereux, J., Paige-Smith, A. and Soler, J. (2010) 'Approaches to curricula in the early years', in C. Cable, L. Miller and G. Goodliff (eds) *Working with Children in the Early Years* (2nd edn). Abingdon, Oxon: Routledge/Open University Press.

Nieto, S. (1999) *The Light in their Eyes*. New York: Teachers College Press.

OECD (2006) *Starting Strong II: Early Childhood Education and Care*. Paris: OECD Publishing.

Olusoga, Y. (2009) '"We don't play like that here": social cultural and gender perspectives on play', in A. Brock, S. Dodds, P. Jarvis and Y. Olusoga (eds) *Perspectives on Play: Learning for Life*. Harlow, Essex: Pearson Education Ltd.

Paley, V.G. (2004) *A Child's Work: The Importance of Fantasy Play*. London: University of Chicago Press.

Paley, V.G. (2010) *The Boy on the Beach*. London: University of Chicago Press.

Pellis, S. and Pellis, V. (2009) *The Playful Brain*. Oxford: One World Publications.

Pound, L. (2009) *How Children Learn 3: Contemporary Thinking and Theorists*. London: Practical Pre-school Books.

Rogoff, B. (1990) *Apprenticeship in Thinking*. Oxford: Oxford University Press.

Rogoff, B. (2003) *The Cultural Nature of Human Development*. New York: Oxford University Press.

Smith, P.K. (2010) *Children and Play*. Chichester: Wiley/Blackwell.

Tobin, J. (2004) 'The disappearance of the body in early childhood education', in L. Bresler (ed.) *Knowing Bodies, Moving Minds*. Dordrecht, The Netherlands: Kluwer Academic Publishers.

Urban, M. (2008) 'Dealing with uncertainty: challenges and possibilities for the early childhood profession', *European Early Childhood Education Research Journal*, special edition on Professionalism, 16(2): 131–5.

Wenger, E. (2006) 'Communities of practice: a brief introduction'. Available at: www.ewenger.com/theory/index.htm (accessed 2 May 2010).

Wenger, E. (2009) 'Learning in the landscape of practice: a story telling and gathering residential with Etienne Wenger', residential workshop, The Open University, Milton Keynes, 3–4 July.

Woodhead, M. and Moss, P. (2007) *Early Childhood and Primary Education: Transitions in the Lives of Young Children*. Milton Keynes: The Open University.

Woodrow, C. (2010) 'Challenging identities: a case for leadership', in L. Miller and C. Cable (eds) *Professionalization, Leadership and Management in the Early Years*. London: Sage.

INDEX